FOREIGNERS IN THEIR OWN COUNTRY

FOREIGNERS IN THEIR OWN COUNTRY

Identity and Rejection in France

Lawrence M. Martin

berghahn
NEW YORK • OXFORD
www.berghahnbooks.com

First published in 2024 by
Berghahn Books
www.berghahnbooks.com

First paperback edition published in 2026

Library of Congress Cataloging-in-Publication Data
Names: Martin, Lawrence M., author.
Title: Foreigners in their own country : identity and rejection in France / Lawrence M. Martin.
Description: New York City : Berghahn Books, 2023. | Includes bibliographical references and index.
Identifiers: LCCN 2023017771 (print) | LCCN 2023017772 (ebook) | ISBN 9781805390886 (hardback) | ISBN 9781805390800 (ebook)
Subjects: LCSH: National characteristics, French. | Colorism—France. | North Africans—France—Interviews. | Black people—France—Interviews. | Asians—France—Interviews. | Children of immigrants--France—Ethnic identity. | Social integration--France. | Belonging (Social psychology)—France. | Race relations—France.
Classification: LCC DC34 .M348 2023 (print) | LCC DC34 (ebook) | DDC 305.800944—dc23/eng/20230427
LC record available at https://lccn.loc.gov/2023017771
LC ebook record available at https://lccn.loc.gov/2023017772

British Library Cataloguing in Publication Data
A catalogue record for this book is available from the British Library

EU GPSR Authorized Representative
LOGOS EUROPE, 9 rue Nicolas Poussin, 17000, LA ROCHELLE, France
Email: Contact@logoseurope.eu

ISBN 978-1-80539-088-6 hardback
ISBN 978-1-80758-105-3 paperback
ISBN 978-1-80539-089-3 epub
ISBN 978-1-80539-080-0 web pdf

https://doi.org/10.3167/9781805390886

To all the people who welcomed me into their homes and shared their life stories, with gratitude and deep respect.

CONTENTS

ACKNOWLEDGMENTS

First things first: I thank my wife, Carol Fisler. Since long before this project began, Carol has been an enthusiastic partner in our friendships and work with people from backgrounds different from our own. During each of my trips to France, she joined in the experience on a daily basis, prodding me from afar to see what I'd missed. Her empathy, intelligence, and good sense enriched my understanding of the people I stayed with and, to be frank, has enriched me as a person. When it came time to write this book, Carol helped me remain true to the complexity and nuances of each person and, as the chapters took shape, to think more flexibly and write more clearly. Although it embarrasses me to share such thoughts with people I don't know—most of the readers of this book—this is the least I can do to show my appreciation for the role she's played in this effort and in so much of our life together.

This book arose from conversations over dinner tables with strangers who chose to talk about their lives with me. Fatiha Mennis was the first, becoming a friend and champion of this enterprise. During the two years that followed, when I stayed with people throughout France, dozens of people sat down with me and spoke in detail—sometimes in painful detail—about what they had experienced. Many asked me to make sure to include them in my account of these conversations. Since then, more than a few have asked when the book would be published. Later than they imagined, this is finally happening. I hope they feel I've done them justice.

This book, like many others, is the culmination of a process to which many have contributed. It began with Paris Aslanidis, Marcia Inhorn, and the late Pieter Muysken, who expressed enthusiasm and provided guidance, even when I had so little to show for my efforts. As the chapters finally appeared, a number of other friends pitched in. If the reader finds something of value in this book, it is probably thanks to them and to Carol. David Damrosch was my mentor and most astute critic throughout. Cécile Whiting and Sally Nelson reviewed draft after draft, providing criticisms and suggestions that were always on the mark.

In writing these words, I realize how much I owe to other people. This includes my extraordinary children, Pete and Lydia. Thank you all.

INTRODUCTION

In July 2015, I stopped in France on the way to do research for an ethnography course I was to teach at Yale that fall. I stayed with an Airbnb host who had emigrated to France from Morocco nearly thirty years earlier, and we talked for hours. She spoke superb French, lived in a carefully maintained downtown apartment, had multiple degrees from French universities, and worked as a business consultant. Still, she had to deal with people who acted as though she did not belong in France.

Our conversations sparked a project that would continue until this book went to press. I returned to France in August 2016, choosing to stay with Airbnb hosts whose online profiles suggested family roots outside of Europe. (In the US, this might be called reverse racial profiling.) Wherever I stayed, I was struck by how readily my hosts talked about their lives, often at length and with deep emotion. These conversations led me to the research protocol I followed throughout this project. Before each of my next six trips to France, I chose one or two metropolitan areas and sent messages to potential Airbnb hosts explaining that I would be visiting their city not for tourism or business but to speak with them about life there. Many reacted positively. Abbas wrote back, "Your project sounds very interesting, and it will be a pleasure if I can help you," and Olivier wrote, "This sounds very interesting!" With each host who wished to participate, I booked a night or two in the extra bedroom or apartment they rented out. As the trips progressed, reviews on my Airbnb profile from prior hosts piqued the interest of others. When I inquired about staying with her, Aya wrote, "The comments left by other hosts make your project sound appealing, so I'll happily take part."

During these trips, I took public transportation from one home to the next, carrying my duffel bag and backpack. Upon arrival, I would give my host a detailed description of the project and the interview I hoped to conduct, answer any questions they had, and then ask if they wanted to participate. I would also ask if they were comfortable having the interview recorded. Virtually everyone was enthusiastic. During the next day or two, we would conduct the interview, but also share meals and talk about whatever came to mind. If the host lived with family members, I would get to know them, too. Some hosts took me on walks in their neighborhood or introduced me to friends, and one brought me to a family cookout in the country.

I continued traveling to France until I had spoken with people of varying backgrounds throughout the country. In all, I conducted interviews in and around nine cities: Bordeaux, Lille, Lyon, Marseille, Nantes, Nice, Paris, Strasbourg, and Toulouse. While some of my hosts lived within the city itself, others were in suburbs, nearby towns, even exurbs. I recorded 156 hours of interviews with a total of sixty-six people and had hundreds of hours of informal conversations. On the few occasions when I had mistakenly chosen an Airbnb host of European origin, I interviewed that person, too, to see what would come of it. During my few hours off, typically during a host's workday, I walked around town, observing the scene and talking with people.

The interviewees trace their roots to many parts of the world: nine countries in sub-Saharan Africa, three countries in Northwest Africa, three islands in the Caribbean, and thirteen countries in Asia and South America. As with people of non-European origin in France generally (see Tribalat 2015: 21–23; Breuil-Genier, Borrel, and Lhommeau 2011: 33–35), the great majority of the interviewees originate from former French colonies, though some originate from former colonies of other European countries or from countries that had not been colonies. I say "originate" because many of the interviewees have lived their entire lives in France; it was their parents or grandparents who had come from elsewhere. Many spoke of themselves in this way, for example, as *d'origine sénégalaise* (of Senegalese origin). I also use the umbrella term "colonies" to cover the various forms of European control of foreign lands and people, including protectorates, territories, mandates, and, in the case of Algeria, *départements* (where the great majority of indigenous people were controlled by Europeans).

Originating from such different places, the interviewees have different cultural backgrounds and physical appearances. As discussed below, most categorized themselves according to three perceived physical types—Maghrebi, Black, or Asian—each of which is associated with a presumed geographical origin. For Maghrebis, this is the "Maghreb" of Northwest Africa; for Blacks, usually sub-Saharan Africa or the Caribbean; for Asians, the countries of East Asia. They also range in age, from their late teens to early seventies, and in their economic circumstances and temperaments. While some interviewees were better off than others, almost all would be considered middle class by Americans.[1] I interviewed both men and women, though slightly more men. The interviewees live in or near cities of different sizes throughout France. While some came to France in early adulthood, most grew up in France, and a few come from families that settled there well before they were born. Ironically, some interviewees have deeper roots in France than former Interior Minister and then President Nicolas Sarkozy, whose father came to the country as a young man and whose mother's father came as a teenager.

The interviews followed a flexible protocol. We began with an autobiographical overview, during which I did not interrupt or ask questions. This continued for however long the interviewee wished, ranging from ten minutes to more than an hour. One began with his grandparents, who had become French citizens, and concluded his account three generations later, with his adult son. After the autobiographical sketch, we would return to the various periods of the interviewee's life, from childhood to the present. While some interviews were completed in only one session, exhausting both of us, most required two or more sessions. At the end of each interview, I asked my only predetermined questions: Was there anything the interviewee wished to add? Had I said anything insulting? Here, as throughout each interview, it was important for the experience to be collaborative.

Each interview was a conversation. While I asked questions, interviewees were free to speak at whatever length they wished and say whatever they thought important. Olivier described the experience as an "interesting way to interrogate myself," and Nassim said that his interview "allowed me to understand things." I asked each person to set me straight at any time. I assured each that I would not share the recordings with anyone and that I would not reveal their real names or where they live when I published the results. All the names in this book have been changed, and no interviewee's city or town is identified.[2] In a few places, I shifted minor details to protect a person's privacy. After I returned to the United States, I sent the interview recording to each interviewee who had requested it. No one ever asked me to keep what they said confidential. To the contrary, many asked me to include their accounts in whatever I published.

The interviews were often emotional. Some people cried or took breaks to compose themselves. Samuel said that his interview "churned up memories of great misfortune," but that he "had to put it all in place. Telling you certain things," he added, "helped me enormously." Vincent said that his interview was "the first time I've thought about" various aspects of his life. François was "proud" of having participated in the project, and Olivier told me that he found the experience "very interesting, very exciting." Tarek, who suffered grievously during his adolescence, said that his interview was "the first time I've told anyone about this. It gave me the right to tell my story." At the end of his interview, Tarek added:

> It was a pleasure to take part in this exchange. I hope that a great number of people will do this and that you'll succeed with your project. You spoke to me about writing a book. If one day you write and publish a book, I would very much like to read it. I hope you distribute as many copies as possible.

And Thomas said:

> It has given me pleasure to share my experiences. I hope you recount them. And if what you write helps people to be open-minded, that is the ultimate goal; to be open-minded and avoid psychological barriers. It would be as if I succeeded along with you.

Months after his interview, Vincent emailed me, saying:

> Our encounter was very powerful for me. It's funny to know that someone halfway around the world knows me better than my close friends. I have had a lot of highlights in my life. Our time together is one of them.

Such comments inspired me to keep making these trips and then spend more than three years writing this book.

Of course, the interviews did not happen in a vacuum. In France, attitudes toward non-European immigrants and their descendants are often intense. As readers of this book will likely know, many people in France complain about the purported behavior of such people, particularly those who live in the notorious *banlieues*. (While *banlieue* simply means suburb, the word is often used as a shorthand for the broken-down housing projects called *HLMs* or *cités* located on the outskirts of French cities.) In 2005, following the deaths of teenagers who had run from the police in a Parisian *banlieue* and the ensuing upheaval, then-Interior Minister Sarkozy famously vowed to use high-power water hoses to "clean out the scum."[3] In 2020, Interior Minister Gérald Darmanin went even further, speaking of the *ensauvagement* (roughly, becoming savage) of people who live in these communities. A series of large-scale terrorist attacks that rocked France in 2015–16 (the same period as my first trips) hardened feelings throughout the country. Mostly committed by self-described Muslims, these and later attacks have been used to stigmatize entire categories of people, usually labeled "Muslims," "Arabs," or "Maghrebis."

People of non-European origin are often criticized for their supposed failure of *intégration*—not the same word as "integration" in English, but more like "assimilation" or "fitting in." As Gérard Noiriel (1996) and others have chronicled, France has long been a country of immigrants. Until 1945, the vast majority came from elsewhere in Europe. Within a generation or two, people in these families had usually learned French, adopted core French values, and lived according to French norms. They had integrated themselves into the larger society and, having done so, came to be seen as French.[4] Many claim that the non-Europeans who have come to France since about 1945 have failed to do the same. Even worse, some argue, are these people's children and grandchildren—people who have spent their entire lives in France—who have purportedly refused to integrate themselves into French society. Speaking the nonstandard French of the *banlieues*, they are said to lack French values and to behave in antisocial, if not criminal, ways. Although most of these so-called "second-" and "third-generation immigrants"—a revealing oxymoron—are French citizens, many critics contend that they do not deserve to be seen as French. The problem, they claim, is not where their families came from, their religion, or their physical appearance, but their failure to integrate into French society.

Testing the validity of this position—that being accepted into French society has everything to do with *intégration* and nothing to do with physical appearance or religion—was the central goal of this ethnographic project. But rather than pursuing the airy abstraction of acceptance into French society, I decided to focus on the experiences and feelings of each interviewee. Had they worked to integrate themselves into the language, values, and norms of people they see as unquestionably French? If so, had they succeeded? Did they feel accepted? Especially among interviewees who grew up in France, questions of identity were central. Did they feel French? Did they feel that people whom they accept as unquestionably French see them as French? How have these feelings evolved over time?

As this book will show, the answers to these questions varied enormously. The level of acceptance felt by the interviewees ranges, to put it colloquially, from mostly through sort of, sometimes, in some ways, with some people, in some circumstances, to not at all. One near-constant, however, was the interviewee's identity in the eyes of others: even a person who feels French, and who has mastered the language, values, and norms of people they see as indisputably French, confronts a barrier grounded in their non-European physical appearance. To their dismay, the great majority of interviewees feel that they are seen as Maghrebi, Black, Asian, etc., *rather than* as French. With this identity comes a raft of social and economic consequences, including stereotyping, bias, and outright discrimination. More painful still is the emotional cost many reported, particularly in feelings of inferiority and a fear of rejection.[5] The most dramatic consequence is visited upon those who have spent their entire lives in France: if you are not seen as French, then what are you? The answer, according to many, is brutal: you are a foreigner in your own country.

Perhaps because almost all of the interviewees were Airbnb hosts—people with a room or apartment to rent, and thus participants in the larger economy—it turned out that the majority had attended French universities and subscribed to what they saw as French norms and values, notably *laïcité* (today largely seen as the exclusion of religion from the public sphere).[6] Although some were Muslim, none wore religiously oriented clothes like veils or skullcaps in public. Their homes were like other homes I have visited in France. Dozens of interviewees spoke explicitly and repeatedly about their success in integrating themselves into what they saw as the French way of life, with a few declaring that they had become "*plus français que les Français*" (more French than the French).

I should be clear about my own views here. I do not see such devotion to fitting into someone else's norms as inherently virtuous, and certainly don't think that conforming to the norms and whims of those in a dominant position should be a condition for acceptance. But this is an ethnographic project grounded in the accounts of flesh-and-blood people who have the feelings and attitudes they have. I listened as carefully as I could to these people as they spoke about their lives—about their goals, experiences, and feelings about issues that were important to them—and have tried to communicate their accounts faithfully.

As with the interviews, this book focuses on what individuals have experienced during their lives and how they have made sense of these experiences. This does not mean that the book is narrow in scope. To the contrary, by listening carefully to dozens of people who feel they are like millions of French people in virtually every way other than their non-European appearance (and, for some, religion or name), and then by reporting and synthesizing what they said, I have had a chance to provide an in-depth view of this important segment of people in France today. Their experiences may be relevant throughout Europe and beyond.

While the interviews were wide-ranging, they always included two issues: the interviewee's personal identity (how they think about themselves) at various periods of life and their sense of social identity (how others see them), particularly whether they felt accepted by those whose French identity they accept. These are hardly simple issues, and ambiguity, nuance, contradiction, and uncertainty—all the variety of human experience—came into play. Nor are these issues static. Like everyone else, the interviewees have gone through different stages of life. They have grown up and been educated, joined the work world, and held a variety of jobs at different levels. While some have remained single, most have married or entered into long-term relationships and have had children, even grandchildren. Some have gotten divorced or separated from their partners. They have lived in different neighborhoods, some in different cities. During the same period, France has undergone changes, too, including economic uncertainty, terrorism, and disputes relating to non-European immigration and the absorption of later generations. Through this sweep of time, each of the interviewees has had experiences that changed how they see themselves and how they feel others see them.

Since I was an inextricable participant in this process as both a visitor and interviewer, I should describe myself. I am in my late sixties and am considered "White" in the United States. As will be seen, various interviewees alluded to my skin color and the texture and color of my hair during the interviews, usually in comparison to their own or that of their family members (in some cases, noting that my skin is darker than theirs).[7] Obviously but also importantly, I was from elsewhere; someone who arrived by prearrangement in their home, joined them for meals and conversation for the day or two I stayed there, and then departed. Particularly during the interviews, which were conducted apart from other people, they spoke with me about issues that many had not discussed with people they know, including neighbors, friends, and coworkers with whom they interact every day. Further, I am not a member of French society. This was evident from my accented French and my unfamiliarity with the prejudices that anyone living in France would know. I did not think ill of the interviewees; indeed, I was eager to learn about life from their own perspective.

My own background should also be noted. Although I was born and raised in New York City, my father came to the United States as a young child, and my mother was a child of immigrants. While growing up, I heard stories of the bias they had faced in the US. During my twenties, I lived off and on in West Africa and did doctoral studies in anthropology. I then became a lawyer. Over the last fifteen years, I have returned to my original interest in other societies and ways of life, traveling to various countries, particularly Morocco and Mali, to listen to people talk about their lives and concerns. I have also worked closely with West African asylum-seekers in New York and taught an ethnography course.

OVERVIEW OF EXISTING ETHNOGRAPHIES

In recent years, there have been at least twenty-two book-length ethnographies focusing on people of non-European origin in France. These are Beaman (2017), Boucher (2010), Bowen (2017, 2010), Chuang (2021), Domergue (2010), Fernando (2014), Fleming (2017), Kastoryano (1986), Keaton (2006), Killian (2006), Kobelinsky (2010), Larchanché (2020), Mahut (2017), M. Mazouz (1988), Provencher (2017), Rigaud (2010), Selby (2012), P. Silverstein (2004), Slooter (2019), Sourou (2016), and Tetreault (2015).[8] Many are of high quality and all contribute to the literature about the populations they address. Even taken together, however, these ethnographies leave some imbalances and gaps:

- More than half of these ethnographies focus substantially or exclusively on Paris or its *banlieues*.[9] This leaves areas throughout France—including the metropolitan areas of Lille, Lyon, Marseille, Nantes, Nice, Strasbourg, and Toulouse—largely unrepresented.
- The majority focus either primarily or exclusively on Maghrebi people.[10] Only three focus on Black people.[11]
- Only a few of these ethnographies cover more than one geographical area in France or more than one social category of people (e.g., Maghrebis).
- Many target very specialized populations. These include asylum applicants at a residential center; people who sought services at a psychiatric services center; people who sought services at an intercultural center; people of Laotian origin living in Montpelier; people who recently left a single African city to settle in the Paris area; fourteen teenage girls living in a Paris *banlieue*; and people of Martinican or Guadeloupean origin in the Paris area.[12]
- While most focus on poor or marginalized people—an extremely important segment of society—only a few address those who have made their way into the middle class.

Another limitation arises from the studies' methodologies. While many are rich in detail, few seem to have had extensive recordings to draw upon. This may be understandable, particularly among groups or in public places, but many important details are lost in even the most thorough field notes. These may include patterns of speech and word choices, shifts in affect, and signals of interactional dynamics. By contrast, a large library of recordings allows the ethnographer to listen, listen, and listen again after fieldwork is complete, as I did during the first two years of the Covid pandemic. Recordings also allow the readers of this book to "hear" much of what was said through hundreds of direct quotes. I hope these passages provide an immediacy, and perhaps a deeper understanding, of the interviewees' lived experiences than any paraphrasing could.

PIVOTAL TERMS

Since this book focuses on the interviewees' accounts, the words they used in describing themselves and others require special attention. This is especially true where words have a different meaning from what English speakers would understand by their apparent English equivalent (what the French aptly call "false friends").

Français. While *Français* (feminine: *Française*) means "French," of course, most interviewees use the word in a distinctive way. People of non-European origin who were born and raised in France—people who may speak only French, who fully share French values, and who feel themselves to be French—are usually *not* referred to as "French." Except when speaking of their own sense of identity—many said, often emphatically, "I am French"—most interviewees reserved the word for people who have all these attributes *and* a perceived European physical appearance.[13] Throughout this book, I will follow these interviewees' way of speaking, putting "French" in quotes where needed to communicate the kind of person they see as indisputably French.

Various people pointed to the importance of skin color, together with the associated hair texture and color, shape of nose, eyes, etc., to being seen as "French." These include interviewees who grew up in France and are fully integrated into French values and norms of behavior, even those who say they are French. This way of speaking arose repeatedly. For Caroline, "a French person is White." If Jean refers to someone as "French," he said, "implicitly, I'd be saying that he's White." Karim thinks that it is "impossible" to be French without being White. Tsiory believes that any children he has in France would never be considered French because French people are "White, White, White." Slapping his arm, François said bitterly, "to be French is in the skin."

Hiba's interview brought home the equation of skin color with being seen as French. She and her husband are of Berber (rather than Arab) origin, she says, and their son has the same relatively pale skin as they have. Laughing, she put her arm next to mine and said, "You're darker than me. My son is more French than you!" That my life story and accent make it obvious that I'm American was not at issue. For Hiba, her son is "more French" than I am because his skin is lighter than mine.

Of course, being "French" is not an absolute; some people are neither entirely "French" nor entirely something else. A person with lighter skin may be seen, in Hiba's words, as "more French" than someone with darker skin. The same sliding scale may operate with regard to religion (some consider Catholics to be more French than Muslims), name (European names are said to be more French than non-European names), and behavior (one interviewee eliminated his "expressive" gestures, he said, in order to be "more French"). But to be seen as indisputably French, almost all said that one must have a European appearance.

Maghrebis, Blacks, and Asians. Because the interviewees used the terms *Maghrébins*, *Noirs*, or *Asiatiques* to describe themselves and people they identify as like them, I use the translations Maghrebis, Blacks, and Asians for such people.[14] As discussed below, the main basis for being seen as Maghrebi, Black, or Asian is a person's perceived physical appearance and assumed geographical origin. But one must be careful when using these terms. Despite their grounding in a perceived physical appearance (and thus the terms' seeming objective reality to the interviewees), there is nothing essential about them. In other words, there is no biological or genetic basis for being seen as Maghrebi, Black, or Asian—or, for that matter, as French, European, or White. These are all social categories.

Race, racisme, and raciste. The interviewees used *racisme* and *raciste* much as Americans use "racism" and "racist," but that was not true of *race*. The highly contested status of race in French society is apparent from how the interviewees used—and did not use—the word. Jean, who identifies himself as Black, said that "although there are people who speak of the black race, there is no black race. There's only the human race." But apart from Jean's rejection of a "black race," few people used the word *race* except to report times "French" people used it at their expense. Lina and Khira both reported being called "dirty Arab" or "dirty race" over the years, and Sami complained that people used the slogan "France for the French" to talk about "the White race." One day, a classmate of Elise's blurted out, "*nique ta race*" (roughly, "fuck your race").

Even if the word *race* was rarely used, the interviewees frequently described themselves and others according to perceived physical types. The word they typically used was *faciès*.

Faciès. While *faciès* (also *faciès* in plural) can be translated as "facial appearance" or "facial type," interviewees used this word to refer to a physical appearance thought to be characteristic of people who originate from a certain region of the world. The different perceived *faciès*—all stereotypes—were readily described by the interviewees. An "Arab *faciès*," they said, entails dark skin, curly black hair, and brown eyes. Maghrebis may have either an "Arab *faciès*" or a Berber *faciès*, like Hiba's, with stereotypically lighter skin. The *faciès* of Blacks is said to include very dark skin color, coiled black hair, and a broad nose. Like other Asians, Henri has, in his words, a "Chinese face," and Tsiory spoke of his "slanted eyes." A European *faciès* is said to involve pale skin, straight blond, red, or brown hair, a pointed nose, and eyes of any color.

One's perceived *faciès* is pivotal to one's social identity; that is, to how one is seen by others. Thus, while immigrants whose *faciès* are seen as European can become "French" once they or their children speak unaccented French and adopt French values and norms, this is not true for people from Africa and Asia, who, as Nadia said, "have a different *faciès*." Both Nour and Olivier are not seen as "French" despite their French values and behavior because, each of them reported, of "my *faciès*."

Some of the interviewees (and even more of the interviewees' children) have one parent of European origin and one of non-European origin. Such people, known as *métis* (feminine *métisse*; of mixed parents), would physiologically have a mixture of *faciès*, but, according to the interviewees, that is not how they are seen. Where the *faciès* of the parent of non-European origin is still evident in someone's appearance, he or she is seen as that kind of person. François's children are *métis* and, although they were raised by their "French" mothers, he says that they are seen as Black rather than French. Abdel, whose father is "French" and mother Maghrebi, said that he is seen as Arab because of his "Arab head." The case of Henri and his son is instructive. Henri, whose mother is Asian and father "French," is seen as Asian because of what he called his "Asian *faciès*," but he said that his son, whose mother is "French," has a "European *faciès*" and has been able to present himself as "French."

Depending on the context, the word *faciès* will be translated as "physical appearance" or left in the original French.

Typé. While *typé* (feminine: *typée*) can be translated as "typed" or "typical," interviewees use the term in a distinct way: having the *faciès* characteristic of a familiar "type" of person. Maghrebis use this word to refer to someone who looks Arab. Samuel said that he has been "*typé*" since childhood, so is seen as "an Arab, not French." Elise said that she is only "a bit *typée*," while her brother Abdel, with his "very curly hair and beard," is "more *typé*." Asma's supervisor at work refused to use her Maghrebi first name, saying "Arabs, they're too much. What's more, you're pretty, not at all *typée*. You'll be Nicole."

To be more *typé* is to be less "French" in the eyes of others. For Clément, who is Black, a truly French person is "White, without color, not *typé*." And being more *typé* makes life more difficult. Vincent said that his son, whose mother is "French," has had fewer problems because "he's less *typé* in an Indian way."

Whites. The noun White (*Blanc*) is simple to translate but complicated in how it is used. As discussed below, the interviewees use the word "French" to index the (presumed) fact that the person being referred to would, *unlike the interviewee*, be seen as White. But, apparently unlike "French" people, the interviewees also use the word White for "French" (or "European") people. This was most pronounced among interviewees who identify themselves as Black: they used White interchangeably with "French." A few of the Maghrebi, Asian, and other interviewees also used White in this way, although far less frequently.[15]

Français (or Française) de souche. This expression, roughly meaning "of French stock" or "French to one's root," refers to a person whose family has been in France for generations. Vincent, Karim, and others used this term to describe their choice of romantic partners or spouses. Emphasizing that his girlfriend "had no foreign origin at all" and that "physically, she represented the French woman," Samuel called her a "*Française de pure souche*." The term also arose when interviewees spoke of the National Front slogan "France for the French."[16] According to Fouzia, "When people say 'France for the French,' they mean 'France for the *Français de souche*.'" Excluded are people like Fouzia, who were born and raised in France and live like "French" people, but don't have a European *faciès*.

Intégration and assimilation. *Intégration* is the process by which an individual fits into a group of people, as when a new student fits into her new school or a person acts in accordance with a group's social norms. With his non-*banlieue* clothes, behavior, and language, Jean said, "I'm very well integrated." Yuka is sure she has "integrated" herself into her "French" community because, she said, "in my everyday life, when I go out, when I do something, I do it like other people." Since it might cause unnecessary confusion to translate this word as "integration," which Americans generally use to describe people of different "races" living in the same community or attending the same school, this book will often leave *intégration* in the French.

Unlike *intégration*, the French word *assimilation* will be uniformly translated as "assimilation," since the English word has much the same meaning. Although largely out of date in France (*assimilation* having been largely supplanted by *intégration*), it was used by a few interviewees. Abbas complained that even when people from outside Europe "try to integrate themselves, to assimilate," French people "continue to reject them." And Karim said he has done everything possible to "assimilate" into French society, but still feels that he will "never be accepted by the French."

THE LITERATURE RELATING TO RACE IN FRANCE

Lurking behind the interviewees' use of these words are issues that have received enormous attention in the academic community. Is it meaningful to talk about race in France? If so, what does race mean in that context? What are the perceived races in France today, and how are they interrelated? Is it significant that the interviewees rarely use the word *race* except in recounting insults by "French" people?

Instead of providing a full-blown literature review, I focus on what is important to this ethnography: the writers who are most helpful in understanding what the interviewees mean by such words as *race*, *faciès*, and *typé*, and such categories as *Français*, *Maghrébin*, *Noir*, and *Asiatique*. The eminent sociologist Stuart Hall lays the groundwork. In a speech given in 1996, Hall described race as a "floating signifier" that

> *works like a language*. And signifiers refer to the systems and concepts of the classification of a culture, to its practices for *making meaning*. [They] gain their meaning . . . in the shifting relations of difference, which they establish with other concepts and ideas in a signifying field. Their meaning, because it is relational, and not essential, [is] different in different cultures, in different historical formations at different moments of time. (Hall 2021: 362; emphasis Hall's)

Hall argues that race is founded on a presumed "Nature = Culture" equivalence. Even though race has been debunked scientifically, as a cultural concept it "is made to follow on from nature, to lean on it for its justification" (367). And because race is simultaneously culture and (presumed) nature, "these two systems . . . correspond with one another, in such a way that it is possible to read off the one against the other" (367). In another essay, Hall provides an example from Europe: "'Blackness' has functioned as a sign that the people of African descent are closer to Nature, and *therefore* more likely to be lazy, lacking in higher intellectual faculties, driven by emotion rather than Reason" (Hall 2000: 223; emphasis his). "[T]he body is a text. And we are all readers of it. . . . We are readers of race, that's what we are doing, we are readers of social difference" (Hall 2021: 369).[17]

The interviewees' use of the terms *Maghrébin*, *Noir*, and *Asiatique* (translated here as Maghrebi, Black, and Asian) exemplifies Hall's theory. Although they live in different parts of France and come from an enormous range of personal and family backgrounds, these people spoke in essentially the same way. For them, someone who is thought to look like an Arab or Berber is labeled Maghrebi. A person with dark skin and coiled hair, perhaps with a wide nose and thick lips, is seen as Black. Someone with a "Chinese face" and "slanted eyes" is seen as Asian. And while individuals vary widely in physical appearance—Elise described her brother Abdel as more *typé* than her, François is darker than his *métis* children—they are all classified according to the same relational system. Anyone can be "read" physically as a certain type of human being within this system and be presumed to have certain "natural" qualities, such as temperament and level of intelligence.

As will be seen in the chapters to come, this classificatory scheme has deeply affected the interviewees' lives. Hall's description of how Blackness functions in European societies is played out among the interviewees in France who are seen as Black, both in grossly demeaning stereotypes and ways in which they report being treated (chapter 2). Similarly, people who are seen as Maghrebi or Asian are thought to be a certain way naturally, and many interviewees report being treated accordingly (chapters 1 and 3).[18]

But what about ethnicity, which Hall describes as the "discourse where difference is grounded in cultural and religious features" (Hall 2000: 223)? Aren't Maghrebi, Black, and Asian all, to an important extent, cultural as well as racial categories? While this question cannot be fully addressed until the end of this book—after these categories and such related issues as religion are discussed in detail—it is worth bearing in mind that people lumped in the same category may trace their origins to different cultural traditions, and that many of the interviewees are culturally far more similar to "French" people than to their forebears in distant countries. Hall's theory of the relationship between ethnicity and race should be cited, as it will prove to be instructive:

> [T]hose who are stigmatized on ethnic grounds, because they are "culturally different" and therefore inferior, are often *also* characterized as physically different in significant ways. . . . The more "ethnicity" matters, the more its characteristics are represented as relatively fixed, inherent within a group, transmitted from generation to generation, not just by culture and education, but by biological inheritance. . . . Biological racism and cultural differentialism, therefore, constitute not two different systems, but racism's two registers. (Ibid.; emphasis his)

This leaves the category of people seen as "French." Here the sociologist Colette Guillaumin's theory of racism in France proves useful. Writing in 1972, Guillaumin points to "the occultation of the Self, of which [White] people have no spontaneous awareness" (Guillaumin 1995 [1972]: 50).[19] The "racism prevalent in France," she contends, "recognizes only others and not itself. . . . It offers its own completely adequate explanation of lived experience, one that is literally so blindingly obvious that it prevents its proponents from also seeing, specifying and designating themselves as a race" (52). This racism "is so deeply ingrained in our social system that it distorts language to its own ends" (51). White is "used mainly adjectively," while such words as Black and Asian "have become nouns" (ibid.).

A number of anthropologists and sociologists have recently focused on the anomalous position of Whites in French society. Citing Guillaumin, Didier Fassin notes how the French language reveals "what people would rather hide—racism" (D. Fassin 2006b: 34). Only recently, Didier and Eric Fassin write, have some people "come to realize that the people called 'French' turn out to be 'white'" (D. and E. Fassin 2006: 9). Sarah Mazouz builds on the thinking of W.E.B. Du Bois and Frantz Fanon, as well as of Guillaumin and Fassin, in distinguishing between the concepts of "racialization" (the "logics by which racial hierarchies are produced") and "racisation" (the "process by which a dominant group defines a dominated group as constituting a race") (S. Mazouz 2020: 48–49; see Cohen and S. Mazouz 2021: 5–9). Controlling the process by which others are seen as (inferior) races, Whites are "racialized but in no way racized" (S. Mazouz 2020: 49). "Whiteness is invisible" (Cohen and S. Mazouz 2021: 8).

While these writers help explain why people seen as White speak of themselves as French rather than White, the interviewees' use of the word French is more nuanced. Many, such as Samuel, Nour, Hiba, Clément, Anna, Isabel, Henri, and Shayan, say "I am French" and yet, when referring to others, use the same word to indicate that the person has, *unlike them*, a European *faciès*. This is what Samuel, Nour, Anna, Isabel, Henri, and Shayan meant when they spoke of their spouses or partners as "French," often following up this reference with a physical description. Similarly, those like Henri and Samuel, who had such a parent, described that parent as "French."

Further, French was *not* the word these people typically used when referring to themselves. Samuel has spent his whole life in France, has had a successful career among "French" people, and now lives in a wealthy neighborhood where, he said, "90 percent of the people are French." And while he responded, "I'm French," when I asked about his personal identity, he referred to himself as Maghrebi or Arab throughout two days of conversations and five hours of interviewing, often emphasizing his "Arab" appearance. Other interviewees did much the same, saying "I'm French" when asked about their identity, but usually referring to themselves as Black, Asian, or Maghrebi in other contexts.[20]

The sociolinguistic concept of "shifter" helps explain this choice of words. The reference of a term "shifts" regularly, "depending on the factors of a speech situation" that are presupposed by a "rule of use" when the speaker "indexes" something distinct in that situation. (M. Silverstein 1976: 24–25; see Gal and Irvine 2019). The circumstances and conditions being "indexed" by people like Samuel will be illustrated throughout this book: though they view themselves as French according to an ideology of Frenchness grounded in such non-physical qualities as a lifetime spent in France, adherence to such values as *laïcité* and *intégration*, and the quality of one's French, they are prevented by their *faciès* from being accepted as French socially. They may feel French, but, as they know too well, they aren't seen as French. Their *social* identity—Black, Asian, Maghrebi, etc., rather than French—is routinely indexed, and implicitly acknowledged, in their choice of words. Samuel's romantic relationship with a "French" woman—in his words, a "blonde with blue eyes!"—made him feel that he had entered "into the world that didn't want me." In ending the relationship, Samuel said, she "put me back in my place as a Maghrebi."

Where did the concept of race and the different categories of race come from? While this issue has also generated a vast literature, the historian Pap Ndiaye helps contextualize the interviewees' experience. "The modern notion of 'race,'" he says, "was invented to justify colonial domination, particularly slavery" (2008: 76; 2009: 48).[21] At least from the time of France's colonial conquests, "to be French was to be white" (2008: 84). "Whiteness was an index of normality and universality. It served as a criterion of civilization" (2008: 77), while "the populations being subjugated were defined as non-white and non-civilized" (2008: 84).

The salience of race did not dim as time went on. As Ndiaye reports, "during the period between the two World Wars, the racialization of French identity went hand in hand with a celebration of colonial exoticism, [serving to] distinguish the civilized from the non-civilized, the 'us' from the 'them'" (2008: 88). But this is not just history; "the imaginaries of racial stereotypes" dating from colonialism "persist over time" (2009: 55).

The question remains: does the concept of race really apply to France? Many argue that it does. In making this argument, historians like Ndiaye draw on centuries of French history, including France's involvement in the slave trade, its fabulously profitable exploitation of enslaved people in the Caribbean colonies, and its vast colonial empire, but also the nineteenth and early twentieth century pseudoscience of race advocated by such Frenchmen as Arthur de Gobineau and Georges Vacher de Lapouge, the World War II Vichy government, and Jean-Marie Le Pen's National Front party (see, e.g., Noiriel 2006 and 2010; Beaud and Noiriel 2021; Ndiaye 2008; and Bleich 2004). Others argue that France has been a champion of race-free thinking and, sometimes, race-blind governance during the same period. They, too, have a rich history to cite, including the 1789 Declaration of the Rights of Man and the Citizen, the French Constitution, the 1978 law prohibiting the collection of statistics based on race,[22] even the national motto "Liberty, Equality, and Fraternity" (see ibid.).[23] Both sides are right at least in one way: for more than two centuries, two diametrically opposed ideologies have been powerful forces in French thought and action.

As will be seen in the chapters to come, these ideologies struggle against each other today in the lives of the interviewees. In Stuart Hall's way of thinking, races configure much of the social world in which they live in the form of a classificatory system by which people are "read." In France (a case of less concern to Hall), people are read as either White, referentially called "French," or as Maghrebi, Black, Asian, etc. Grounded in a stereotyped *faciès* that sets each of these presumed types of people apart—with the most *typé* appearance as its archetype—each individual is "read" as being one or another of these categories. With this socio-physical identity comes a presumed biological identity that is, in turn, presumed to correlate with certain behavioral tendencies. That is the world the interviewees must inhabit. But, at the same time, the great majority of interviewees reject much of this way of thinking. At least one of them rejects the classificatory scheme itself, and those who accept it overwhelmingly reject its presumed "Nature = Culture" linkage. Often citing the strain of French ideology by which all people are equal and undifferentiated, these interviewees reject the stereotypes, biases, and outright discrimination that attach to their social identity.

CHAPTER OUTLINE

The interviewees' vast richness of experience posed a challenge in organizing this book. For the initial chapters, I chose to group the interviewees according to the categories that they themselves use. Two of these categories, Maghrebi and Black, were especially salient: throughout their interviews, people continually referenced these identities when discussing their lives in France and in describing how they felt that others, especially "French" people, saw them. Chapters 1 and 2, respectively, focus on interviewees of these two identities. The remaining categories were far less fraught. Asians (*Asiatiques*, who are seen as having an East Asian *faciès*) constitute a third category. And then there are the interviewees who originate from different parts of South or Western Asia. They do not fall into a distinct group, but, because of their non-European (non-White) *faciès*, they too are not seen as "French." Flagging the stigma that attaches to Maghrebis and Blacks in France, a number of these interviewees made clear that they are not confused with such people. The absence of this stigma among both Asians and people who originate from South or Western Asia provided the logic for discussing both groups in chapter 3. As one of the interviewees said, apart from people with a European *faciès,* there are three types of people in France: Maghrebis, Blacks, and everyone else.

Each of these chapters begins with a detailed profile of one interviewee, followed by a dozen or so shorter profiles, all using the interviewee's own words as much as possible.[24] The demeaning stereotypes, especially of Maghrebis and Blacks, are presented as plainly as the interviewees reported them. Much of what they said was painful to hear and may be painful to read. The profiles tell only part of the story, however. Since each profile provides a sense of only one person's life, the profiles in each chapter are followed by a discussion of similarities of experience among interviewees of that group. For example, chapter 2 addresses discrimination that many Black interviewees reported enduring in various aspects of life. Recognizing that people who share a social identity often have similar experiences—after all, they all live in France and are seen as Black (or Maghrebi, Asian, etc.)—is vital to understanding the conditions they face.

The rest of the book, chapters 4–6, addresses experiences that are shared by people across all non-European *faciès* and presumed origins (transcending the categories of chapters 1–3). Chapter 4 discusses feelings of inferiority and the fear of rejection among all categories of interviewees. This involves both the "colonialism in the head" reported by some and its flip side, the feeling of superiority many sense among "French" people, which they attribute to the persisting effects of colonialism. Chapter 4 also notes the lack of any feeling of inferiority or fear of rejection among most of the interviewees and summarizes the strategies they use to avoid these corrosive emotions. Finally, it reports a striking pattern among the interviewees who originate from countries that had not experienced colonial control by Europeans: none of them feel inferior to people of European origin.

Chapter 5 is devoted to feelings of romantic desire and the choice of spouse or long-term partner, again across the full spectrum of interviewees. Many interviewees recounted their experiences, even fantasies, with astonishing candor. While men and women sought different qualities in romantic attachments, as well as in spouses or other long-term partners, the majority of both genders gravitated toward "French" people. Where an interviewee chose a "French" spouse or partner, the long-term success or failure of the relationship correlated closely with how comfortable the interviewee felt in French society.

Finally, chapter 6 takes up the experience of being Muslim or assumed to be Muslim. According to the interviewees, Muslims are stereotyped as culturally backward, unwilling to fit into French society, and fundamentally opposed to French values, particularly *laïcité*. This is problematic for many interviewees. Although none of these people resemble this stereotype, they find themselves socially tarnished by it. And then there is the not-so-obvious question of who is Muslim. According to the interviewees, most "French" people assume that Maghrebis are Muslim and assume that non-Maghrebis (or non-Arabs) are not. But neither generalization is borne out by the interviewees: some Maghrebis are not Muslim, and some Blacks and other interviewees are. For both sets of people, however, the issue is not left to their private lives. Many "French" people, interviewees believe, try to ferret out whether they are practicing Muslims in a recurring moment of life in France: when they are offered wine or a pork dish at a social occasion.

The conclusion highlights larger themes in the interviewees' lives and relates these themes to the relevant statistical and scholarly literature. As with this book overall, I hope it fosters a greater appreciation of people like the interviewees, who are fully involved in the life of their country.

Finally, the appendix sets out basic facts about each interviewee—age, gender, country of origin, time in France, education, and employment—and the pages where each is mentioned. Readers are encouraged to refer to the appendix as they read the chapters to be reminded of who a person is and where else in the book that person is discussed.

NOTES

1. While there do not seem to be statistics on the income levels of Airbnb hosts in France, the majority of hosts in the UK earned over £30,500 a year as of 2014–15 (Statista 2015).
2. The omission of where the interviewees live proved less significant than one might imagine. With the partial exception of Paris, the interviewees' experiences relating to their sense of self and acceptance by others did not vary according to the metropolitan area in which they live. Where the size of a city is significant to a person's account, this is noted.
3. The word Mr. Sarkozy used, *racailles*, has a long history. As early as the sixteenth century, its then-current form, *racure*, was used disdainfully for France's urban poor. During the colonial period, *racailles* was used, again disdainfully, for colonized peoples, including Vietnamese and North Africans (Ruscio 2020: 117–19).
4. This is obviously a broad-brush generalization. There are whole categories of European immigrants, notably Roma, who remain marginalized over multiple generations. In some quarters, there are also biases

against Jews and darker-skinned people of European origin, even in later generations. Finally, some people distinguish between families that have been in France—even in a specific community—for generations and families that arrived more recently.

5. Some, of course, have risen above such hurts, showing extraordinary strength. See chapter 4 below.
6. Although this shorthand is not incorrect, as John Bowen (2007: 20–33) explains, there is no generally accepted or stable concept of *laïcité.* Indeed, "there is no historical actor called laïcité: only a series of debates, laws, and multiple efforts to assert claims over public space. . . . In sum," he says, "there is no 'it'" (2007: 33).
7. My physical appearance was hardly incidental to this project. As the French anthropologist Didier Fassim says, "the anthropologist himself cannot elude his own bodily presence in the game of racial unveiling: he is entirely part of it" (D. Fassin 2011: 421).
8. In addition, ethnographies by Didier Fassin (2013) and Sarah Mazouz (2017) focus on personnel in government agencies who interact primarily with people of non-European origin.
9. These are Beaman (2017), Bowen (2007, 2010), Chuang (2021), Fernando, (2014), Fleming (2017), Keaton (2006), Killian (2006), Kobelinsky (2010), Kastoryano (1988), Larchaché (2020), Mahut (2017), M. Mazouz (1988), Provencher (2017), Selby (2012), P. Silverstein (2004), Slooter (2019), and Tetreault (2015).
10. These are Beaman (2017), Bowen (2007, 2010), Domergue (2010), Fernando (2014), Keaton (2006), Killian (2006), Kobelinsky (2010), M. Mazouz (1988), Provencher (2017), Selby (2012), P. Silverstein (2014), and Tetreault (2015).
11. These are Keaton (2006), Mahut (2017), and Slooter (2019).
12. These are, respectively, Kobelinsky (2010), Larchaché (2020), Sourou (2016), Rigaud (2010), Mahut (2017), Keaton (2006), and Fleming (2017). Another five, Beaman (2017), Killian (2006), M. Mazouz (1998), Selby (2012), and Tetreault (2015), focus exclusively or primarily on a specific cohort of people: Maghrebis in the Paris area.
13. By "European" or "French" I mean nothing more nor less than what the interviewees mean. As discussed below, there is no essence to these words or any other social category, and the only dividing lines between those who qualify as a certain kind of person and those who don't are the ones they draw themselves.
14. While the French adjective *asiatique* means Asian in a general sense, interviewees limited the noun *Asiatique* to people with a physical appearance they associate with East Asia. Thus, while all such interviewees used *Asiatique* to describe themselves, none of the interviewees who originate from elsewhere in Asia described themselves this way. Because the English word Asiatic is outdated and offensive among many English speakers, I translate *Asiatique* as "Asian."
15. Virtually all Black interviewees routinely used the noun White in this way, and this book contains nearly a hundred direct quotes in which

they use this term. By contrast, only two of the interviewees who identify as Maghrebi and four who identify as Asian are quoted as using White in this way, and even they used "French" far more often. One interviewee who spoke of his "Indian *faciès*" and another who originates from Iran used the word White, but only once each.

16. The *Front National* (National Front) party was renamed *Rassemblement National* (National Rally) in June 2018, after most of the interviews were complete.
17. According to Hall, this marker of social difference is far from neutral: "'Race' is a political and social construct. It is the ongoing discursive category around which has been constructed a system of socio-economic power, exploitation and exclusion—i.e., racism" (Hall 2000: 222).
18. The interviewees who aren't seen as Maghrebi, Black, or Asian—those who originate from Turkey, Iran, Pakistan, or India—fall into the residual category of people with non-European *faciès* discussed in chapter 3.
19. Throughout this book, I quote from published translations of foreign-language sources. Where these are unavailable, the translations are my own.
20. Readers may be reminded of W.E.B. Du Bois's concept of "double consciousness" here. Its applicability to France today, especially among people classified as Black, is discussed at the end of chapter 2.
21. Ndiaye 2006 and chapter 2 of Ndiaye 2008 are nearly identical. Where the same quote appears in both publications, I hereafter cite only the better-known work, Ndiaye 2008.
22. Subject to limited exceptions, the 1978 law makes it unlawful "to collect or process data of a personal nature that reveal, directly or indirectly, the racial or ethnic origins" of anyone (Simon 2008: 19).
23. Although it is often argued that "Republican" ideology has been race-blind, at least during the colonial period this was largely untrue (see, e.g., Bancel and Blanchard 2017a; Ndiaye 2008: 83–84).
24. Since people spoke spontaneously, sometimes changing direction mid-sentence, some of the quoted passages in this book have been edited or condensed for clarity. Similarly, since some people spoke about the same subject at different points in their interviews, some quotes have been combined.

PART I

ONE

MAGHREBIS

Making Their Way in French Society

As most readers of this book will know, the Maghreb region of Northwestern Africa, particularly Algeria, Morocco, and Tunisia, and the people who trace their origins to the Maghreb, known as Maghrebis, play a major role in the history, demography, and politics of France. A general background may still be helpful.

The modern period of French involvement in the Maghreb dates back nearly two centuries, to 1830, when France began conquering the coast of what is today Algeria. Almost immediately, the economic opportunities opened up by France's control of this region drew large numbers of European settlers. In 1848, with the conquest of northern Algeria complete, France absorbed this area, with its cities and expanses of arable land, as *départements*; that is, as administrative units of France itself. But unlike the *départements* of mainland France (the "metropole"), Algeria's population—primarily composed of Arabs and Kabyles, a Berber ethnic group—was subject to two profoundly different legal statuses: the European settlers were French citizens, while the vast majority of Maghrebis were French "subjects" with virtually no rights.[1]

By 1871, there were almost 300,000 people of European descent living in Algeria. This number increased to 800,000 by 1914, and to more than a million by 1960. Familiarly known as *pieds-noirs*, these people dominated commerce in the coastal cities, especially Algiers, and ultimately owned almost 90 percent of the arable land, which they hired Maghrebis to farm for extremely low wages. The mass of Maghrebis—by the 1950s, totaling almost ten million—were left with few rights and meager economic resources. Beginning in 1954, a bloody war of independence wracked Algeria. As the struggle intensified, it roiled

French politics so severely that it contributed to the collapse of France's Fourth Republic in 1958. A 1961 demonstration by Algerians in Paris was met with brutality by the police, who killed more than one hundred demonstrators. Finally, in 1962, after eight years of war and approximately 300,000 deaths, Algeria became an independent country. About 800,000 *pieds-noirs* fled to mainland France, together with about 90,000 Algerians who had fought on the French side, known as *harkis*. Even after resettling in France, many former *pieds-noirs* maintained a deep disdain toward people of Algerian origin.

France's involvement with Tunisia and Morocco was shorter, less intrusive, and less violent than with Algeria. France forced Tunisia to become one of its "protectorates" in the early 1880s. Control of Morocco came later and more gradually. France established zones of influence in parts of Morocco in 1904 and made it a protectorate in 1912. While France developed significant economic interests in both Tunisia and Morocco, neither developed a European settler community on the scale of Algeria. Tunisia and Morocco gained independence in 1956 without significant violence.

During the thirty years following World War II—both before and after these countries had gained independence from France—large numbers of Maghrebis came to France for work. With France experiencing economic growth and a chronic labor shortage during the so-called *Trente Glorieuses*, French companies actively recruited manual laborers, especially Berbers, from the Maghreb. While many of these people returned "home" to retire, others remained in France. France closed the door to economic migrants in 1974, when its economy fell into recession, but two years later instituted a policy permitting "family reunification," which drew large numbers of the workers' wives and children to France. Net migration from the Maghreb continues through the present. Of the 63 million people living in mainland France in 2011, an estimated 3.8 million people (6 percent) were of Maghrebi origin (Tribalat 2015: 9).[2]

The term Maghrebi is not limited to immigrants from the Maghreb or people living there. As discussed in the introduction, the term is used in France for anyone who is perceived as Maghrebi, and thus is presumed to have a Maghrebi origin. The main basis for this social identity, interviewees reported, is a person's *faciès*: those whose Arab or Berber *faciès* is discernible will be seen as Maghrebi.[3] This is the case with Nour, Fouzia, Zhora, Samuel, and Abdel, even though each of them was born and grew up in France and has little attachment to the Maghreb or Maghrebi culture. People of mixed Maghrebi and "French" parentage, like Samuel and Abdel, are also seen as Maghrebi if they are thought to look Maghrebi. A recognizably Maghrebi name may also suggest a Maghrebi identity, though this assumption apparently can be neutralized where a person (like Selma, as discussed below) has a European *faciès* and European parentage.

Although many "French" people harbor particular ill will toward people they identify as Algerian, including those who have spent their entire lives in France, this attitude extends to other Maghrebis. According to the interviewees, many "French" people see Maghrebis as stubbornly clinging to a religion and way of life that is antithetical to French norms. Maghrebis supposedly indulge in criminality and abuse France's generous benefits programs. Even those who were born in France are thought by some to stick together, adhering to *communautarisme* (roughly, keeping apart from the rest of French society) rather than *intégration*.

Attitudes toward Maghrebis became particularly harsh following a series of terrorist attacks in France in 2015–16. On 7 January 2015, French-born brothers of Algerian origin attacked the Paris offices of Charlie Hebdo, a political satire magazine, killing twelve people and injuring eleven.[4] On 13 November 2015, coordinated attacks in Paris at the Stade de France soccer stadium, the Bataclan theater, and several bars and restaurants resulted in 130 deaths and 416 injuries. Planned by the Islamic State of Iraq and Syria (ISIS, also known as ISIL or Daesh), the perpetrators of these attacks were Arab Muslims. On 14 July 2016, a Tunisian man living in France rammed a truck into a crowd of people celebrating Bastille Day in Nice, killing eighty-six people and injuring 458. Since 2016, there have been more than twenty terrorist attacks in France. Although none were as destructive as the 2015–16 attacks, some—particularly the 2020 beheading of Samuel Paty, a high school teacher who had purportedly shown disrespect for the prophet Muhammad—have gained harsh news coverage. Most of these attacks have been blamed on "radical Muslims," and many of the assailants were described as Maghrebis or Arabs.

Today, millions of Maghrebis in France are relegated to rundown public housing projects in the poor, ethnic communities that surround French cities. Many of these people are deeply marginalized from French society—geographically, economically, politically, and culturally—and do not speak, act, or dress according to traditional French norms. The interviewees for this project are different. Almost all have been well-educated in francophone schools (most at French universities), speak "good" French, believe in core French values, including *laïcité*, live in middle-class, mixed communities, and dress and act like the "French" people around them. Unlike some people in the poor, ethnic suburbs, the women are not veiled, and the men do not wear skullcaps in public.[5] They have jobs within the larger French economy and work with "French" people.[6]

ZHORA

"Your project interests me, of course," read the message that Zhora sent me the morning before my arrival, so we met in time to discuss it at dinner. I took the metro to her home, a small but carefully maintained house in town, and we talked about the project and her life. The interview began the next day after breakfast and continued at her kitchen table or in the living room for much of the day. Zhora was at turns hurt, angry, nostalgic, and proud. She often laughed at the incongruities of her life.

Now in her early fifties and divorced, Zhora lives on her own after raising three children. Her parents, both Berbers from Algeria, had never planned or even wanted to come to France. At seventeen, her father-to-be escaped the life of a shepherd by taking a job with the French army as a gardener at a military post, but evidently did not realize that this made him a *harki*. "How young, how naive" he must have been, Zhora thought. This was in 1961, shortly before France lost the war. The French army evacuated in 1962, leaving behind most of the *harkis* to be killed by the victorious Algerian army. Zhora's parents-to-be were lucky: they escaped on the last helicopter out of Algeria. Their first child, a son, had been born that morning.

The family began their lives in France at a former World War II internment camp, where armed French guards kept the Algerians from escaping. "It was winter and there weren't even blankets, nothing," Zhora's parents would later tell her. Her father was then recruited to be a miner elsewhere in France, and he was shipped to the city near the mine. The family soon joined him, settling in a poor, immigrant community in the *banlieue.* Zhora was born two years later, and other children followed.

While neither parent spoke French at first, they insisted that their children speak only French at home. They would declare, "We were Algerian, but we're no longer Algerian. We will be French." They also insisted that their children get excellent grades at school, telling them, "You are brilliant. You must succeed. You will leave this life of menial labor."

Zhora did well, and her older brother was "first in his class." Impatient to make a success of himself, her brother left school at sixteen to start his own business. It soon failed, leaving him bitter; he claimed that "an Arab can't succeed because business is reserved for the French or the Jews." Her brother disappeared without a word, even to his family.

Zhora went in a different direction. Even as a young teenager in her poor, isolated community outside the city,

> I always felt free inside. To be who I was, I knew I had to get away. It was like a corral, with the horses inside. There might be horses that are happy in there, but there's a horse that says to itself, I don't want to be in this enclosure. The others don't mind, but I see the countryside outside. I will go out there. I'll jump over the fence and go toward the horizon. So I jumped over the fence.

As soon as she turned sixteen, Zhora transferred to a high school in the city and moved into a small student apartment. A government grant covered her expenses until she turned eighteen. She then "took any job at all," and finished high school at night. "I cleaned houses, I took care of kids, of old people." Zhora enrolled in the local university, and to support her studies she took a lowly job with the metropolitan government "collecting trash and cleaning offices." At the time, "I was the only Arab government worker among three thousand, the only one. I was very young."

People working in the offices she cleaned kept calling her *bougnoule,* a highly insulting slang term for Maghrebis or, more generally, Arabs.[7] They did this "even in front of their supervisor." Zhora wondered, "Why do they call me a *bougnoule*? What did I do? Did I fail to do my job, to be respectful? I've done nothing wrong."

When this name-calling didn't stop, Zhora asked the supervisor how he could let it go on, but he only replied, "They don't really mean it. Why make a scandal?" Finally, Zhora "went to the big boss to tell him what was happening," but his only response was to fire her. By chance, someone who, she said, "knew my whole story" intervened, and she was called back to the boss's office. There, a secretary told Zhora, "You're not fired, but don't come back, *bougnoule*." She went back to work and was treated as she had been before.

Zhora continued with her studies and began to date. Initially interested in Maghrebi men, she discovered that they weren't as "free" as she was, so she turned to "French" men. At twenty-two, she married a man with "red hair, blue eyes, and white skin" from a family that was "French on both sides." After becoming pregnant with their first child, Zhora left college to raise her family.

As a mother, Zhora butted up against the same problem over and over. Although she has the relatively pale skin and smooth hair sometimes seen among people of Berber origin, people who didn't know the family assumed that her children weren't hers. They had "blond" hair and "pale" skin, she said, "especially when they were kids." Zhora laughed as she thought of the family's return from the annual summer vacation, when she "was darker and they were even blonder." But it wasn't funny when people assumed she was "either their babysitter or a housekeeper, never their mother." Of all the times she remembered being asked for proof of parenthood, the time a train conductor wondered aloud whether she had "kidnapped" her children brought fresh disgust and fury.

There was also trouble in the family. Zhora's mother-in-law often spoke disparagingly of Arabs. When she used the word *bougnoule* in Zhora's presence, Zhora told her, "Mother, don't ever say that in front of me." Her mother-in-law replied, "Oh, that's not an insult. Everyone says it. It's no big deal."

About fifteen years after her older brother's disappearance, Zhora learned that he was alive and still living in the same city. When the two met, her brother told her that he had transformed himself: "I changed my identity," he said, because "I was sick of the racism." He had changed both his first and last names, married a "French" woman, and gone into business as a "French" person. He and his wife, who knew his secret, had settled in a part of the city far from his original family and had three children. His new business has been a success. "Since I changed, God be praised, business has gone well. I no longer have money problems. Everything goes well for me."

Zhora was furious. "You say that people are racist, so you'll change flags. That's your strategy," she told him, but she'd do no such thing. People "treat me as a *bougnoule*, but I face it." While her brother is "not very *typé*," she explained to me—the whole family is of Berber origin—Zhora imagines that people suspect the truth but do not confront him or his family about his charade.

Although she was hurt by her brother's absence—their mother had died without even knowing he was alive—Zhora suggested that the two families get together. Her brother refused, explaining that neither his children nor his in-laws know that he isn't "French." Showing her a photo of his family, he said, "To my great misfortune, my middle daughter looks just like you. Look at this photo. Every morning, when I see her, it's you who I see." He was right, Zhora said to me: "I swear, Larry, it was my very portrait." She told her brother, "You wanted to forget me? Well, you see me every morning. God has punished you." The families have never gotten together, and Zhora has never met her niece.

Zhora continued to work at the same municipal government where she had once cleaned offices, taking professional training courses and standardized exams to gain more skilled positions. She now serves as a land use specialist on projects where the municipality is acquiring private property for public purposes such as roads and community centers. While she is respected for her expertise, the sting from her early days remains:

> Today, you see, Larry, when someone sees me, it's funny, but I think I unsettle them because, in the beginning, when they saw me, they called me *bougnoule*. That hits me, knowing the life my parents lived, how they suffered, and then to be called a *bougnoule*, it's not right.

Problems at work occasionally crop up. During a recent legal training class at her office—"imagine a big conference room with everyone"—the instructor spoke of a neighborhood that had been "invaded." Zhora recalled:

> Everyone understood what she meant. I waited for a reaction. I couldn't say anything because of who I am. I didn't want to make a scandal. I waited for my supervisor to say, "Madame, please use a different way of speaking," but she said nothing. The instructor kept saying "invaded, invaded, invaded." Everyone frowned—they understood—but no one said anything.

At the coffee break, Zhora spoke with her supervisor, who told her, "Yes, it's not right what she said." Still, the supervisor declined to do anything because, she explained, "It's delicate."

There have also been problems relating to social and economic class. "Some lawyers and other jurists have made me know that I'm 'a little shit' because I'm not from the middle class." Even though, she says, "it's gotten me in trouble with my boss, I tell them, 'I may be a little shit because I was born into the working class, but you're lucky to have the poor to make money from. Don't spit on them.'" Some of these lawyers switched their files to others in the office, but they returned to Zhora after a couple of years. She told them, "We'll start from zero. We'll respect everyone. Me, I respect the poor because I know where I come from." Then "we work together again. I treat them as equals."

A few months before our interview, Zhora got into a dispute on the street. She was about to move into a parking space, but another car suddenly took the spot. When she complained in her accent-free French, the man in that car responded, "What are you going to do about it? If you're not happy, go back to your country, dirty *bougnoule*." Although many people witnessed this incident—"everyone was there," watching him insult her—"no one did anything." Zhora said nothing to the man. At such times, she tries to "remain a master of myself and leave such people in their smallness."

Some incidents are less extreme. She and her mother-in-law once ran into a friend of her mother-in-law on the street. After everyone had exchanged greetings, the friend said, "You have a charming housekeeper." A recurring problem involves deliveries. "You see that I have a pretty house in a residential neighborhood," Zhora told me. "Sometimes, I order something, like from

Amazon. And it's always like this. When I answer the door, the delivery man asks, 'Is Madame here?' or, 'Is the owner of the house here? I'm looking for the person who lives here.'" When Zhora says that she's the owner, the man responds, "Sorry, I thought you were the cleaning lady. No problem."

Religion is a simple matter for Zhora: "Me, I'm an atheist." (I had noticed that she had wine and served a pork dish at dinner the night before.) But she did not raise her children to follow her lead. Just as "it's been my choice about how I'll live my own life, I never chose a religion for my children. When you're an adult, it's for you to decide, not me. It's as if you gave them a sexual orientation. No!" As it turned out, her son became religious after moving out of the house at age twenty. "My daughters are atheists and my son is Muslim." That's fine by her, she said, though complications arise when her son comes home to visit. She tells him, "You want to pray, fine, you can pray in your room, but not the rest of the house. That's my domain." And when her son brought home a girlfriend who was veiled, Zhora told her, "Take off your veil. There are no veils here."

Zhora thinks that her children can also decide whether they are French or something else. Although she had retained her Maghrebi name, each of her children has a French first name as well as their father's French last name. "People often ask me why I didn't even give them a middle name that reflects my origins. That would be ridiculous. Their name is French. Why would I make trouble?" Their appearance is closer to the French norm as well. Even in adulthood, their skin color is relatively light, while their eye colors range from blue to brown. She thinks that even the younger daughter—"the one who you can now tell is *métisse*, though you'd need a keen eye" to see it—is probably seen as "French."

Now young adults, Zhora's children have chosen their own identities. "My son would say, 'I'm not French, I'm Arab and a Muslim." While she accepts this, it strikes her as odd since her family was Berber, and Arabs were the original "invaders" of Berber lands. Both her daughters have embraced French identities, though she thinks they draw the line at anti-Arab insults. Zhora believes that if the older daughter, who has "strawberry blonde hair and very white skin" as well as a French name, "hears an attack on Maghrebis or Arabs, she'll say: 'Stop right there, I'm Arab.'"

While Zhora thinks her children can choose their identities, she cannot. The reason is simple: "My identity is on my face." But even if she can't decide how others see her, how does she think of herself? She speaks only a few words of the Berber language Tamazight, and no Arabic at all. "I'm incapable" of speaking these languages, she says; "I'm blocked." She was born in France and grew up speaking French. She lives and works among "French" people, married a "French" man, and raised children in France. Still, Zhora says, "I never say I'm French." Why not, I asked. She answered, "I don't have a feeling of belonging."

Zhora kept coming back to this issue. At one point she told me, "the only thing I say is that I'm Kabyle"—a person originating from the main Berber region of Algeria—"I'm a woman and a Kabyle, that's it." At another point she was less certain: "I don't know who I am, I don't know who I am, I confess to you, I don't know who I am." It was only while writing this profile that I realized that she had expressed her feelings most fully during the first few minutes of the interview. In an emotional whisper, she explained:

> I don't feel I'm in a country. I don't feel that I'm of any country. That's the problem. The problem is with a piece of land, that's what's missing. Religious people say, "From dust one comes and to dust one returns." A person wants to belong to some dust.

MAKING ONE'S WAY IN FRANCE

Although the Maghrebi interviewees recounted a great variety of experiences, a single theme arose again and again: to be truly accepted into French society, they must do away with whatever reflects their Maghrebi identity. Although the interviewees are already like "French" people in their language, habits, and values, they must also eliminate any clothing or public behavior that is associated with Islam, have a European *faciès*, and have a first and last name that is French or at least European. According to the interviewees, this process might be partial at first—for example, one can eliminate all public signs of being Muslim—but it would only be complete in their children or children's children, through the reduction in Maghrebi *faciès* (where

Maghrebis have children with "French" spouses or partners) and the assumption of European names.[8]

This process is less extraordinary than it might seem: once called assimilation and now *intégration*, the absorption of immigrants has been a mainstay of modern French history. Beginning long before the influx of people from non-European countries following World War II, millions of people from elsewhere in Europe took this route to acceptance, much like Europeans who settle in France do today. For them, the path to incorporation into French society was straightforward, even if many faced intense bias in the beginning. They needed to start behaving according to French norms and learning to speak French; their children and grandchildren, in turn, would conform more closely to French norms and speak without an accent. The rest of the transformation was far quicker and easier for Europeans than it would be for Maghrebis: their *faciès* were usually close to what is seen as a French *faciès*, their religious background was typically Catholic, rather than Muslim, and their names were already European.

One of my Airbnb hosts showed how quickly this transformation can happen. Originally from Portugal, rather than outside Europe, as I had expected, Mariana was seven when her family moved to France. She learned French within months, was Catholic by birth and upbringing, and has relatively light skin and smooth hair. From the start, she felt accepted in the village where she grew up, and now, living in a nearby city, is seen as "French" by those who do not know her background.

Although it takes more time for Maghrebis to be fully assimilated into French society than it does for Europeans like Mariana, it is possible for people of Maghrebi origins to become nearly indistinguishable from "French" people within two or three generations. This is not to say that a particular individual will choose this path or that one's social identity is a binary choice between Maghrebi and "French." Zhora and her family illustrate some of the choices one might make. Zhora decided to keep her Maghrebi names, both first and last. Remaining unashamedly Maghrebi, she has always participated in the world around her—including a workplace dominated by "French" people—and fought for respect.

Zhora's older brother and her children illustrate other choices. Her brother tried to become "French" by cutting all ties with his

Maghrebi family, changing his first and last names, marrying a "French" woman, and presenting himself as a "French" person. Because he is not *typé*, he may have largely succeeded, though Zhora imagines that people around him suspect the truth. Zhora's children are differently situated: they have a "French" father and *faciès* that combine both parents' *faciès*, have French first and last names, and were raised in a largely "French" downtown neighborhood. Today, her daughters apparently see themselves as French and are largely or entirely seen that way by the "French" people around them, while her son has taken a different path, identifying as "Arab" and becoming the only practicing Muslim in the family.

The Maghrebi interviewees vary enormously in their backgrounds and life stories. Along with some of the richness of each person's life, the following profiles show how each person deals with issues of identity. To keep these accounts from becoming a blur, the interviewees are grouped according to three general approaches to life in France: (a) interviewees who have become, or were raised to be, as similar as possible to the "French" people around them; (b) interviewees who have developed strategies for achieving success in French society while maintaining a distinct Maghrebi identity; and (c) interviewees who have pursued a slower path in French society for both themselves and their children.

(a) *As French as Possible*

At least eight of the interviewees have become, or were raised to be, like the "French" people around them in language, values, and norms. While this has allowed them to participate in the larger French society and economy, it has not been enough for them to be seen as French.

Samuel. I met Samuel at his handsome apartment in the historic center of town, where he lives on his own. He was dressed like a successful man on his day off. An enthusiastic host, he cooked most of our meals during my two-day stay with him—the cuisine was French—and we talked almost nonstop. Our formal interview totaled almost six hours. It contained many surprises.

Now forty-three, Samuel was born in France of a "French" mother and Maghrebi father. "Swarthy" at birth, he said, Samuel was given a French first name to lessen the "racism" his maternal grandmother thought he'd face in life. His last name is Maghrebi, however, and he was raised in a Muslim household, his mother having converted. Being "*typé*" since childhood—Samuel described himself as "dark-skinned with brown hair and brown eyes"—he was seen as "an Arab, not French." Unlike most of the Maghrebis interviewed for this project and counter to his manner and appearance today, Samuel grew up extremely poor in a deeply dysfunctional household. At sixteen, he dropped out of school and left his parents' home.

Although explicit insults were rare while he was growing up, he said, "with my face" prejudice was a fact of life. One day, when he was walking down the street, "a woman from the window of an upper floor threw some ham down on me, calling it 'a *bougnoule*'s supper.'" As one of the few Maghrebis in school, he felt like the "black dog" of the class. Recounting these childhood experiences brought Samuel close to tears, but he pushed on: "It's not so bad if I cry a little. It clears the soul." The problems continued into adulthood. When he tried to file an application at city hall, the official there "threw my documents on the floor like I was a dog." During a parking incident, he was called a "damned *bougnoule*." Remembering that "this kind of thing happened often enough," he began to cry.

Samuel worked at fitting into French society. During his teenage years, an employer taught him how to speak, act, and dress like a respectable "French" person. "He educated me. Because of him I speak as I do today. He taught me good manners." Samuel had a series of jobs in restaurants and cafes and then as a door-to-door life insurance salesman. By his twenties, he had "started to feel more and more French." When he was about thirty, he got an entry-level job in the entertainment industry. Working day and night, Samuel said, he became "one of the best" in his field and won various awards. By the time I met him, he was living in an overwhelmingly "French" neighborhood in "one of the richest parts of town."

Two themes of Samuel's life will be discussed in later chapters of this book. Always drawn to "blondes with blue eyes," he has had a turbulent love life, as will be discussed in chapter 5. Meanwhile, his devotion to Islam has swung from intense as a child to absent as a young adult and back to intense in recent years (see chapter 6).

Early in his twenties, Samuel had two daughters with a woman of mixed "French" and Algerian parentage. They have his Maghrebi last name, but French first names. The older daughter, who is now twenty years old, "doesn't look very Arab," though he thinks it's evident that she has "origins." She has decided to be "a rebel" and, full of resentment, "dresses and behaves like a girl from the *banlieue.*" Samuel believes that she does this to make a statement: "You want to see me this way, well, then that's how I'll be." For him, "it's a vicious circle," since the more she acts that way, the more she's seen that way. His younger daughter, who is now eighteen, is "blonde with blue eyes," and, unlike her sister, has "many French friends. She doesn't have a problem with that." People probably assume that she "has origins, but that's less important, since she looks French. She's more accepted."

The spike in anti-Maghrebi and anti-Arab attitudes since the 2015–16 attacks has had a dire effect on him. "An Arab in France," he says, "is a potential terrorist." Although he dresses and behaves well, Samuel became uncomfortable in public. "I no longer take the metro because of how people looked at me. It was incredible." Even in his own neighborhood, "I've started to lower my eyes to avoid frightening people."

Samuel became emotional toward the end of his interview. There are now just two types of people in France, "the Arabs and the French." This sharp division eliminates people like him, who feel themselves to be French and live like "French" people, but who are Muslim and of Maghrebi origin. "We look for a place for us, but there is none. We are lost."

Elise and Abdel. Siblings in their twenties, Elise and Abdel were born and raised in France. Their mother Lina, who is profiled later in this chapter, had left Morocco to attend college in France, married a "French" classmate, and started a family. Her husband was successful in business and the family was well-off.

Although the marriage ended in divorce, Lina and her children continued to live in the handsome, overwhelmingly "French" neighborhood near the center of the city where I met them. Having raised them to be French rather than Moroccan, Lina says, "my children are French." After all, they had a "French education, dress in the French style, and have a French father." They also have their father's French last name. But Lina raised her children to be Muslim, and thus to be "Muslim and French at the same time."

While Elise and Abdel do not recall many insults growing up—Elise says that their Catholic school would not tolerate such behavior—it was not unknown. As noted in the introduction, a girl once told her "*nique ta race*" (roughly, "fuck your race"). This was a "brutal insult," both because of the coarseness of *nique* and the "signification of the word *race*." In the interview, Elise also spoke about insults directed against her mother by her paternal grandfather (Lina's father-in-law).

Now young adults, Elise and Abdel are strikingly different from each other. Elise, whose first name and last names are both French, works as an investment banker. She has long, smooth hair, and, while her skin is "a bit *typé*," she says, people "can't tell that I have an Arab origin."

By contrast, Abdel has an Arab first name and is "more *typé*." With his "very curly hair and a beard," Abdel says, he has "an Arab *faciès*." Their religious identities are the reverse of their first names and physical appearance: Elise remains devoutly Muslim, while Abdel is completely unreligious.

Both Elise and Abdel have had problems fitting in with the "French" people around them. As a practicing Muslim, Elise abstains from pork and alcohol and fasts during the month of Ramadan. Whenever a "French" person notices this, she says, she is asked whether she's Muslim, and, when she can't sidestep this question, she's forced to "justify" herself. These interactions undercut her professional relations—client entertainment entails copious amounts of wine and other alcohol—and cause friction in her social and romantic life. As reported in chapter 6, some people act as if she is less French, or as if she's doing something wrong. For her, "it's a battle every day."

Abdel's issues are rooted in his *faciès* and first name. Although he feels "culturally French in quotes," as an adolescent he was often stopped by the police because of his "Arab head." This infuriated him. These days, when people get to know him, they often say things like "You're not an Arab like the others," or "You're the only Arab I think well of." Although "made in a friendly way," these comments upset him since they reflect "a monumental separation between the garbage that people think Arabs are and the person who's Arab but behaves like a French person." He's not seen as "French" because of his *faciès* and first name, nor as "Arab" because of his behavior. And feeling neither one nor the other, he has concluded that a person's identity is "something of a fiction." After becoming fluent in other languages (German and English, but not Arabic) and traveling extensively, he thinks of himself as "a citizen of the world."

Abdel spoke about French history with unrestrained fury: "People have forgotten everything about colonialism."[9] France "took people out of their own countries to fight in its wars—wars they had no connection to—and to be killed." Later, France put Maghrebis in public housing projects outside the cities, "parking them in boxes, telling them to stay there." Now "French" people complain that "France no longer belongs to the French." They say such things as "We're in France, we're in a White country, so why are there mosques?" And offended by how many French-born Maghrebi kids in the poor *banlieues* reportedly behave, they say that "Arabs are monsters and terrorists, they do terrible things," and they "want to throw these people out." To Abdel's mind, "it's hypocritical."

Estranged by the growing "intolerance" (as Elise says) and "racism" (as both Elise and Abdel say) in France, both siblings moved to other countries as young adults—Abdel to Greece and Elise to Switzerland. It was only by chance that they were visiting their mother when I stayed at her apartment.

Nassim. Now thirty, Nassim and his family left Algeria for France when he was one. They settled in a small city with "very few foreigners," by which Nassim means people with "dark" skin. "These were the years I suffered the most from racism," he recalls. Often the only "foreigner" in his class, he would be "pushed around" by the other children. "When something was stolen, automatically everyone looked at me." He still remembers when, at the age of six, he was sent to the neighborhood bakery for a baguette and the proprietor "wouldn't even look at me."

As an adolescent, Nassim went about becoming "more likable," particularly "more French." He became "obsessed with mastering the French language," he said, and began to eat pork and drink wine "like everyone else." He dated only "European" girls. By young adulthood, people remarked that he had become "almost French."

Adjustments to his physical appearance were an important part of this process. To be "like the French" with their "smooth hair," Nassim says he kept his "curly" hair short and used chemical relaxers. When I commented that his hair is still smooth, he laughed aloud, and said, "Thank you!" Although his skin is "not as white as French people," he says, "I'm paler than other foreigners." In fact, "I'm mostly White." Driving the point home, he put his arm next to mine and laughed again: "I'm lighter than you!"

Nassim's efforts to become "more French" reached their peak a few years ago. He did his best to be French, to be accepted as French, at the company where he worked. By this time, he dressed, ate, drank, and acted French. Many of his colleagues deferred to his expertise in French, asking him to correct important memos. Some professed surprise at his background, saying, "You were born in Algeria?" A letter from the company's Director of Operations in support of his citizenship application in 2014 confirmed this perception:

> [Nassim] has always shown such an attachment to France that all his colleagues are convinced that he already has French nationality. . . . Since his arrival at the company, he has shown, time and again, that he has established very strong ties with France. . . . He has allied himself with the traditions and habits of our country better than anyone. . . . As I often tell him, he is "the most French person I know."

This letter made Nassim "very happy." But even as he was promoted at the company, becoming its youngest manager, he experienced increasing stress. This spiked following the 2015–16 attacks, when almost everyone at his company, even the president, he says, insisted that "I condemn the attacks, totally and absolutely" and make clear that "I'm not a terrorist." He understood how the others viewed him. "At this point I realized the difference: why me rather than the others? Why? It came to a point that I experienced a physical reaction. I was stressed, very stressed."

Realizing, Nassim says, that "I had betrayed my identity and my origin, I abandoned it all." He left the company and broke up with the "French" woman he'd been dating. He learned to read and write Arabic and became a practicing Muslim. No longer does he eat and drink like "French" people. He is now engaged to a religious Maghrebi woman.

As the interview drew to a close, Nassim looked back at his life. "I had passed the exam" of becoming "more French than the French," but this came "at a personal sacrifice." It was all unnecessary. "I could have been another person, in sync with my two cultures, even if this made me socially less acceptable in France." Whatever the future holds, "the Nassim of today is not a mask."

Nour. Born in the same large French city where she still lives, Nour has always considered herself French. Almost fifty, she now lives in a downtown apartment with her seven-year-old son. We met in the nearby apartment she rents through Airbnb. It was her day off from work, and she was dressed in close-fitting jeans.

Although Nour's parents had come from Algeria, the family lived in a "French" neighborhood of a large city for most of her childhood. Everyone went to the local French schools, which, she says, inculcated "French values." "It was very fluid, very pleasant" back in the 1970s," when people "were less frightened." She felt accepted from the start. "Those were the best years of my life."

Within the family, there was a sharp divide between the generations. Her parents, devout Muslims, were nonliterate and at first did not speak French. Nour and her siblings spoke only French with each other and their friends. She "didn't have any feeling of belonging to Algerian culture" and didn't care about Islam, eating pork when her parents weren't looking and ignoring the Ramadan fast each year. As adults, she and her siblings married or partnered with non-Muslim, non-Maghrebi people: "All my brothers and sisters are with French people."

Nour attended college, where she got a teaching degree. She had no trouble fitting into the schools where she worked, since both the students and faculty were "of different ethnicities." She then switched to a position with the local public transportation system, where she has encountered problems with some of the "French" staff she supervises, as discussed later in this chapter.

Nour's romantic relationships have all been with "French" men, and one is the father of her son. Unlike Nour, her son has French first and last names, and he is *métis*, a mixture of his two parents' *faciès*. He's had no trouble fitting in so far; she and her son live in a mixed neighborhood, and he attends a school with a wide range of children. Following the 2015 terrorist attack at the office of the journal *Charlie Hebdo*, she and her son marched in the "I am Charlie" demonstration against the attack and in support of freedom of speech.

Nour has always been certain about her identity: "I'm French. I was born in France and grew up in government schools with the values of the Republic. France is my country." She says that the words assimilation and *intégration* "make no sense" in her case because "my frame of reference is France." Still, some people see her differently: "Because of my first and last names and my *faciès*, some people make very clear to me that I'm not French." Although French by conviction, values, habits, culture, experience, and birth, Nour occasionally described herself as a "foreigner" during the interview. When I asked why—she hadn't noticed this—she answered, "because, in the eyes of people who see me on the street, I'm not French." People sometimes ask what she "truly" is.

Fouzia. Fouzia was born in the early 1960s in the same French city where she still lives. Originally from Algeria, her parents had been in France since the 1930s and did not follow Muslim practices, except to avoid pork. She has the "light skin" and "smooth" hair associated with Berbers.

Fouzia learned French when she began school. She heard insults like "dirty Arab" and "Arabs are thieves," though these weren't addressed directly at her. It was more of an "atmosphere" of bias, she says, which "sent me back to my ethnicity, to my origins." French people felt a particular "rancor" toward Algerians because of the bloody Algerian War and its aftermath. "Even if a person has fit in, she's implicated in these prejudices."

Over the years, Fouzia socialized with "French" people, she said, if only because her "social and cultural milieu" did not include Maghrebis. She was one of only two Maghrebis in her high school class and then became a nurse. Her coworkers, neighbors, friends, and the men she dated were "French." She bought an apartment in a "good" French neighborhood. French became her primary language and she forgot much of the Algerian Arabic she had known as a child. She has never been religious.

Fouzia has a nineteen-year-old daughter by a "French" man. Her daughter looks mostly "French," she says, and has a non-

Maghrebi name, including a "typically French" last name. Fouzia thinks that her daughter feels French, though she has heard that it's now stylish at her daughter's school to claim a bit of Maghrebi origin.

Although Fouzia is "French of Algerian origin," she feels she's still French: "Even if you're not 100 percent French, you're still French." And so "it's hurtful when you hear people say 'France for the French'"—a long-time motto of the right-wing National Front political party—because they mean only people of European origin. Using France's 2018 World Cup champion soccer team as an example, Fouzia explained, "They were French in name, but because of their *faciès*, their skin color," some people said that the players were "Africans, not French. It's bizarre, but that's the way it is." For many "French" people, France "is a history of religion, of continents, and of *faciès*." People who trace their origin to Africa or Asia "have different *faciès*" and different religions.

Olivier. A twenty-four-year-old university student, Olivier shares an off-campus apartment with other students. After I had put my bags in the extra bedroom he rents on Airbnb, he said that he wanted to be interviewed elsewhere. We settled outside a nearby McDonald's. After two hours of intense conversation, he went into town for the night, but was interested in doing another session. We resumed the interview the next morning outside the central train station before I left for another city. For much of his interview, Olivier held the digital recorder and talked directly into it.

Although Olivier is of Moroccan origin and grew up in Morocco, his father was born in France, and his parents met as university students there. Olivier has been a French citizen his whole life and has spoken both French and Moroccan Arabic since childhood. After graduating from a French government high school in Casablanca, he moved to Montreal and then to France. In France, he has transformed himself into someone just like the "French" people around him, changing "whatever's visible, for example, clothes, accent, way of speaking, and even my opinions about certain things." His friends are all "French," and he speaks "perfect French without any accent." He also began to use a French name; more than an hour into the interview, he revealed that his real name isn't Olivier, but Ali. When I commented that he dresses like the stereotypical "French" man—

like "Jean-Christophe," I joked—he replied, "I feel reassured. It's working."

"On a more profound, a more psychological level," Olivier said, the process of adopting French ways "has been very subtle. The last thing that could be changed is my *faciès*. It's the last thing, the thing that escapes me." I asked whether he'd want to be magically transformed, so that his *faciès* were no longer his own, but that of "Jean-Christophe." "It wouldn't bother me at all to look like Jean-Christophe," he replied. "I wouldn't have any problem signing a paper to become Jean-Christophe." Indeed, if "other Maghrebis were asked the same question, if they were being honest, 99.9 percent would say the same thing."

As the interview continued, Olivier began wondering whether he's been fooling himself about how much his external transformation has affected his character. While earlier he had said that he's just wearing "a mask" in France, and that he hadn't undergone "plastic surgery," now he wasn't so sure. He senses that the changes go deeper, even though he "didn't see it" at the time. Olivier had "always been frightened to look into such things," he said, so "it's only now, when I think of my own case, that I see that I've changed."

Asma. Now fifty-seven, Asma has always considered herself French, even though she spent her first four years and a few years as a young adult in Tunisia. Since early childhood, she has always had "only French friends" and a "French mindset." She's a French citizen, has "no accent," and lives entirely in French ways. This includes eating pork and drinking alcohol; the evening I arrived at her apartment she had set out charcuteries and aperitifs. She has never been a practicing Muslim.

Asma had "always dreamed of marrying a French man and having a French daughter." She made this dream come true, marrying a "French" man she had met at a bank and having a daughter, to whom she gave a distinctly French first name to go along with her husband's French last name. Life hasn't been easy. When she was pregnant, her father-in-law derided her—"Whatever you do, your child will be a *bougnoule*"—and neither he nor her mother-in-law, she says, has "ever seen their granddaughter." The invitations and photos Asma sent them were returned unopened. Her husband "betrayed" her, and they divorced. Since then, "he's never seen his daughter."

As a single parent, Asma raised her daughter to be totally French. "No one knew that she had an Arab mother. Not her teachers, not her friends, no one." Islam was never a factor in her upbringing, and now that her daughter is an adult, she is an atheist. Since Asma is not "very *typée*" and her former husband is "French," she thinks that her daughter is able to present herself as "French." In the photo she showed me, her daughter has straight, blonde hair (which Asma says she dyes) and fairly light skin. To maintain her social identity as "French," her daughter never revealed the ethnicity of her mother to schoolmates or to her bosses at work. "No one knew that she had a Tunisian mother." Asma isn't bothered by this. Her daughter tells her that "there are racists everywhere," and Asma agrees. "People here are idiots, they're completely racist." Her daughter recently moved to New Zealand.

Throughout her interview, Asma spoke about feeling French but being seen as Maghrebi. With Olivier's comments fresh in my mind (his interview had been a week earlier), I asked how she'd feel if she woke up some morning and discovered that, magically, she had blonde hair and blue eyes. She replied, "I'd love it. It would let me live as an equal. If I were a blonde with blue eyes, I'd live like the people in our country. I'd be very happy."

(b) *Strategies for Becoming Successful in France Without Trying to Become French*

While the interviewees profiled above would like to be seen as French, other people I interviewed have taken a different approach: they conform to French behavioral norms, but do not identify as French or hope to be seen that way. Having grown up in the Maghreb, they either hold firmly to their original identities or are indifferent to the whole issue. Each has developed a strategy to succeed in France without being French.

Rania. I arrived at Rania's small but cozy apartment in the early evening. Looking like a professional woman after a day of work—wearing jeans and her hair pulled back, but still with makeup on—she did not fit the cliché of what she turned out to be: a devout Muslim woman from the Maghreb. During a home-cooked Tunisian dinner, her interview later that evening, and breakfast the next morning, Rania cheerfully described how she navigates work at a high-tech French company while remaining true to herself. She often laughed at how odd but enjoyable it all was.

Now twenty-eight, Rania was an only child in a poor family in Tunisia. At school, she was "very intelligent" and "studied all the time, always the first in my class." Rania was admitted to the country's elite high school and did "super well" in her high school diploma exams. At this point, she says, "the government offered me scholarships to attend universities in Germany or France, but I said no. I couldn't leave the country with my parents there." Instead, she did two years at a preparatory school and two more at "the best IT school in Tunisia." Only when France offered a scholarship that allowed her to support her parents did she agree to go. She received a "double diploma" and a master's degree at a French university after two years, and then started a six-month internship at a tech company in a large French city. The company offered her a job after only three months, and she has worked there ever since.

Rania has always been a devout Muslim. Inspired by a dream she had at the age of twelve, she began veiling herself even though her mother did not do so. She continued to be veiled throughout her university years in France, but after some time with the tech job, her supervisor told her that while the company had no problem with her being veiled, it would make clients uncomfortable. After speaking with her mother—who said, "Take it off, take it off!"—she decided to remove the veil. She soon went further. To succeed in the work world, she decided, a woman must be "well-made-up, well-perfumed, well-coiffed." She straightened her hair, began dressing stylishly, and applied makeup every workday. She also adopted the distinctive accent of people from the city where she lives and works, and she would change her first and last names if that were useful. "Why not? None of this matters to me."

Even as she dresses and behaves like the French people around her, Rania is unapologetic about being Maghrebi and Muslim. She openly adheres to all Muslim dietary restrictions. When one of her French superiors joked about how Maghrebis are thieves, she joked back about how, as he's told everyone, he sneaks high-priced meat out of supermarkets. After the 2015–16 terrorist attacks, "when everyone came to me as if I were responsible," Rania made them agree that there are many other people like her. She told them, "Okay, so there are the good and the bad."

Rania has been very successful during her four years at the tech company. Her immediate supervisor has been an important source of support. "He helped me a lot, helped me fit in. He taught me a lot about work, but also about life. He's like my father." She has been promoted every year. "What matters to me," she says, "is competence." Some colleagues "are jealous, saying 'Why her, why do you give her these responsibilities when she's not even French,'" but others treat her "like family." With her ever-increasing salary, she has no trouble supporting her parents back in Tunisia.

Rania's dual life—adhering to big-city, professional French norms in public while remaining devoutly Muslim in her private life—is reported at length in chapter 6. She does not aspire to be French in *faciès* or religion, but she succeeds in all ways that matter to her.

Lina. As already noted, Lina is Elise's and Abdel's mother. Raised in Morocco, she was a university student in France when she met and married a "French" student and started a family. Now fifty-nine, she proudly proclaims, "I've changed nothing, I remain myself. I've always said I'm Moroccan, to everyone and up to the present. I'm also Muslim and will remain Muslim until my death."

But Lina's life has been more complicated. When members of her family back home opposed her marrying a European man even though he would become Muslim, she decided never to return to Morocco. She told them, "You'll never see me again." During the years that followed, she raised her children to be both Muslim and French. Lina is a French citizen, "speaks very well," and lives in a well-off neighborhood near the center of town. Since her former husband was a successful businessman, she was able, she says, to "indulge my taste for luxury." She has virtually no Maghrebi friends.

Lina's pride in maintaining a Moroccan identity has helped her deal with what she sees as racism all around her. French racism, she said, "goes back many years to colonialism," when "the Arab countries of Northwestern Africa were colonized by

France." Sometimes store personnel refuse to respond to her greetings. "On the street, in supermarkets, I see the look, the hatred." Although she once "almost cried," she now stares right back at them. "I return their hatred until they lower their eyes." When she hears "dirty Arab" or "dirty race," she thinks about how "Arabs are a thousand times cleaner than the French." (As I had already noticed, her apartment was impeccably clean and orderly.) With a bitter chuckle, she added, "I know that the French are hyper-dirty."

Since many "French" people see only a person's "physical appearance," Lina says, she's seen as the "swarthy foreigner." And for them, "a foreigner remains a foreigner forever." To deal with such people, she turns racism on its head: while conforming to *haut bourgeois* French norms, she remains proud of her Moroccan identity. "Racism exists, but it doesn't touch me."

Salma. Salma was my Airbnb host during both of my trips to France before this project began, and she invited me back to her home once it was underway. During my later visit, I interviewed her for six hours, and she lined up two other people who were interested in participating. She remains a good friend of mine.

Now in her mid-forties, Salma grew up in an elite family in Morocco that was essentially unreligious, one that lived "more like Europeans than Moroccans." In her early years, she attended private French-language schools where many of the other students were European. Salma came to France almost thirty years ago for her university education, ultimately completing the level just below the doctorate in business. She became a business consultant and a French citizen. She is careful with her clothing: "When I go out, I have a European look, with good taste."

Even in France, Salma lived in a "cocoon" that protected her from prejudice. Now amazed at her naivete, she recalls, "I heard the word 'racism' for the first time in my life when I was twenty-eight." That changed in short order. Having some free time, she began to do volunteer work with the organization SOS Racisme, putting her management skills to use. As Salma explained, SOS Racisme worked to protect "victims of racial discrimination" by, for example, sending applicants for housing who were identical except for being "French," Maghrebi or Black, and then litigating the differential results. "It was another world, as if I had arrived at the planet Jupiter."

Salma was soon volunteering full-time for non-profits, particularly SOS Racisme and Ni Putes Ni Soumises (Neither Whores Nor Submissives). During her five years as the head of her city's Ni Putes Ni Soumises chapter, she organized volunteer support systems, such as temporary housing, employment opportunities, psychological services, and occasionally lawyers, for women who had fled their homes because of beatings by older brothers and husbands. She was often in her city's notorious *banlieue*, a world far away from her comfortable central-city neighborhood, getting to know "the people and their problems." After working "seven days a week, every week" for eight years, she realized that she had reached her limit, that her health and finances were near the breaking point. She wound down her responsibilities and went back to business consulting, forming a company of her own.

During one of our conversations, I told Salma that a number of the "French" people I had met around town had told me not to set foot in that city's *banlieue*. They said there was nothing of interest there, and, with its drug dealing and violence, it was too dangerous to visit anyway. While I was buying a house plant for a friend, a downtown florist told me that he had never been there; indeed, that he'd never think of going. Salma offered to take me on a tour of the *banlieue* and we went there at least twice, stopping at cafes and the like. Once we drove into the notorious public housing project on a hill, encountering young men hanging out in a dead-end driveway we had entered. Salma greeted them matter-of-factly and we continued without incident.

After resuming her business consulting career, Salma became conscious—for the first time—of the prejudice she encountered as a Maghrebi and a woman. Sometimes she is overtly challenged by "French" men at training sessions. Rather than yielding to their intimidation, thereby accepting an inferior position, she presses forward with the material she is there to teach. If still challenged, she holds her ground, asking, "Do you want competence or do you want a French person? If you want a French person, well, I'm the wrong one for you." As "the equal of anyone and everyone," she won't be bullied into subservience.

Achraf. I met Achraf through Salma. Now sixty-three, Achraf has been "in a more or less privileged milieu" his whole life. He was raised in a commercially successful family in a well-off neighborhood in Tunisia that had both Tunisian and French people and came to France for university studies. Already fluent in French, at ease with French people, and completely unreligious, Achraf says that he fit into the university's social world of partying, drinking, and dating. After getting his degree, he married a woman "from a traditional French family, pure French and bourgeois," and went into business for himself. From the start, he did business with all types of people: "Europeans and Jews from North Africa," as well as "Indochinese, Syrians, Armenians."

Achraf and his wife settled in a small French town where, he said, "I was very well received, very well accepted." Perhaps because he had the means, "no one ever posed the question" of his origins. Already managing his family's real estate holdings in Tunisia and his own holdings in France, Achraf invested in restaurants and other businesses. During our interview, he looked like any successful "French" businessman on his day off—with a high-quality sports shirt and smooth, carefully combed hair—except for the darker hue of his face.

Achraf spoke candidly about his reception by the local social, political, and business community. A successful entrepreneur, he easily "integrated" himself into this world; indeed, politicians and others "eagerly" seek his opinions on various issues. But "I'm no fool," he said twice during the interview. "There are people with the same name as me, but not the same financial means—people in the ghetto, living in government housing projects—who have problems."

Although he became a French citizen decades ago, Achraf says he's never thought much about whether "I'm Tunisian or I'm French." He has his business interests in France, and "an inheritance, houses, and land holdings" in Tunisia. He goes to Tunisia, only a short plane ride away, every year. Meanwhile, he and his "French" wife raised their three daughters to be simply French. Now adults, they don't speak Arabic, don't go to Tunisia, and have no background in Islam. *Métisse* and raised in well-off circumstances, they've "never had a problem" fitting in.

(c) *Pursuing a Slower Path in French Society*

What about the Maghrebi interviewees who have not sought to be seen as French, like those profiled in section (a), or developed a strategy to excel in French society, like those profiled in section (b)? The answer is simple: they have pursued a slower path in French society, working in modest jobs, marrying other Maghrebis, and raising children not so different from themselves.

Khira. Like many of the interviewees, Khira lives in the suburb of a city, but in circumstances altogether different from the dirty and ramshackle housing projects where Maghrebis are assumed to live. Khira's house was neat and well maintained. She lives on her own, though one of her adult daughters, also an Airbnb host, lives nearby.

Khira's parents came to France from Algeria in 1954, when she was four. Though she spoke Arabic with her parents, who never really learned French, Khira "spoke French very well" from an early age. The family was not very religious. With "light" skin and "non-kinky hair," she says, "I'm not very *typée.*" And while "French" children occasionally called her insulting names, "I didn't feel inferior" since "I'd learned in geography class that I was a member of the White race."

Although Khira had hoped to become a journalist, she entered into an arranged marriage at age sixteen to a Maghrebi man, and had four children in quick succession. She raised them at home, then trained to become a secretary. During the decades that followed, she encountered discrimination in getting hired and, once hired, she never achieved parity in salary (as discussed later in this chapter). Now in her mid-sixties and retired, she is more religious than when she was growing up, praying five times a day and fasting during Ramadan. This hasn't altered how she's seen by others. Indeed, because of how she speaks, dresses, and looks, people are occasionally surprised by her origin. Khira's identity is clear in her own mind: "I've always been both Algerian and French."

Her children have spent their entire lives in France. They are fully French "in their clothing and ways of acting" and are not "too *typé,*" she says, because her former husband is not *typé* either. Nevertheless, their first and last names are Algerian. Khira thinks that they feel French, but she does not know whether they are seen that way.

Hiba. Although Hiba has had a challenging life (both her husband and sole child are disabled), she was full of verve during our time together. She laughed often. It was only when she spoke of the sad times in her life or the prejudices some people have shown that her voice dropped and her eyes misted up.

Hiba was born in Morocco. When she was seven, she and her mother moved to France to join her father, who had gone there in the 1960s to do menial labor. They settled in a government housing project, and she learned French at school. She had "frizzy hair," unlike the "beautiful hair" of the "French" girls at school, she says, and "white skin, though a little tan." Although she had dreamed of becoming a journalist or UN interpreter, her father decided that she would study sewing at a vocational school.

At eighteen, Hiba entered into an arranged marriage with a Moroccan man. They had a son, who her mother raised while Hiba took care of the four children of a "French" family. Scrimping and saving, she was able to buy the apartment that became the Airbnb where I stayed—"It's my baby!"—and then the small house where she and her family live. Now forty-seven, she works for individuals, mostly taking care of their families and managing their small real estate properties. Though a devout Muslim, Hiba fits in since she behaves "like a French person."

When she hears the slogan "France for the French," Hiba feels that "I'm excluded even if I've lived here 150 years. I'm on the sidelines. The problem is that this is my country. I can't do otherwise." She thinks that there has been "more racism" in France since the 2015–16 terrorist attacks. People on the street sometimes say "dirty Arab" or "stupid ass," and "frankly, I hear the neighbor behind me even today" saying these things. "It's bizarre. I'm French, I'm in my country, sincerely," but, when all is said and done, "I'll never be accepted."

Much like Zhora, who suspects that people can tell that her brother isn't really "French," Hiba thinks that Maghrebis cannot transform themselves in just one generation. "You can't be like Spanish or Italian people." Even if your skin is relatively light, as Hiba's is, and you are baptized, you still must "change your whole identity." You have to "change your name, drink and eat pork like a real Christian, and marry a French person." You have to "change everything, renounce everything. You have to renounce the name of your parents, your origins, who you are." But after all this, she says, even if you "erase everything, you'll never get in. Among true French people, it's always, 'Ah, he has origins.' That's not erased."

At the end of the interview, Hiba spoke about her adult son, who has spent his entire life in France, but whose names, both first and last, are distinctively Arab. I asked whether he feels French. No, "he'd never say he's French." He'd say, "I'm an Arab, and I'll remain an Arab, since they don't accept me as I am."

Sami. Now fifty-five, Sami grew up in Tunisia. After graduating from high school, he settled in France, where he earned a diploma in electronics and opened a repair shop in an ethnically mixed town near a large city. He has lived and worked there for the last seventeen years. The community has all kinds of people—"Africans, Tunisians, Moroccans, and Algerians, plus the French not far away"—and his clientele includes all of them. He repairs their electronic devices, like smartphones, and has good relations with everyone.

Sami is "Tunisian, not French," and though he has the right to become a French citizen, he has no intention of doing so. Sami first married a woman he described as "Algerian," even though she was born in France, and they had two daughters. They divorced, and he is now married to a Tunisian woman who lives in Tunisia. He goes there often. He is also a devout Muslim and regularly attends the local mosque. Taking a break from our interview for his evening prayers, he was kind enough to invite me to join him there.

Sami's two daughters, now twenty-one and nineteen, were born in France and educated in French schools. They now live with his ex-wife. They are "French by nationality," he says, but "do not feel French French. They are Tunisian." They speak Arabic as well as French, have both Tunisian and French passports, and spend each summer vacation in Tunisia. Living in the same multi-ethnic community as Sami, they are rarely insulted, though "some people are aggressive" with the daughter who is veiled.

Sami thinks that "racism has increased in France" since the rise of Jean-Marie Le Pen and his right-wing National Front party, but that such politicians, he says, "don't make me afraid. What can they do? We live in a country of rights. People who would do racist acts are sick, that's all."

I ended Sami's interview by asking if there was anything he wished to add, as I did with each interviewee. The following is an excerpt from his response:

> Foreigners build France; France was built by foreigners. There were thousands of Moroccans who died during the war in France, for France. French people don't want to admit the positive things that foreigners have done. French people also don't want to admit the negative things that they've done. They killed a million Algerians in Algeria; they killed thousands in Tunisia. They have not recognized all the wrongs they committed in foreign countries, the colonization, the Maghrebi countries they colonized. All the wealth they seize back home. Tunisia, I think, doesn't get even five percent of the profits. France doesn't want to change the contracts. How can they say that the foreigners must go home when their wealth comes here? They live with it. They need to reflect on this.

THE SOCIAL, ECONOMIC, AND PSYCHOLOGICAL COSTS OF BEING MAGHREBI IN FRANCE

Over and over, interviewees described the high price they pay for being seen as Maghrebi in France. Even those who feel fully integrated say they must deal with the many consequences of being Maghrebi. These include the social costs of this identity—including harsh stereotyping, public humiliation, and discrimination in employment and housing—and, for some, severe psychological stress.

The Social and Economic Costs of Being Maghrebi

Many "French" people see Maghrebis in stereotypical ways. According to the interviewees, Maghrebis are thought to be thieves, drug dealers, and drug users. Those who do not abstain from alcohol are thought to be heavy drinkers. Maghrebis follow "strange" customs. Husbands are said to beat their wives and to force them to be veiled. Men, especially young men, are seen as dangerous. Maghrebis are thought to be "invaders" in France who scam the country's generous social welfare system. Summing this up, one interviewee put the image of Maghrebis pungently: they're seen as "scum, thugs, pieces of shit."

Many of the interviewees think these stereotypes hold some truth when it comes to the impoverished Maghrebis, especially young males, who live in the rundown public housing complexes in the *banlieues*. While Abdel believes that "if I'd grown up under those circumstances, I'd have ended up the same way," he says he's "always the first to be annoyed" by young Maghrebis "from the ghettos" who "swear to God while drinking alcohol, who insult women and hit people." He understands why "there's been an increase in crazy racism" in France. For Samuel, "the worst thing is when I see young Arabs in the subway or on the street saying anything they like, doing anything they like, like insulting French people, breaking things, and yelling." Olivier complained that "with them it's always a mess. They live like the racists say." Indeed, Olivier admits that he has "a tendency to be racist" toward those people.

Other interviewees expressed a more nuanced view of Maghrebis in poor neighborhoods, perhaps because they had once lived there. Both Zhora and Khira grew up in poor, largely Maghrebi *banlieues* and both remain proud of their parents and the other decent, hard-working people who live there. Although Zhora's parents weren't literate in any language and originally spoke no French, they wanted to fit into their new country. They insisted that Zhora and her siblings succeed in school and educate their own parents: "You will learn French at school and teach us when you come home." Khira's parents, who were also illiterate and did not speak French at first, raised their children to be proud of themselves, despite the family's poverty and the insults from some "French" children. Having "never felt inferior" to "French" people, Khira pressed forward with her own life and, as an adult, with raising children to be full participants in French society.

Unfortunately for the interviewees, many "French" people apply their stereotypes of Maghrebis to people like them. Samuel "can understand their attitude" because they "don't distinguish between me and them. Physically," he says, "I look like them." And so, "we're the first victims of all the offensive things they do." Olivier complains, "Because of them, society considers me inferior to French people. When I'm speaking with a French person, I immediately feel a doubt, a kind of judgment."

A few interviewees spoke about how the harsh image of Maghrebis has entered into their own ways of thinking. Riding the subway at the time of the 2015–16 terrorist attacks, Samuel found himself "terrified" at the sight of "a Muslim, a brother, bearded," with a sack on the floor. Olivier says, "Even I, I have reservations, to be honest, a different feeling when I see Jean-Marie than when I see Youssef, Ali, or Mohammed. There's a difference, even I feel different" about such people. Ironically, Olivier's real name is Ali.

Terrorist attacks attributed to "Arabs" and "radicalized Muslims" have only made things worse. Mohamed remembers watching news reports of the 11 September 2001 attack on New York's World Trade Center with other university students from Morocco, thinking, "This is going to be blamed on us." After each of the 2015–16 attacks in France, Ibrahim felt "stigmatized" and forced to "justify" himself. People asked Elise, the investment banker, "Why do you do this?" Even today, Samuel feels he's seen as a "potential terrorist because of my physical appearance."

Feeling that they're seen to be like the Maghrebis of the housing projects—that they're "put in the same sack," as some of the interviewees phrased it—they try to distinguish themselves in various ways. Many talked about the importance of speaking "good" French and behaving "as one should." Samuel was reminded of how clothing affects people's reactions. "Just yesterday," he remembered, "I was wearing an old T-shirt and old pants because I'd been doing some cleaning and I realized that I was seen as someone from the *banlieue*." Olivier said that he's especially polite when he's in a "French" neighborhood, saying, "Please, if you don't mind" and the like to avoid being "seen badly."

Although the interviewees do not act like the Maghrebis of stereotypes, many fear being humiliated in almost any public place. Ibrahim and others reported being turned away at bars and nightclubs, even as the "French" people around them are admitted. Many interviewees feel that, when they enter a store, the staff treat them like potential shoplifters. "One can become paranoid being followed in stores," Mohamed said, but "that's the reality." Karim complained that "they don't see my diploma in a store." Cashiers often refuse to respond to Lina, even after she has repeatedly greeted them politely. Youssef, Mohamed, Samuel, Karim, and other Maghrebi men talked about women pulling their bags and phones close to their bodies on the street or in public transportation.

Ayoub recounted a particularly painful experience that began when a "French" man kept insulting his friend at a local bar.

Ayoub finally stepped forward, saying, "Stop this shit or I'll really explode." The French man left, but returned with a policeman, claiming that Ayoub had said he had a "bomb that would explode." Ayoub was taken to the local police station. Although there was no bomb, for the next ten hours, he was interrogated by various police officers who tried to get him to admit he had threatened the man with a bomb. Ayoub stood by his denial and was finally released. But because of France's continuing state of emergency, Ayoub explained, he had no right to call a lawyer and afterwards could not seek redress.

When Abdel was a teenager, he was often stopped and frisked by the police. "The moment I went into town with my friends, if I was wearing a baseball cap and with my Arab head, Bam! I was stopped. Immediately." When Nassim started driving at eighteen, "the police stopped me all the time," he says, while "my French friends said that they were never stopped." As will be seen in chapters 2 and 3, Abdel and Nassim were not the only interviewees who endured frequent police stops based, they think, on their appearance; Lucas (who is Black) and Fatih (who is of Turkish origin) reported similar experiences.

Police bias in these police stops, known as *contrôles des identités*, has been demonstrated through statistical testing.[10] In 2007, the Open Society commissioned a study that found that "Blacks were overall six times more likely than Whites to be stopped by the police," and "Arabs were 7.6 times more likely." An "equally important determinant . . . was the style of clothing worn by the stopped individuals. Although those wearing clothing typically associated with French youth culture (including 'hip-hop,' . . .) made up only 10 percent of the people available to be stopped, they made up 47 percent of the people actually stopped" (Open Society Foundations 2009: 10).[11] Other studies from the same time period resulted in similar findings (see Lozès and Lecherbonnier 2009: 35–39).

Discrimination in Employment and Housing

Discrimination in employment was a recurring theme in the interviews. Many interviewees have had trouble securing jobs commensurate with their qualifications, and a few have gone years between jobs. When they get a job, some are paid salaries far below those paid to "French" people at the same level. A few have encountered overt insults at work.

Interviewees confront a major problem when they apply for a job: the résumé. In France, résumés routinely include the person's name, photo, and address. The significance of this was explained by an Airbnb host I had assumed to be Maghrebi. She had posted no photo of herself (a way Airbnb hosts who are not "French" avoid bias from prospective guests), and both her first and last names seemed Maghrebi.[12] When I arrived at her apartment, I was proven wrong: from a longtime "French" family, Selma has pale skin and long, smooth hair. But my mistake was actually a common one: as she explained, many "French" people also assume from her name that she is Maghrebi. She realized that this could pose a problem a few years ago, when she was applying for jobs. Fearing that this name on her résumé would make potential employers think she's Maghrebi, Selma attached a photo so "my name wouldn't count against me." The photo leaves "no doubt," she said, that she is "French." Otherwise, her résumé "would have gone into the trash."

Selma's fears are not imagined: a number of Maghrebi interviewees talked about their résumés going "directly into the trash." Early in his career, Nassim discovered how quickly this can happen. Hoping that his excellent French and choice of clothes would improve his chances of getting the posted position, he personally delivered his résumé to a company's hiring office. A few minutes after he'd left, he realized that he had forgotten to say something and went back. But it didn't matter: "They'd already thrown my résumé into a trash basket."

Khira was once assigned to an employment counselor to help her find a job. Frustrated by her lack of success, the counselor allowed her to listen while she spoke by phone with a potential employer. On the call, the employment counselor described her as fully qualified for the job, as well as professionally oriented and dressed ("yes, she wears heels"), but with Khira's obviously Maghrebi name, the counselor couldn't even get her an interview. Hanging up, the counselor told Khira, "I'm sorry, but I wanted you to see how this happens."

A number of interviewees are stuck working at menial jobs. Even after receiving both a bachelor's and master's degree, Mohamed had trouble finding a job above the level of farm hand or restaurant kitchen help. An employment counselor advised him to seek such a job anyway because that was the kind of work he had done as a student. This hurt Mohamed, he recalled, because it "suggested that I wasn't up to doing more."

Even when they were hired for one or another job, many interviewees encountered problems. The detailed profile of Zhora at the beginning of this chapter illustrates how bias can dog a person throughout her career. Zhora feels she's dismissed as a *bougnoule* even today, more than thirty years since she started working at a government office and even after she has reached a paraprofessional position through passing civil service exams.

Once she was finally hired, Khira worked for many years for the same employer. Even though this went well, she said, "I was paid less because I'm a foreigner." (In fact, Khira has lived in France since she was four and has been a citizen since 1992.) She periodically requested the same salary as the "French" people in her position, but without success. This salary differential stung most when she discovered that a "French" woman at the same level was paid substantially more than her, indeed, "six hundred euros a month" more. "One feels betrayed not to be given the respect one deserves," she said. "I wanted to cry."

When Asma began a job in a nursing home, her direct supervisor told her, "Starting tomorrow, I will call you Nicole." When Asma asked to be called by her real name, her supervisor refused, explaining, "All those Arabs, those Maghrebis, they're a little dirty. They have lice." On the surface, Asma's current supervisor is the opposite. "He'd never say anything intolerant about Maghrebis." Still, he treats her differently from the "French" employees: "He doesn't even say hello," she is sure, "because I'm an Arab." Her doctor has authorized a medical leave because of her emotional stress, but Asma feels she must quit.

Finally, there are the problems encountered by the few Maghrebi interviewees who have risen to management positions. A college graduate with experience in school administration, Nour was hired by the local commuter train company to supervise a team of "controllers" who enter buses to check for passengers who have not paid the required fare. Among the employees of this company, "there are many, many who are racist." Once, when a subordinate discovered a fare-beater, he called out to her, in front of the other members of her team and the passengers on the bus, "Hey, here's a cousin of yours." Although the company management sided with her in a complaint she filed about the incident, Nour said that such behavior "hurts me sometimes."

Housing discrimination is also a problem. When Ibrahim was looking for an apartment from a government agency, he requested one that would be near his job, but was only offered an apartment in an overwhelmingly Maghrebi community far away. Similarly, Mohamed "called about an apartment and was given an appointment to see it," but a problem arose after he gave his (Maghrebi) name. The landlord "called back the next day to say that the apartment had been rented." Mohamed then asked his wife, who has a European name, to call. "When she asked if the apartment was available, the answer was yes."

One may wonder whether the interviewees' feelings of discrimination correlate with the actual incidence of discrimination in France. While this issue is outside the scope of this ethnography, it merits at least a brief discussion. The landmark Trajectories and Origins study by the French national research institutes INED and INSEE[13] provides the necessary statistical information. Regarding employment discrimination, the results of this study "suggest that the respondents' felt and reported experiences are in fact correlated with 'objective' indicators of inequality" (Meurs 2018a: 80). They also reveal a higher level of perceived discrimination from people like the interviewees: "the more attractive, in theory, a respondent's profile, the more positively they respond to questions on feelings of discrimination" (105). This applies to both the chance of being hired and average wages earned by people of comparable qualifications (80–106). "Descendants of parents from the Maghreb" reported approximately 12 percent more employment discrimination than people in "the mainstream population."[14]

The Trajectories and Origins study also covered housing issues (see Pan Ké Shon and Scodellaro 2018). While housing discrimination is less often reported than employment discrimination, it remains a problem for immigrants, especially from Africa, including the Maghreb (Pan Ké Shon and Scodellaro 2018: 161). And while the children of immigrants from Europe "have become invisible"—just one generation removed from immigration, they "can no longer be distinguished from the mainstream population"—this is not true for children of immigrants from elsewhere (162). Among Algerians, "reported discrimination does not decrease significantly from one generation to the next," and the situation is only slightly better among the children of Moroccan and Tunisian immigrants (162).

The Psychological Costs of Being Maghrebi in France

A number of interviewees reported anxiety relating to issues of identity or acceptance. Statements already quoted in their profiles capture these feelings. Zhora said, "I don't feel I belong in my own country; I don't know who I am." Samuel despairs for people like him: "We look for a place for us, but there is none. We are lost." Following each of the 2015–16 attacks, when Nassim felt he had to show "French" people that he's not a terrorist, he "experienced a physical reaction" because he "was stressed, very stressed." And although Olivier and Asma make a point of living like "French" people, their Maghrebi appearance makes them feel excluded. "The last thing that could be changed is my *faciès*," Olivier said, but he knows he cannot do this. And because Asma isn't "a blonde with blue eyes," she knows that she can't "live as an equal" in France.

Maghrebi interviewees who were not profiled in this chapter also expressed distress. While both Ibrahim and Mohamed both feel excluded by French society, each feels particular concern for their young children. Ibrahim is so sure his children "will never be accepted in France" that he lectures his oldest, a son who's only five and speaks only French, "You are not French, you are Algerian." Choking up, Ibrahim said, "I cry," but he feels that it's better for his son to learn this lesson now than when he grows up and faces what Ibrahim has experienced. Mohamed thinks that when his toddler gets older, "French" kids will shun him because his "skin is too dark." This worries him: "My son was born in France, he's being socialized in France." He has to feel French. "If he's not French, then what is he? It's enough to make a person schizophrenic."

Karim, who will be profiled in chapter 4, claims that he has done everything to be "assimilated" into French society—becoming "more French than the French"—but to no avail. "It's unjust to think you have to be like this, but in the end you'll never, ever be accepted. You will never be a part of it." And so, he says, "I feel like I have no country."

CONCLUSION

As this chapter has shown, the Maghrebi interviewees are firm believers in *intégration*. They speak "good" French, champion French values, live in middle-class communities, and dress and act like the "French" people around them. They wholeheartedly participate in French society, and, to the extent that discrimination does not block their way, they live and work with "French" people. Most have degrees from French universities. Many have married or partnered with "French" people and raised their children to be French. Two of the interviewees are the children of these relationships. All of the women interviewees are independent in thought and action. Even Islam does not distance the interviewees from French values: many are unreligious, and even the practicing Muslims are vigorous adherents of *laïcité*.[15]

Yet even the interviewees who have spent their entire lives in France and consider themselves French do not feel that they are seen that way. Despite all she has done through the decades, Zhora is not accepted as French: "My identity is on my face," she says, and even today many "French" people see her as a *bougnoule*. Although Samuel has had a successful career in the French entertainment industry, speaks and behaves like the "French" people around him, and lives in a well-off downtown neighborhood, he feels that "French" people will never accept him because of his *faciès*. There are two types of people in France, he explained, "the Arabs and the French," and "an Arab in France is a potential terrorist." Abdel, who is *métis* and says he is "culturally French"—he grew up in a bourgeois "French" neighborhood and attended private schools with "French" children—is nonetheless seen as an "Arab" because of his "Arab *faciès*" and Maghrebi first name. Fouzia attended high school and nursing school with "French" students, worked for decades among "French" doctors and nurses, bought an apartment in a "French" neighborhood, and has had a daughter with a "French" man, but she still feels a divide. For many people, France "is a history of religion, of continents, and of *faciès*." For them, Fouzia says, she is not French.

As this chapter has shown, even for people like the interviewees, to be Maghrebi in France is to face chronic bias, discrimination, and ugly stereotypes. Still, it could be worse. The next chapter addresses the experience of being Black in France.

NOTES

1. Algeria also had a substantial indigenous Jewish population. From 1870 until Algerian independence (apart from the years of the Vichy regime), the French government accorded French citizenship to most of these Jewish Algerians.
2. This number does not capture all people of Maghrebi origin because, in keeping with French statistical practice, it represents only the first two generations in France, i.e., immigrants and their French-born children (Simon 2008: 12). Of the 3.8 million cited here, 1.9 million originate from Algeria, 1.4 million from Morocco, and 0.5 million from Tunisia (ibid.).
3. "Arab" (*Arabe*) is often used interchangeably with "Maghrebi." Thus, Maghrebi interviewees—even those of Berber origin—frequently refer to themselves as Arabs or report hearing "French" people refer to them or others in this way. "Arab" appears to be used for various discursive reasons, though a common theme involves insult (as when a "French" person says "dirty Arab") or the harsh way they feel many "French" people view them (as in "I'm an Arab, and I'll remain an Arab, since they don't accept me as I am"). See Ruscio 2020: 27–30, which details stereotyping and disdainful use of *Arabe* going back to Charlemagne.
4. Two days after the *Charlie Hebdo* attack, Amedy Coulibaly, a French-born man of sub-Saharan origin, attacked a kosher supermarket in Paris in the name of ISIS, killing four people and taking fifteen hostages.
5. While millions of Muslim women around the world wear a veil or a scarf covering their hair, this isn't dictated in the Qur'an or most hadiths (sayings of the Prophet Muhammad), and many Muslims do not consider this a religious obligation.
6. While this chapter focuses on Maghrebis, there are Arab people in France who do not originate from the Maghreb. Only one of the interviewees who has lived in France more than a few years fell into this category. Now in her sixties, Leila grew up in western Syria, worked for a "French" family in Lebanon, and then moved to France when they did. Leila's non-Maghrebi origin has not factored into her life in France. Indeed, she married a Maghrebi man and has lived in much the same way as the Maghrebi interviewees.

7. Later in her interview, Zhora said that "*bougnoule* was not originally about the Arabs," and she was right. Evidently derived from *bou-gnoul*, "black one" in the Senegalese language of Wolof, *bougnoule* was used as a derogatory term for Blacks during the colonial era (see Centre National de Ressources Textuelles et Lexicales, Portail lexicale, Lexigraphie, "bougnoule." https://www.cnrtl.fr/definition/bougnoule, retrieved 9 December 2022; Ruscio 2020: 50–51). None of the Black interviewees mentioned hearing this term directed at them, though one non-Maghrebi interviewee did. Paul, who is of Korean origin, reported that "a xenophobe once called me *bougnoule*. That's a term used against Maghrebis, not Asiatics," he said. "It made me laugh." But see Ruscio 2020: 52–53, reporting its use for Vietnamese and Chinese people.
8. This is not to say that they are seen as *Français de souche*, people who can credibly claim generations of French identity.
9. According to various researchers, it's less a matter of forgetting France's colonial experience than suppression or even aphasia. See, e.g., Verges: 2014; P. Silverstein 2018: 1–10; Bancel and Blanchard 2017b.
10. Punning on this term, Abdel and others call these stops *contrôles au faciès*.
11. Abdel experienced this himself. When he was dressed like "someone of the ghetto," he was stopped "loads of times," but, he adds, when "I'm dressed in a suit, I won't be stopped by the police. It's simple."
12. Complaints of discrimination by Airbnb hosts—including the refusal by some French hosts to rent to Maghrebis—reportedly caused Airbnb to require hosts around the world to sign a non-discrimination agreement. See "Airbnb. Plus d'un million de personnes n'ont pas voulu signer une charte de non-discrimination" (2020).
13. These are the Institut national d'études démographiques (INED) and Institut national de la statistique et des études économiques (INSEE). Conducted throughout France in 2008–09, the Trajectories and Origins project employed 566 interviewers and administered nearly 22,000 questionnaires (Simon, Beauchemin, and Hamel 2018: 1).
14. If only because of France's legal constraints on the collection of statistical information relating to race (as discussed in the introduction to this book), the Trajectories and Origins study used rough proxies for such social categories as Maghrebi, Black, and Asian. For example, the "descendants of parents from the Maghreb" did not extend to all their descendants, but only to one full generation, i.e., only the French-born children of Maghrebi immigrants. Similarly, "the mainstream population" encompassed everyone in later generations, including people of such social categories. The same proxies were, by necessity, used for Blacks (the proxy being people who came from sub-Saharan Africa or the overseas departments and their children) and others, including Asians and others originating from Asia. Further, statistics grounded in original nationality—the people from one or another country and

their descendants, whether or not limited to one generation—do not capture the categories actually used in social life. As an expert on such statistics notes, "The gap between statistical categories and the terms used in everyday discourse is huge" (Simon 2008: 12). Concerning these issues generally, see Simon 2008.

Another study, using a different set of data and a different methodology, focused on differentials in the employment rate between French-born people with at least one parent who had been born in North Africa versus French-born people (of whatever background) whose parents were both born in France (Rathelot 2014). Much like the Trajectories and Origins study, it concluded that the employment differentials "should be mostly attributable to [the former group's] ethnicity, and not to differentials in residential location or observable characteristics" (136).

15. See above and, more extensively, chapter 6.

TWO

BLACK IN A WHITE WORLD

Although they vary greatly in their ages, appearances, family histories, cultural and national backgrounds, and lives in France, the interviewees who trace their origins to sub-Saharan Africa or the Caribbean report that they are seen as part of a distinct category. French-born people whose *faciès* suggest a European origin are called "French," while people with a *faciès* suggesting sub-Saharan African origin are called "Black." The interviewees' own way of speaking reflects this: even though many consider themselves French, they refer to people with a European *faciès* as "French" or "White," but to people like themselves as "Black."[1]

BACKGROUND

France has long been involved with sub-Saharan Africa and people who trace their origin to sub-Saharan Africa. From the sixteenth to the nineteenth centuries, France and other European countries were active in the transatlantic slave trade, with (White) Europeans buying Black African people, primarily from other Africans who had seized and brought them to ports on coastal Africa. Europeans then transported these people under brutal conditions across the Atlantic Ocean to the Americas. The enslaved Africans were then sold again to people of European origins, who put them to work farming land in areas that European countries had seized and turned into colonies. These included the French colonies of Martinique, Guadeloupe, and, until 1803, Haiti, where the treatment of plantation slaves was particularly harsh. The vast majority of slaveholders were White; the vast majority of slaves were Black. The exploitation of enslaved Black people generated enormous wealth for White people, both in these colonies and in metropolitan France. France prohibited involvement in the international slave trade in the early nineteenth century, but slavery in the French colonies was not definitively banned until 1848.

Sub-Saharan Africa was largely free of European domination until after the transatlantic slave trade had ended and slavery had been prohibited in the Americas. It was not until the "Scramble for Africa" in the late nineteenth and early twentieth centuries that most of sub-Saharan Africa was conquered by European powers, and only then did France establish its massive and far-flung colonies there. The people who lived in these colonies were controlled by French administrators, soldiers, and traders, and were proselytized by European missionaries. France used its supposed "civilizing mission" to justify the subjugation of the "natives" in its colonies throughout the world. As former French Prime Minister Jules Ferry argued in 1884, when the Scramble for Africa was getting underway, "the higher races have a right over the lower races" because "they have the duty to civilize the inferior races" (Ferry 1897: 156).

France's centuries-long involvement with slavery and colonialism deeply affected French thinking in the metropole. There developed a "racialization of French identity," Pap Ndiaye argues, that "aimed to clearly distinguish the civilized from the uncivilized, the 'us' from the 'them'" (Ndiaye 2006: 55). "Whiteness," the mark of the civilized, became "constitutive of the French national identity" (56), and blackness was its antithesis: "The furthest, strangest, closest to the order of nature [were] the Blacks of Africa" (55). Human zoos and other displays intensified this imagery, sending "Blacks back to an infrahuman state [through a] system of racialization that made the Black the Other par excellence, the absolute opposite of the White" (Ndiaye 2008: 205).

Colonialism did not end until the middle of the twentieth century. France's two main colonies in the Caribbean, Martinique and Guadeloupe, were absorbed into France as "overseas" *départements* in 1946. Most of France's sub-Saharan African colonies became independent in 1960. Large numbers of Black people from sub-Saharan Africa and the Caribbean began coming to mainland France in the 1970s, and the influx has increased in the decades since then (Blanchard, Dubucs and Gastaut 2016: 30–31, 36–37). Because French law prohibits the collection of data according to race, there are no reliable statistics for the number of Black people in mainland France today. Estimates reviewed in one source ranged from three to seven million (Gourévitch 2009: 56–57).[2]

Ndiaye has written extensively on "the Black condition" in France (see Ndiaye 2008). "Being black is neither an essence nor a culture, but the outcome of a social relationship: there are Blacks because they are considered Black" (Ndiaye 2008: 69; 2009: 45; see 2008: 38, 48–49). Being seen as Black—and seeing yourself as Black—nevertheless affects one's way of thinking. Ndiaye reports that "interviews conducted with black people [in France] bring to light a specific social experience of the black minority: to be Black is a preoccupation, a worry, in contrast to the fact of being White" (Ndiaye 2006: 61).[3] Of course, individual Black people can limit this preoccupation and take control of their own identities, and various interviewees have done so.

Much like Ndiaye (2008: 205) and other scholars, the interviewees reported a raft of stereotypes of Blacks in France. At least six interviewees said that Blacks are likened to monkeys, and two spoke about Blacks being "treated like monkeys."[4] Even when not caricatured as subhuman, interviewees report that Blacks are routinely dismissed as "unintelligent" or "stupid." They are thought to "smell bad" and be "dirty," as well as "uncivilized," "impolite," "lazy," and "chronically late." The men are considered generally "docile," while the women are "vulgar" and sexually lax.

Interviewees reported similar stereotypes of people living in sub-Saharan Africa. Black Africans are seen as "savages," "uncouth," "ignorant," and "uncivilized." They are dismissed by some as "banana-eaters" who live "like animals" in "primitive conditions," even "in trees." Interviewees also complained that the French media denigrates modern-day sub-Saharan Africa. One said that "when the media speaks of Africa, it's always about war, it's always about barbarism." On television, Black Africans are always "dirty, sick, and poor."

The image of Black Africans among Whites came up when I stayed with Selma, an Airbnb host from a longstanding "French" family whom I had mistakenly assumed was of non-European origin because of her name. On the wall of Selma's kitchen was a vintage advertisement for Banania, a children's cocoa-based drink, depicting a Black colonial soldier with cartoonish features saying, in comically broken French, how good the drink tastes.[5] Next to this was another vintage advertisement, depicting a White man whom Selma described as "very well-dressed, in a suit and hat." This man is culturally "advanced," she said, "not at all in the same category" as the Black man in the other advertisement. Ironically, Selma works as a guidance counselor at a vocational school with a high percentage of Maghrebi and Black students, and she spoke feelingly about the problems they encounter in navigating French society.

One's skin does not need to be black for one to be categorized as Black in France. According to the interviewees, the term Black (the interviewees used the word *noir*) is not only applied to people whose *faciès* is typical of sub-Saharan Africa, but also to those with a mixture of European and African *faciès*, who are called "*métis*" (of mixed parentage). François, whose French-born children have White mothers, is categorical about how his children are seen: "They are *métis*," and "the *métis* are Blacks." The same is true for *métis* people in mainland France who originate from the overseas *départements*. When Lucas's grandparents from Guadeloupe (whom he described as having "*café au lait*" skin) bought a house in a French village, he said, "it was the first time" people there "had ever seen a Black." Similarly, Emmanuelle, a *métisse* woman from Guadeloupe, spoke of herself as "a Black."[6]

THOMAS

As I walked from a commuter railway stop outside town to Thomas's Airbnb address, I was struck—as I had been with many interviewees in the *banlieues*—by how much his community differed from the stereotype of how people of non-European origin live. Rather than the large, broken-down government housing projects (the *cités* or *HLMs*) so often talked about, I passed well-maintained walk-up apartment buildings, small houses, and neighborhood shops. It was the same when I went out for pizza that evening and when I walked around town the next morning.

Unlike most of my hosts, who let out an extra bedroom in their own homes, Thomas rented out an apartment near his home. He had asked me to arrive by mid-afternoon. As soon as he had shown me into the apartment (which was small, but newly renovated and immaculate), he wanted to begin the interview. When I turned on the recorder, he said:

> Thank you, Larry, for having proposed this interview. When you first contacted me, I found the concept very interesting and open-minded. Then, when I read what the other Airbnb hosts had written on Airbnb about their experiences, I decided I'd participate, too. I decided to take the time to do this interview.

Our interview began, as they all did, with an autobiographical sketch. But while some people summarized their lives in ten or fifteen minutes, Thomas—though only twenty-nine—spoke uninterrupted for an hour and a half. He began with his parents' early adulthood. They came to France from the Democratic Republic of the Congo, a former Belgian colony, when his father was twenty and his mother seventeen. "Life wasn't easy," and his parents "worked very, very hard" at whatever jobs they could find. His father worked as a garbage man, and both parents handed out flyers on the metro. "They also took care of old people who were often sick, so they got sick, too." Unable to pay rent, "they lived in abandoned apartments. It was very difficult."

As the years passed, his parents made their way; they got better jobs, rented a real apartment, and had four children. Thomas and his siblings didn't know about their parents' financial difficulties while they were growing up. "They protected us from all that. We never wore torn clothes or went to school hungry." But his parents were clear in their expectations:

> My parents told us every day—every single day—"You must push ahead in your studies." My father always told us that he didn't have the chance to get much education, so we had to work hard at school. "You must go as far as you can. If you don't, it will be very hard for you."

Although the family lived at first in poor *banlieue* neighborhoods, his parents "protected us," Thomas said. "It was a good childhood, and we were a united family." But the outside world could be challenging. Thomas still remembers when, as a young child, he told his father how he had been treated unfairly. "That, my son, is just the beginning" was all he said in response. His parents went as far as they could in their jobs; his father left menial labor to drive a taxi, and his mother became a chambermaid at a five-star hotel. Along the way, Thomas said, they "experienced a lot of racism, personally, racism that was strong. They were called 'dirty Blacks' for no reason, things like that."

As the children got older, Thomas's father became more pointed in his advice:

> We are not White. Even though you were born in France, you won't be considered a true French person. You must work harder than the others because of racism. If working twice as hard isn't enough, work four times as hard. If that's not enough, work eight times as hard. And if you fall, get back up.

Thomas's father had a succinct way of describing working life in France: "Whites in the office, Blacks collect the trash." But while he and their mother had to live by this rule, their children could escape. "We, his children, must be in the offices too." But it wouldn't be easy; Thomas and his siblings would have to "study to the limit." Their father said that "Whites in the office" was not just a description of who works where, but of "social categories," of where the "power" is. His children would have to work hard to get in.

Along the way, Thomas's father warned that they would meet stiff resistance: "You were born in France, you are citizens, but the more you advance, the more you'll come upon people who want you to fail." Thomas was shocked. "It's not possible!" Their father would explain: "All French people aren't racists, but racism exists. You'll go places because you've worked hard. But some people won't be happy. They'll think, 'Why is he here? Blacks are just store guards and the like. He shouldn't be here.'"

After graduating from high school, Thomas entered a two-year IT program. His first year went well until the third trimester, when the official teacher returned from maternity leave. "I'd never seen her before, but she gave me looks like she was shooting me. Oh!" He had the same teacher in his second year. It was "truly bizarre"—"she did everything to slow me down"—and he was not the only one; the three other Black students were treated the same way. When, toward the end of the year, she predicted to Thomas's face that he'd fail the program's final exams, saying "you won't get your diploma," he was stunned. "Teachers are supposed to encourage students!" But rather than "closing in upon myself," he said, "I worked twice as hard, three times harder than the other students." At the end of year, he passed his exams and graduated.

Looking back, Thomas was struck by his teacher's cruelty. "Consciously," he thinks, she was trying to foster within him a low estimation of his abilities. Her message was, "You can't do it, it's impossible, it's not for you." He says, "Even now when I talk of this, it's incredible."[7]

Having gotten his diploma, Thomas had a decision to make. The company where he had worked part-time during the IT program offered him a full-time job at a good salary. It was tempting, especially since his friends already had jobs and some owned cars. But he decided to continue his education, first getting an advanced IT diploma and then a master's degree in IT engineering. This yielded a management position at a major company. All went well there until, after three years, his supervisor said that the promotion he'd been promised was "impossible."

Thomas was crushed; he had "zero morale, less than zero." Thomas switched companies, but decided to start his own business and threw himself into learning about small-scale real estate investing and identifying apartments that were good investment opportunities. He prepared a proposal showing how a specific apartment would be profitable, but when he went to the bank to seek a loan—"wearing a tie, et cetera, et cetera"—he was turned down. He was also rejected by the second bank, and the third. "They didn't say they weren't lending me the money because I'm Black, but I thought that if I'd been White maybe they would have." He persisted, finally getting a loan from the sixth bank, and then launched his real estate business. It has been hard work, but he's been successful. By the time of our interview, Thomas owned a number of apartments, including the one in which I stayed. He had also married his high school girlfriend and started a family.

As the interview neared its fourth hour, Thomas shared his feelings through these years. Sitting just a couple of feet from me, he spoke with unrestrained intensity, but also laughed often. The experience with his IT teacher "was something new to me. It was the first time my parents couldn't protect me." And though he'd been able to turn his teacher's behavior to his benefit (it "motivated me times ten, times a thousand"), by the time he had gotten his diploma, he realized that his father had been right. In Thomas's words: "I understood that a Black can be French, but only up to a certain level. The higher you go, the more you'll face racism." Later in the interview, Thomas returned to this issue:

> I know that there are French people who consider me a foreigner. They make clear that "even if you were born here, you're a foreigner. You remain a Black. You've succeeded, you've done advanced studies, et cetera, but pay attention: though you were born in France, as you advance, you are less French."

For Thomas, the challenge is to keep racism from undermining his drive to succeed. "What's dangerous for me today is to think that everyone's racist, that when there's a problem it's because they don't like Blacks. That's what's dangerous." When he encounters someone who's racist, he follows his family's approach. "Other families get frightened or hunker down. They say, 'Don't go there because they don't like Blacks.' Our family is not like that. One person might be a racist, but another isn't. There are imbeciles in France, so let them be." Thomas feels that you must always be "positive," believing that "human beings are good even if some people aren't." Don't "cry" about being a "victim" and "don't lose yourself in anger. You need to keep advancing in life."

Thomas turned to the general issue of being Black in France. There are "the true French, the French who are White" and then—he laughed, pointing to his skin—there are "the French who are Black." Although it has been hard to make his way up in the work world—in his father's words, "in the office"—Thomas has never wanted to be White. "No, not once, because of the education my parents gave me. They'd say, 'Never deny your origins.'" And so "I've never envied a White person." While many Blacks feel inferior to Whites, he says, that's not for him: "If you feel inferior, you can't go on living. The goal is to live. There's enough room for everyone." I asked whether he's ever felt ashamed about being Black. "No, never, never. Never!"

We finally ended at 9 PM. Thomas was emphatic about his personal philosophy: "You must have objectives that you'll attain. You must fight and fight again to make your dreams come true."

BLACK IN A WHITE WORLD—INTERVIEWEE PROFILES

The interviewees who are seen as Black vary in many ways. They originate from almost a dozen countries or overseas *départements* of France: in Africa, from Burkina Faso, Cameroon, Republic of the Congo, Gabon, Guinea, Ivory Coast, Madagascar, and Senegal; and, in the Caribbean, from Guadeloupe, Haiti, and Martinique. Some have spent their entire lives in France, while others came as children or young adults. They range in age from seventeen to their fifties. But, despite this variety, they have certain things in common. All originate from places that were once European colonies. Indeed, except for Thomas, whose parents came from a former Belgian colony, all originate from former French colonies.[8] And all must live with being seen as Black, with all that this entails in other people's minds.

Perhaps because of their similar family histories and their shared reality of being seen as Black—intertwined facts of life in France—these interviewees focused on two related themes. Some focused on issues of identity, both how they see themselves and how they feel others see them. Others focused on achieving professional success, in part to disprove the stereotypes of Blacks they encountered in their own lives. Some spoke about both concerns.

The Problem of Identity

Jean, Clément, Anna, Caroline, Lucas, and François spoke about their lives with raw emotion. All are in their thirties or early forties and all share the norms of language, values, and behavior of the "French" people around them. Although almost all of them grew up in France and see themselves as French, this self-image is undercut by their *faciès*, by being Black in a country where the people who are unquestionably French—those who are referred to as "French"—are White. Certain issues came up again and again. Do they feel inferior? Do they feel that "French" people see them as inferior? That "French" people do not accept them as really French? That they are seen as outsiders in their own country?

Jean. Now thirty, Jean has spent his entire life in France. His parents came from Haiti, where his mother had been deeply impressed by the wealth and appearance of American tourists. In France, his family settled in a public housing project in a poor neighborhood, where Jean "saw everything: violence, prostitution, drug addiction," even as a young child. Today, he is a dedicated artist, living with his parents for financial reasons. I met him through a mutual friend.

In person, Jean is far from the stereotype of people in the housing projects. He says, "I'm very well integrated, thanks to my parental education." He makes a point of dressing "in a completely Western way" and having the right haircut. In sum, "I fit into the mold."

From an early age, Jean says, "my parents wanted me to succeed at any price." His mother kept telling him and his siblings that they had to "succeed like the Whites succeed. We always had that comparison: Look at how the Whites succeed, look at how they are. You must do the same. There was this omnipotence of the Whites in our life. This never ended."

Growing up, Jean didn't only want to be like Whites, he says, "I wanted to be White." But as he fell behind academically, he wondered, "What will I do, since I can't succeed in school? How will I be White if I can't succeed at school? If I can't be intelligent?" Hoping to look like a White person, "I would pinch my nostrils and pull my nose forward."

By middle school, Jean saw his mother's logic play out. While most Whites continued on the academic track, he was funneled into the slower school program, the "dark side," with mostly Blacks and Maghrebis. Jean had "a great feeling of desire, of impotence and injustice. It angered me a lot."

His color also put him at a disadvantage in the larger society. In France, he says, there's an enormous difference between a second-generation Black person like him and a second-generation person whose parents came from a European country. "The difference is very simple: they're White. Automatically, that gives them an incredible superiority."

Adolescence was difficult. Other kids would make jokes, he said, "about the color of my skin," calling out, "You're a gorilla" or "You're a monkey." These images come from "the colonial past of France," Jean thinks, and they haven't disappeared. He pointed to the way that "museum exhibits depict Blacks. Look at how they are! Sadly, it's a heritage that comes back over and over and over again."

Jean was also troubled by what he learned in school about sub-Saharan Africa:

> Even if I'm not African, I was ashamed of Africa with its shantytowns and broken-down houses. I couldn't understand it. Why do Africans stay that way? In my head, I criticized them. Why do they live in caves, why do they remain in those primitive conditions? And then there are the wars they fight among themselves. I couldn't understand that.

The contrast with Europe was humiliating. "Then you turned the page and saw the great powers with all their incredible things. Even though I wasn't African, I was a bit like one. I was a little ashamed."

The problem went beyond Africa. At school, he says, "I was also ashamed when they talked about slavery. It was very sad. I felt like I was screwed into my chair and could do nothing. Ow! It really weighed me down. I couldn't understand why the slaves stayed that way." In recounting this scene, Jean spoke about being "ashamed" of the slaves rather than, say, about being furious with Europeans for having transported Black Africans across the Atlantic or for having brutalized them as slaves in places like Haiti, where Jean's parents came from, and other parts of the Americas.

By high school, Jean began to focus on his own art, which he feels has saved him. His twenties were a time of

> enormous evolution, of an opening up and knowledge of myself as an artist. Starting then, I sought out who I am: the Black, the Haitian, my origins. All of this came back in a flash. Because to work as an artist, you have to have these keys, this code.

He also discovered Jean-Michel Basquiat, an American artist whose father was Haitian. Basquiat "totally overthrew" Jean's goal to "be like the Whites, to feel like the Whites." Becoming "a mirror" for him, Basquiat "put me on a road that's mine." Jean began to take "great pride" in himself. "I left the shadows for the sunlight."

Today, Jean sees himself as "a Black artist." Through his art, he is involved in the "struggle against prejudice, against racism, many such struggles, to enter into a world that's more welcoming." But it's an "internal struggle," too. As Blacks, "we can say that we're proud of ourselves, but there's still what's left from the past. We have to struggle against those voices."

During a break in the interview, Jean showed me a portfolio of his pen-and-ink drawings. He spoke about them when we turned the recorder back on. "My characters are primarily Whites," he said, but "starting last year, I've tried to draw Black people. It's very difficult. I'm in a disequilibrium about what I should do." One of the drawings in the portfolio depicts an artist at his easel who is "blond" with "Western features." Another drawing features "two Black men, one who is holding a brush and trying to lift up his friend," while nearby there are "people with pitchforks and torches who want to block their way." The final drawing, which he was still working on, portrays "a young Black man who's lost, who's looking for a destiny, a place to live, because he has no roots, he doesn't know who he is."

Since Jean had referred to some people as "French" during the interview, I asked what he meant by this. He replied, "Implicitly, I'd be saying that he's White." But what about him, I asked. He's lived his whole life in France. Doesn't he consider himself French too? "Yes, I'm French, but internally I'd have a little smile, thinking 'I'm French, but I'm no fool.' I fully understand that in the eyes of many people I'm something else." Then, evoking the history of France's roundups and its shipping of Jews to their deaths during World War II, he said "if the Nazis came back today and rounded people up, despite my French passport, I'd be taken away."

Clément. I met Clément at his modest apartment on the outskirts of town. He was alone that evening—his wife and daughter were away—and eager to talk about his life. Conducted in his dimly lit and quiet living room, his interview continued until midnight and resumed early the next morning. Clément stared into a middle distance as he recounted the many painful times of his life.

Originally from the Cape Verde Islands, Clément's family was living in Senegal when he was born. His father, a veteran of the French Foreign Legion who had gained French citizenship, moved the family to France when Clément was six. After a short time living in a housing project in the city's poor *banlieue*, the family settled in a pleasant house with a garden in a largely White, middle-class community outside the city. Clément's first and last names are European, he is a French citizen, and his family has always been Catholic. He is now thirty-six.

When Clément was about twelve, he and a "blond and blue-eyed" friend went into the town's central cafe to buy candies. Clément was called over to be photographed with a group of men, who then "burst into laughter." This baffled him. After leaving the café, Clément's friend explained what had happened: the men "were ridiculing you. They're with the National Front and you represent the people they want to force out of the country." Clément says he "froze for five minutes. This was the first time I'd been hit full force with the image of my skin color. It really affected me."

While this experience was extreme, Clément often felt "different in the eyes of others." He explained:

> Here's a simple example. I'd go to a store with a friend, blond with blue eyes. The tone toward each of us wouldn't be the same, the welcome wouldn't be the same. Or when we were going someplace or getting on a bus—the simple things of life. Even though I was young, I felt it.

After a while, "I'd play naive to avoid confronting this lack of belonging. I'd hang back or stand at the end of the line."

At school, Clément was "virtually the only Black in class," he said, and "eighty percent of our school was White, they were French." When the subject of slavery came up, "I identified with the Blacks in chains," and thought "people of my origin were the ones who'd been enslaved" by the White students' ancestors. He also felt that the other students had a glamorous history to study—"Napoleon and his many conquests"—while he had "a lack of history." Clément kept wondering, "Why can't I be White like the others? It's unfair."

Geography class provided another painful lesson. There were two types of countries: the "developed ones," like France, and "the poor ones, like Senegal and Mali." From Senegal himself, Clément says he "immediately identified with the poor countries." Such experiences created a "discouragement with what we were being taught." He fell into an "educational malaise."

Clément also began to feel socially rejected. "A friend would go to another friend's house to play a video game, but I could never go. Their parents wouldn't allow it. And when a friend's family would go away for a weekend, others could go, but for me it wasn't possible." The "pity of my friends," he said, made him "ashamed" and "angry."

Feeling "different from my classmates and the kids in my neighborhood," Clément started hanging out "little by little with the kids of the housing projects" outside town. "I needed to belong," he said, and so "I made a change in the palette of my friends. I sought out Maghrebis, Comorians, Senegalese kids because they looked more like me. They wouldn't ridicule me; they wouldn't exclude me."

When he graduated from high school, Clément's father arranged for him to join the French Foreign Legion. This required a ploy. Because the Foreign Legion is limited to people who are not French citizens, it issued Clément an ID card with a new name and new nationality, identifying him as Canadian. This had an astonishing effect:

> When I went out with that Canadian identity, I was immediately more appealing; I was exotic. If I entered a department store or nice restaurant, for example, or a discotheque, the simple fact that my ID card had "Canadian" on it, all of a sudden, made people think, "Ah, this is an exotic Black from Canada." All of a sudden I had more value. And that was super appealing. That Canadian ID eliminated a lot of complexes and opened a lot of doors. It really changed how I was seen. A whole lot.

Just being a soldier helped too: "The military uniform put me in another status." Clément felt like "a citizen who serves my country, not a foreigner they don't want."

Today, those days are long over. The return to civilian life, he says, was "a bit brutal because I lost my Canadian identity and left the army at the same time." Wondering about his "origins" and wanting to learn what he "hadn't learned in school," Clément went to Senegal for four months. Senegal was poor. "That touched me a lot" and "culturally it was a great shock," he reported, but "with time I came to see some things that were more profound." The experience was "very enriching." Clément also fell in love with a Senegalese woman, whom he ultimately married. He returned to France feeling proud. "I had regained my history."[9]

During the years since his army service and trip to Senegal, Clément has held a variety of jobs. For five years, he served as the leader of a small social services team and faced resistance from its White members, as detailed later in this chapter. More recently, he has gone into business for himself, teaching teenagers how to drive. This allows him more autonomy. But even now, despite five years of military service, ten more years as a responsible member of society, and his fully European name, Clément is not seen as truly French. "A French person," he says. doesn't "look Arab or Black." To be "seen as totally French," a person must be "White, without color, not *typé*." And so "I'm French, but not very French."

Clément explained what this means in practice:

> Okay, you're a citizen, you follow the same rules, et cetera, but you don't have the same access, the same rights, the same opportunities. Yes, I grew up in this country, I was educated in this country, I absorbed the culture, but I can't eat at certain restaurants, I can't go into certain stores, into certain discotheques or nightclubs, et cetera. And so I'm French, but not very French.

This last sentence came with a sardonic laugh, much like the laughs that punctuated other moments of his life story.

Clément's situation has been further complicated by religion. As will be discussed in chapter 6, he converted from Catholicism to Islam before marrying his Senegalese fiancée. While this aspect of life is "hyper-enriching," he feels he must hide it to avoid "aggravating" other people.

Anna. A friend of one of my Airbnb hosts, Anna met me for dinner at a downtown restaurant. I explained the project, and she readily volunteered to be interviewed. We met later that week at her apartment in an attractive neighborhood in town.

Anna was born in Burkina Faso, a poor former French colony in West Africa, shortly after her parents, both from Burkina

Faso, were divorced. When Anna was two, her father married a French woman who was working as a volunteer nurse in the country; when she was four, her father and stepmother brought her to France. Now thirty-one, Anna has lived in France ever since.

The family first settled in a town called Le Blanc ("The White")—Anna chuckled at the name—where there were "only two families of color." Her stepmother, she says, became "my mother, the person who raised me, the person I love, the mother of my heart." And so "I had a White mother." Meanwhile, her father had felt estranged from life in Burkina Faso when he was there ("He said he'd always been apart from the others"), and so, she recalls, "didn't give me an African education." There was no African food, music, clothing, or language in the household. "I always had the model of my dad, who wasn't born in France, but who'd totally adapted to France, in his habits and his culture." In sum, "I was very White, I was very French."

During her childhood, Anna remembers being a "mascot" among the other kids, with "everyone wanting to be my friend." She later realized that Le Blanc had not been totally free of bias. Shortly after the family arrived, her parents were forced to switch Anna's preschool because of other parents' objections. In her early teens, she was occasionally called such things "*bamboula*" (a degrading term for Black people; see Ruscio 2020: 31–34) or told "Your mother descends from the monkeys," but only because, she says, "everyone becomes stupid" at that age.

When Anna was sixteen, the family moved to a small French city where there were some Africans. One day an African girl called her a "Bounty" (a French candy that is coconut on the inside and chocolate on the outside). Although intended as an insult, Anna thought that the image was apt. After all, she had grown up in an entirely French environment at home, in school, and in her community. She says, "I was raised as a European in a black envelope. It's the person I am."

After a year and a half of college, Anna entered the work world. As reported later in this chapter, she has faced employment discrimination in at least two jobs. Anna has also lived in different cities. While in Paris, she encountered its large African community, which, she admits, "frightened me a little. I felt like a foreigner among people who look like me." The people were "hardly assimilated at all"; many were "vulgar" in their way of speaking and acting. This conflicted sharply with her own behavior: "I like being reserved." One African custom she did adopt, however, is having her hair braided. Anna has dated only White men.

When I asked Anna whether she is French, she answered, "I feel French." Later in the interview, she explained this equivocal statement: "From my point of view, yes, I'm French. For others I will never be. For certain people I can have a French passport, have lived virtually my entire life in France, live with a French man, and pay French taxes, but I'll never be French." Nevertheless, Anna won't dwell on bias against Blacks. "One can't live in a country thinking that everyone sees us in a bad light."

Caroline. Much like Anna, Caroline is Black but has spent most of her life with White people. Born in Guadeloupe, she came to mainland France with her mother and European stepfather when she was only three. She is now thirty-five. Caroline grew up in a well-off White neighborhood and was often in all-White classes in school. Her mother, she says, disdained the Africans who later moved into town: "Oh, yes, she was racist." Her mother would tell Caroline to stay away: "Don't hang out with the Africans; you'll ruin your life."

Teachers and other kids could be hurtful. In elementary school, White children refused to hold Caroline's hand and didn't want her to join them in the swimming pool. "It was mean." Later, when recent African immigrants were enrolled in her school and put in a separate class to learn French—known to Whites as the "idiots' class"—her teacher suggested that she switch to that class "because I was Black." It didn't matter that she was a native French speaker or that she had been a student at the school for years. Still later, Caroline attended a private school specializing in *haute cuisine*, where she was either the only Black student or one of just two. "The director of the high school was racist; it was intolerable." When a student was to be chosen to represent the school at a nationwide competition, she wouldn't even consider Caroline: "You're Black. We can't be represented by a Black."

Despite these incidents, Caroline thought of herself as White, like her fellow students. "For me, I was like them. I didn't even see that my color was different from theirs." It was only the comments by students and faculty that, she says, "brought me back to reality."

After high school, Caroline worked as a dessert chef at a hotel kitchen and then for the local commuter railway system where she still works. "I've pretty much always lived with French people," she says. "I've always been integrated into my country." Caroline married "a White, a French man" and had two children with him, though the couple is now divorced. Caroline's children do not look like her—she says "they're both White"—and so people assume that she is their babysitter. For them, "I'm never the mother." Having kept her married name, Caroline has the same last name as her children. This has proved useful, since "even after four years," she must show her ID card to pick her children up at school. She also has "a lot of racist neighbors."

Caroline says, "For me, a French person is White," and her best friends are White. "It's true that I'm Black, but I don't see my color. I'm like my friends." And they see her the same way: "My friends often tell me, 'It's true, we forget you're Black. You're White like us.'"

Lucas. I arrived at Lucas's apartment in a middle-class suburb in the late afternoon. He immediately identified himself as Guadeloupean, even though we had just said hello. Lucas invited me to join him for dinner, and we got to know each other while he chopped and cooked. The interview began right after dinner and continued until nearly midnight. Now thirty-eight, he is the owner of a small electrical maintenance and repair business. He has never been married and has no children.

Lucas started his life story not with himself, but with his grandparents. His paternal grandparents came to mainland France from Guadeloupe. They were "*métis*." His maternal grandparents were entirely White, with deep roots in mainland France; in Lucas's words, they were "French French." Turning to his parents, he said that his father had "*café au lait*" skin and his mother was White. Because both of his parents were born and raised in mainland France, Lucas is at least the second generation on both sides of his family to be born and to live in mainland France.

Still, the issue of belonging has been complicated. Just a few minutes into the interview, Lucas spoke of a childhood incident that, he said, "has marked me ever since."

> I was seven years old. I was going out to play with my friends. My mother stopped me, saying that I needed to take my na-

> tional identity card with me. I had been born here, and yet I had to carry my papers when I was outside. I have always found that troubling. It was a shock. I was just a young child who had no idea of skin color; this made me understand that in the world I was different, even though I hadn't felt different.

His White friends didn't need to carry their national identity cards. It was "at this moment" that Lucas discovered that there are people like his friends, who, he says, are "French French," and there are people like him who look different, who are "not totally French." "I was not in the same category of person. I was not what I thought I was."[10]

As Lucas entered adolescence, the issue of identity continued to trouble him. Although he has the same *"café au lait"* skin as his father, Lucas's father "never wanted to talk about my roots." Meanwhile, his "French French" mother taught him "to speak a better French and to respect people," which helped him to "mix in" with Whites. "The fact that I was polite reassured them." Throughout his life, Lucas has been a "chameleon," he says, always ready to "adjust to the type of person that's in front of me."

Police on the street did not see him this way. "During my adolescence I had a big problem" with the police, he said, "because of my *faciès.*" They saw a young man with hair "like the Jackson Five" and "swarthy" skin. "Over and over," the police stopped him and demanded that he show them his national identity card.

The awkwardness of being a "chameleon" was brought home some years later, when a White friend came banging on Lucas's door. His friend was furious with his daughter because she had started dating a Senegalese man. "Vomiting" his disgust with this liaison, the friend evidently had forgotten Lucas's own skin color. At that moment, Lucas said, "it was as if he'd put on the table the core of his personality."

Even today, more than thirty years after the childhood incident that "marked" him, Lucas wrestles with the issue of identity. Not wanting others to decide his place in French society, he suddenly said to me, "If I must be put in a caste" —neither of us had said anything about "caste" or a "caste" system—"I'll be the one to put myself into a caste." He is "Guadeloupean." Lucas said this even though he and both of his parents have spent their entire lives in mainland France and even though his mother, who came from a longtime "French" family, has no connection whatever to Guadeloupe.

François. Unlike all the interviewees profiled to this point, François grew up outside of France. Now forty-eight, François is from a prosperous Catholic family in the capital of Gabon, a former French colony in Central Africa. He remembers thinking of France as "a great country, an intelligent country. It's the White man." France "brought television, it brought the Industrial Revolution, the automobile, et cetera. You thought of France as powerful, as superior."

François attended a French government middle and high school with French teachers and mostly European students. There were "very few Africans." The teachers talked about "fabulous things. There was all this fantasy." He described his emotions at the time:

> You want to be like the Whites, you want to act like the Whites. You want to speak like the Whites, you want to erase any accent. You wanted to have White friends. Even at that age, there's a feeling of belonging, of belonging to the culture that comes from colonization, from White people in France, from your French friends. You want to have a White identity, consciously or unconsciously.

These feelings were complicated by his experience at school. Though he had a "deep-set complex" about Whites being "more intelligent" than Africans, he "had the same grades" as his White classmates.

While still a child, François made a striking discovery. He had not known his father because his parents had divorced very early in his life and his father lived in a different part of the country. When he was about nine, François took an inter-city car to visit his father. There he discovered that his father was *métis*, since his paternal grandfather had been Portuguese. This made François "proud" and explained his own "cappuccino" skin color. It also, he says, "reinforced my desire to identify" with Whites and "to do things like a White."

At twenty-one, François went to France to attend business school, where everything went well. His finances put him on a par with the French students, and he fit in socially. "We went to the same school, and we went out together in the evening. I felt equal to the other students." He spoke "good French," better than many native-born French people, who "speak badly." When a French person asked whether his parents back in Africa spoke French, he responded, "Monsieur, my parents speak a better French than you." He graduated and entered the work world.

It has been twenty-five years since those early years in France. During this time, François has had a variety of jobs, was married once (to a White woman), and has had two other close relationships (also with White women). He has three children. Now separated from the mothers of his children, he lives on his own. He is a French citizen, fully "assimilated," he says, and a Catholic. But while "I live like French people," he says, "I grew up in Gabon. I have an African, a Gabonese identity."

But what about his children? "Take the case of my children," he said, "it's complicated for them." Even though they've been raised by their "purely French" mothers and have spent their entire lives in France, "they're *métis*." And the "*métis* are Blacks."

François became increasingly emotional as he discussed these issues. Even a Black person who "grows up in France and accepts all French codes of behavior and succeeds" is not really French. In France, there are "two morphologies, two typologies," he explained, and "to be French is in the skin." Slapping his forearm more and more sharply—the sound jumps out on the recording of our interview—he added, "It's the skin, it's the skin, the skin. With the skin, they always see our origins."

I asked François whether Blacks can be accepted in France. He laughed, but not happily. "This skin is with us. This skin, when one is here, is terrible. It doesn't matter what you do, it doesn't matter if you grow up in a bourgeois environment in the middle of Paris, you must always justify yourself." He continued, "There are those who feel French" and marry into a French family, but "one day a cousin might get annoyed and say, 'little black one.'" When all is said and done, he says, "French people won't accept us. Consciously or unconsciously, they don't accept us."

"I'm not what you think I am": Pushing Forward in the Face of Prejudice

Thomas's profile at the beginning of this chapter reveals a person who spends less mental energy on his identity, about which he has no doubt, than on making a successful life in France. Thomas is not alone. Charles, Isabel, Amina, Marie, Markus, Daniel, and Philippe do much the same. Unlike all but one of the interviewees discussed in the section above, most of these people grew up outside of France. Fully conscious of the prejudices they face, each is intent on proving, in the words of one, that "I'm not what you think I am."

Like the first group of interviewees, many of whom also push forward even while they think about their identities, each interviewee in this section is unique. Common themes nevertheless emerged in their interviews. What obstacles have they faced? Have they succeeded in their careers? Are they calm in the face of prejudice or are they consumed with fury?

Charles. Charles's wife Ariel picked me up at the airport late in the evening and brought me to the house where the couple lives with their three-year-old son. We talked late into the night and continued through two days of their home-cooked meals, with such succulent dishes as seared duck breast. Charles is profiled here, Ariel in chapter 4.

Now fifty-six, Charles grew up in the former French colony of Martinique in the Antilles section of the Caribbean. Martinique became an overseas *département* of France more than a decade before his birth, and he has always felt French. Like other interviewees who came from overseas *départements*, Charles has been a French citizen since birth. As far as he was concerned, "France was the best country." Looking back today, he says, "I was born French, I am French."

Since early adolescence, Charles has had two passions: judo and mathematics. Judo "forged my personality," he says, and Charles excelled in it, becoming the Martinican judo champion for each age group from fifteen through twenty-one. He also excelled in math, even in the demanding science track of his high school. Realizing that he would have to go to mainland France to become more than a high school math teacher, he decided to make the jump. He knew that computers were the key to the future, and he wanted to pursue this future.

At twenty-one, Charles left for mainland France to study information technology. Although he had always considered himself French while growing up in Martinique, he had had little experience with Whites. In mainland France, Charles quickly discovered that many did not consider him French: "There are many, many, many people who are prejudiced against Africans, Antilleans, and Arabs. Against everyone who isn't French. I say openly and clearly that French society is very racist." Charles persisted in his professional plans. He finished his IT training and has worked at consulting firms ever since. He is now the head of a project team.

This has been a good match for him. In tech, "intellectual competence, not skin color, is what's valued" and the people are more open-minded than elsewhere. They "are at least as educated" as him and have been "exposed to other cultures." Tech people also have professional freedom: with recognized skills, they can change companies when they feel unappreciated. Charles has done this three times.

Judo continued to be a major part of his life in France. "In competition you're there to win" and you're not alone.

> Bizarrely, after all we've said about French society, sport is universal in France. You are a member of a club, not judged at all about appearance, by your exterior color, but only by your abilities. I was never, I say never, judged by my origins or the color of my skin in judo.

Psychologically, "sports give a person the strength to do battle and to resist." For Charles, this strength has been helpful "with regard to *intégration*, racism, et cetera, since it's easier to attack someone who's weak than someone who has force of character." Coming to my room after one of our interview sessions, Charles added that his physical presence has helped, too: he is "one meter ninety" (six feet, two inches) and "muscular."

Charles refuses to be put off by racism, he says, "so long as I'm not attacked intellectually or physically." No one has ever tried to attack Charles physically, but he recalled two times when his intellect was questioned on racial grounds. In high school in Martinique, a White math teacher considered the Martinican students a bunch of "little *nègres*" (an insulting term for Blacks; see Ruscio 2020: 95–102), saying, "You'll never succeed in life; you're all welfare cases." Charles's only recourse was to do well on his exams, and "since it was math, rather than French or philosophy, the teacher couldn't cheat on the grades." Charles easily beat out the teacher's pet, a White boy.

The second incident occurred during an IT assignment in Guadeloupe. A White colleague from mainland France rejected Charles's solution to a technical problem, saying, "An Antillean does not teach me my work." During a larger meeting the next day, the same man said, "You Antilleans don't know how to do things; you don't know how things work." Charles spoke up, telling the man, "I simply explained something you didn't know. I didn't question your competence. Don't question ours."

Despite Charles's strength of character, living with racism has been difficult. Whenever he discussed the subject, Charles's booming voice grew softer, his face sagged, and his shoulders pulled in. But he refuses to live thinking with the notion that racism is behind every slight or setback, and he won't be thrown off track: "There are obstacles, but the obstacles, you go around them or you jump over them. Every morning that you wake up is a chance to make your life."

Isabel. From the beginning of her interview to the end, Isabel was emphatic about everything: her family, her values, her pride, her hurt, and her resoluteness.

Now forty-one, Isabel grew up in extraordinary circumstances. Her father was an army general and then the Minister of Defense of the Republic of the Congo, a former French colony in Central Africa. Her family lived in an enormous house in a military complex, and the children were not allowed to go into the outer world. French was the language of the household—"since the cradle, we spoke only French"—and she never learned an African language. The family was deeply Catholic.

Isabel's father expected that his children would meet the same exacting standards as his officer training program in Europe. He was emphatic about life in Europe. While a person can make much of himself there, Blacks had to fight every step of the way. Having "suffered from racism," he told Isabel:

> In Europe, there'll always be people to let you know you are Black, that you will remain Black. People will think you're inferior. So, a Black must always be the best. A Black must prove, "I'm intelligent. I'm not what you think I am." If you don't, you'll be crushed.

At sixteen, Isabel came to France to attend a Catholic high school. Gifted in clothing design, she then studied *haute cou-*

ture at an elite private school. Her father paid the tuition there, he told her, "on the sole condition that you are the best." She became a French citizen at twenty. After getting her diploma, Isabel worked at an international fashion house and then returned to her former school as a faculty member. She married a "French" man and had two children, but the couple then divorced. Despite the hard times followed—Isabel cleaned hospital rooms and worked as a security guard at an airport and a housing project—she pushed forward. There could be no help from her father: back in the Congo, he had been assassinated, and his assets had been seized by political rivals.

Ultimately, Isabel was able to open a store in a stylish neighborhood downtown, where she sells clothes made from African cloth that she designs and sews herself. (Most of our interview was conducted in the store during breaks between customers.) Although her business has been relatively successful, the experience has not been easy. One morning, when she arrived at her store, she was greeted by the words (in French) "Dirty *Nègre* Go Home" written with fecal matter on the plate-glass window.

Siblings of Isabel who have settled in France have also experienced rejection. She recounted an incident involving one of her brothers, who is a lawyer in Paris. He and his White girlfriend had wanted to get married, but he needed to get the approval of her father, who is a judge. Meeting privately with Isabel's brother, her father told him that, though he seemed to be a fine young man and promising lawyer, the marriage would never happen. The reason was clear to both of them.

Meanwhile, Isabel feels no affinity for African people in France who have not adopted French ways. When we were having lunch at a restaurant near her shop, an African woman launched into a boisterous conversation at the table next to ours. Isabel was visibly put off. She explained why afterwards: the woman's behavior revealed a "lack of education"; it was as if she were still a "savage" in Africa.

Isabel has raised her children to be French. Both are *métis* with fully French names and have never been to Africa. Once, when one of them said something foolish, she reproved him, saying, "Now you're thinking like an old African villager." As with her father and herself, Isabel's children must excel, and so far they've met this standard. "In all they do," she said, "they're best in their category—in sports, in school, they're the best."

Isabel is sure of her identity. Her voice swelling, she declared, "I'm proud of being myself, of being Black, because God made me that way. I'm Congolese by origin, but I'm French by adoption. I've lived here for years, and my children were born here. Above all, I'm French." In the face of the rejection she sometimes experiences in France, Isabel made her point with characteristic bluntness: "I'm French whether people like it or not."

Amina. Amina picked me up downtown at the end of her workday. She was wearing a black business dress and had the stylish haircut and makeup of an urban professional. We had dinner at a restaurant near the Airbnb apartment she rents out and then, back at the apartment, began her interview at 10 PM. We didn't stop until 1:30 AM. Since there was still more to discuss, Amina kindly met me two days later at my next Airbnb apartment.

Now thirty-eight, Amina is from Cameroon, in west-central Africa. The daughter of a former ambassador, she grew up in "comfortable" circumstances in a small city. Though everyone in her family spoke French fluently and admired France, she had no "complexes," she said, relating to the country or the people. And since she didn't know Europeans in Cameroon, she wasn't exposed to their attitudes toward Africans. "I was very protected by my mother until I left for France."

After completing high school and two years of business school in Cameroon, Amina went to France to finish her education. Until the day her plane landed in France, Amina says, "the only contact I had with racism was the television program about Kunta Kinte" (the enslaved hero of the American television series *Roots*) "and films about slavery in Brazil." She discovered racism firsthand on that first day in France. Needing to transfer at a metro station, she approached a young couple on the platform to ask for directions. She greeted the couple, but they didn't respond. When she greeted them again, they looked at her, she says, "as if I were transparent and said nothing." By chance, a French woman then approached the same couple to ask for directions. They responded readily.

Since Amina arrived in France after the school trimester had begun, her professor suggested that she borrow the class notes of another student in the class. None of her classmates were willing to help. Later that year, an African student in another class offered Amina a theory of why French students were dismissive toward Africans. French children, she said, grew up learning that "Africans live like animals in trees, that they're monkeys, and so for them it's unthinkable to see a Black at a university." It was outright absurd for a Black person to be at an expensive business school like the one they attended. After getting poor grades in her first trimester, Amina decided that "the only way to take my revenge against these fools was to get very high grades. If they thought I'd come down from a tree, that I couldn't be as intelligent as them, the only way to prove that we're equal was to beat them in school." Beginning with the next trimester, she did just that.

After getting her business diploma, Amina got a master's degree in IT and did advanced studies in business intelligence. This last step was crucial. In business intelligence, she says, competence is the only thing that matters: "You either know it or you don't." In her first job in this field, she worked extremely hard and "learned a lot," even at the cost of a "burnout." After this, no one could doubt her abilities. "Clients pay a lot" for business intelligence services, she says, so it doesn't matter "if you're Black, White, et cetera."

Amina ultimately switched from corporate employee to self-employed consultant. She explained why, using the bank where she currently works as an example. There, she works on a project with about a dozen other technical consultants—mostly Maghrebis and Blacks—who are stationed in a single, large room. The bank officials to whom they report are different; the "great majority are French." Working apart from them, Amina and the other non-French consultants are largely protected from their biases.

Although her career is going well enough, being a woman, she says, "is an extra handicap. It's a problem for all women in France." There are incidents "etched in my memory" that Amina says she originally thought occurred "because I'm Black," but that she later realized were "because I'm a woman." Being a woman and a Black are not the only challenges Amina faces. As discussed in chapter 6, she is also Muslim. With a deep laugh, she said, "To be a woman, Black, and a Muslim is not a promising route to a great career."

Almost twenty years have passed since her first days in business school, and Amina remains angry. The senseless rejection she faced from French students that first trimester, she says, "fed my rage. I must absolutely succeed. And the rage I had then is the same rage I have today because I'm in the same battle. My sole revenge is to succeed." Amina is determined to make her way in France. "I won't accept being a victim. I detest people who play the victim."

Marie and Markus. Marie invited me to her house in an attractive suburb for a family Sunday dinner. Dressed in a bright dress of African cloth, she welcomed me warmly, and we sat down to a large Cameroonian meal of chicken, plantains, and rice. The conversation was spirited, with everyone at the table taking part. When I described my project, Marie said she'd be happy to participate and her son Markus, although only seventeen, asked to participate, too.

Now fifty, Marie comes from an extremely well-off family in the commercial capital of Cameroon. Her family was devoutly Catholic. She and her siblings "grew up with White neighbors," she says. "We went to church together, we played together. I never saw a difference between myself and a White." Their father "insisted that we speak a good French to be seen well in the community." They attended a Jesuit high school with a mixed European and Cameroonian student body, where "everyone was equal." At their church, on the cross, "Jesus was a Black." Meanwhile, the family was proud to be descended from those who had resisted colonial conquest, "from the king who had said 'no' to the Whites and died." Marie laughed while talking about those happy years.

After high school, Marie's father paid for her to be trained in France as a midwife. Although she had intended to return to Cameroon to practice midwifery after her training, the situation in Cameroon had changed by the time she got her diploma. Her father told her that the political and economic crisis that Cameroon had just experienced left the country "without a future," and that she should make her future elsewhere. But she was also "blocked" in France because non-citizens were prohibited from practicing midwifery.

Marie decided to stay in France, resolving to "build something" there. She took whatever jobs she could find, at one point working as a cleaning woman. In the meantime, she had two children with men from Africa, Markus and his older sister, and adopted two children, one a Cameroonian nephew with disabilities. Life "was a struggle." Finally, thirteen years after she had gotten her midwifery diploma, she gained French citizenship and began her career as a midwife. She worked at a hospital, then opened a practice of her own, where her patients are both White and Black. She is the only Black midwife in her city.

When her children were still young, Marie decided to resolve the issue of identity. Though she could live with ties to both France and Cameroon, her children could not. They were born in France, would be raised in France, and would have to make their way in France. For them to have a "stable identity," they'd need to be French. And to eliminate ambiguity, she said, "I decided to become French so I could transmit this to my children."

I asked Marie what being French means to her. "To be French," she said, "is to participate in the life of France." For her, this involves providing the best and most caring treatment for her patients. Some suffer from postpartum depression, so she works closely with them during the weeks and months following birth. Marie also remains active in her church and helps recent immigrants. She maintains good relations with her neighbors, who are mostly White retirees. "When I moved in, I went to everyone and said 'Hello.'" Marie thinks that, for her children, being French also means participation in the life around them: "They do sports, they interact with others, they go to church and school, they have friends." In a school with mostly White students, Markus excels academically and athletically. She thinks that he and his older sister (who now lives in another city) are simply French: "They are in their own country."

Marie's interview ended just in time. After a hurried telephone call, she changed into a tailored black dress and drove off to see a patient.

Markus and I then started his interview. Now a high school senior, he has sometimes had to face ridicule. He's been called, he says, "piece of shit" and "monkey." Even though he has spent his entire life in France, he's been told to "go back to where you come from." He has also been harassed by online trolls. None of this matters. He says, "I've always thought of myself as French. I grew up as a French person, I eat like a French person, and I've been educated as a French person. To be French is not a cliché."

For Markus, being French is not a "White person with a beret," but "to share French values and ideologies, to have the freedom to think," and to participate in France's democracy.

Although life is "a struggle every day," Markus feels no need to justify himself. He says, "I am what I am." He focuses on his goal of becoming an airline pilot.

Daniel. I met Daniel and his girlfriend Justine at their apartment in town. Within minutes, we had settled into their sunny living room with their cat to begin the interview.

Growing up in the Ivory Coast, a former French colony in West Africa that continues to have a strong French presence, Daniel says that he had the same attitude as those around him: Ivorians "always felt inferior" to the French. But he was freed from this attitude in his early twenties, after he had arrived in France and began working with French people. "I realized that everyone is equal." The only difference, he thinks, is that Europeans start out knowing more.

A few years later, Daniel took a factory job in the city where he now lives. He moved up three levels within a year. Then, when he was poised to become a team captain, a White employee blocked his promotion because the White employee, Daniel says, "couldn't tolerate a Black in a management position." Learning of this, a manager at the company pushed the promotion through. The manager—a man from Senegal—told Daniel, "I want you to show them that we Africans are not what they think." Daniel has thrown himself into the new position, motivating his team and "getting the job done."

Turning an anti-Black stereotype on its head, Daniel is struck by how hard many Africans work in France. He certainly does. "In all the domains in France, if there isn't an African involved, it won't work out."

All has not been easy in his personal life. Daniel can ignore being followed in stores or being called "dirty" by a young child—he laughed as he remembered that incident—but biased comments can hurt. An earlier relationship with a White woman ended after she referred to a government minister as a *nègre*. Justine, who is also White but grew up in Martinique among Black Martinicans, seems free of bias.

Now thirty, Daniel is happy with his life. "I have my job and apartment, I play soccer, and I've been with Justine for six months." Looking at Justine with playful affection, he added, "I hope it goes on. Voilà, voilà."

Philippe. Within fifteen minutes of my arrival at his apartment, Philippe was discussing Rousseau, Voltaire, and other figures of the French Enlightenment. His intellectual passion did not flag during the six hours of conversation that followed. The next day was much the same.

Now thirty-four, Philippe grew up in a remote part of Guinea, a former French colony in West Africa. Although his parents spoke little French, he was sent to the capital, Conakry, for high school and college. There, he excelled in French literature and philosophy, which he read voraciously. He remembers the time well. "I was very literary, I very much enjoyed reading." He also began to "dress French," develop a "French mentality," and take on a "French identity." As Philippe increasingly "imitated" French ways, he became less Guinean; as he realized later, he'd become "*déraciné*" (uprooted or alienated from his original culture). At this point, he was "a French person in an African body." As "every African who's sincere" would admit, he said, he had an "inferiority complex." He added, "It's incredible—all the Guineans I know are impressed by Westerners."

After two years of college in Guinea, Philippe went to France to study law. This move had a surprising effect on his intellectual life. It was in France that he dove into the works of Frantz Fanon and started to read African literature. At first, he said, "it was hard to read African novels. It was not like reading a novel by Flaubert or Stendhal. These I understood easily." He also became an avid reader of Russian literature while he continued to "devour" French literature. In the meantime, he got his law degree and an advanced degree in transportation law.

Reading Frantz Fanon forced Philippe to acknowledge his "inferiority complex," but also made him understand that "the problem is not of inferiority, but of identity." Fanon taught him, he said, "not to be ashamed of my Africanness, of who I am. I accept it with pride." Fanon "makes each person responsible for himself." While Fanon's argument made Philippe "realize that I had over-idealized the French," it did not require him to "pass from one extreme to the other," from feeling purely French to feeling purely African. For Philippe, the task is instead to "conjugate the two" and "find an equilibrium." By doing so, he could "have the two cultures and not be forced to seek refuge in only one."

Even after getting his advanced law degree, Philippe was unable to find a job in that field. For the last six years, he has worked instead as an activities counselor and administrator in middle schools. He refuses to attribute his inability to find a law-related job to racism because, he says, there might have been "superior candidates for each of the jobs I sought." He has the same feeling about social relations, refusing to attribute the "coldness" he has felt from some French people to racism. "If you don't like me, well, you don't like me. It's not racism." Interactions that other people might readily interpret as racist—when the parents of two French girlfriends refused to accept him, or when a real estate agent told him that no apartments were available but then told his French girlfriend that there were apartments—Philippe instead attributes to "a lack of comprehension." He says, "It's possible that I have experienced racism. I just refuse to see it that way." He refuses to see himself as a victim, and certainly not the "eternal victim."[11]

At the end of the interview, when I invited Philippe to add anything he'd like, he said:

> For someone who's been exposed to two different cultures, the best way to feel good in one's skin, to not feel lost, is to assimilate both cultures, to encompass both. It is the acceptance of the two cultures that has allowed me to feel reconnected with myself.

A few months after our interview, I received an email from Philippe: he had accepted the position of magistrate in Guinea and was planning to return there. A year later, Philippe sent an update. Although he had returned to Guinea, he wrote, "I had to come back" to France because "I was threatened" by the Guinean government.

DISCRIMINATION, "SUBTERRANEAN" BIAS, AND "INTELLIGENT RACISM"

For the interviewees, at least, just being seen as Black in France forces a person to face serious obstacles, particularly discrimination in employment, education, housing, and daily life. Collected below are the specifics of these obstacles, as reported either by the interviewees profiled above or by other people I interviewed or spoke with during this project. The chapter concludes with the subtlest of issues: how "French" people communicate bias toward Black people in France without saying it openly.

"Racism is most evident in the work world"

The most commonly reported consequence of being Black in France involves employment discrimination. Over and over, interviewees spoke of their difficulties in getting hired for anything above menial or entry-level jobs. They found this galling since almost all of them were completely fluent in French, educated (in many cases, through a university bachelor's or master's degree), and comfortable with the social norms required for managerial or professional work. Some interviewees talked about submitting hundreds of résumés to no effect. (Because a résumé in France includes a photograph on the first page, a Black person's *faciès* is immediately evident.) Even when a résumé yielded an interview for the open position, the face-to-face interview typically resulted in a rejection.

Interviewees reported that, instead of working in managerial or professional positions commensurate with their credentials, many Black people are forced to work as office cleaners, security guards, or nightclub bouncers. According to Djibril, some Whites "think that a Black belongs" in a menial job because they "don't have the necessary intelligence" to do anything more. "There are people," he says, "who think that there's a certain kind of work for Blacks and a certain kind of work for Whites." Or, as Thomas's father put it: "Whites in the offices, Blacks collect the trash."

Even those who get an office job hit a barrier. According to Isabel, "In France, Blacks aren't accepted in offices beyond a certain level. They're merely tolerated." There's "always talk behind their backs. They're always criticized." Even working at a staff-level job can be a problem when there are Whites at the same level. According to Isabel, many Whites in the workplace have an attitude that "if you're Black, you must always be lower than me." And Amina says she has faced a "hostile work environment" from her White coworkers.

Emmanuelle's brother was the only Black member of the graduating class of a "very highly regarded" business school in France, she reported, and he was the last in the class to find a job. "It was very difficult for him," she said. "At first, he didn't understand." Finally, after seven or eight months, he was able to find a position, but only as "manager of a small grocery store."

Even more problematic is the (apparently rare) situation in which a Black person supervises White employees. After five years of military service, Clément was hired to lead a small community service team. With Whites on the team, he said, "I had to justify that I had a right to that position." He thinks that he succeeded, although, he added, "with more difficulty than if I'd been White."

Thomas recounted two contrasting experiences with teams managed by a Black person. When Thomas supervised his own team at the company where he once worked, he did not experience resentment from team members. There were no White members on his team; "there were none, none at all." It was different earlier in his career, when he was a trainee with a team that had White members. The Black leader of that team, he remembers, was "treated very badly."

A number of interviewees reported times when an expected or promised promotion at work failed to materialize, though prejudice was rarely explicit. Anna recounted two painful instances. When the airline for which she worked as a flight attendant was hiring pursers (chief flight attendants), she applied for the position. Although her job performance had been excellent, Anna was turned down, she was told, because "the quota for people of color had already been met." Later, when she worked for the national train company, Anna sought a promotion that would allow her to work on the trains, backed by a stellar personnel file and her manager's support. She was offered a promotion, but only to the position of train controller—the only position on a train that involved no customer contact.

Career progress is difficult. One problem the interviewees face is a lack of mentors. Discrimination against Blacks means that, as Amina explained, "there are few who have really succeeded who can take us by the hand." Thomas's father warned him, "The higher you go, the more you'll face racism." Similarly, Isabel said,

"When one is the best, that's when the struggle begins." And Djibril feels that many Whites "don't want Blacks to have access to certain positions" or to "reach a certain level of wealth."

Many interviewees have adopted strategies to sidestep workplace discrimination. One is to get training in a rigorous discipline where, as Amina phrased it, "only capability matters," and then pursue it vigorously. Examples of this approach include Charles's and Ariel's careers in information technology, Amina's in business intelligence, and Alejandro's in biochemistry. But a job grounded in objective expertise does not make bias disappear. At one point, Charles's White superior made it clear that a Black person could never know something that he didn't. Only at the highest levels might there be no prejudice. Alejandro earned a doctorate in biochemistry and now works as a research scientist at an international laboratory where equally highly educated professional colleagues from various countries evince no bias toward him.

Working for yourself is another strategy for escaping workplace bias. Many interviewees have taken that route, especially after frustrating experiences with organizational employers. These include Clément (driving school), Thomas (property management), Amina (business consulting), Marie (midwifery), Lucas (electrical installation and repair), Isabel (clothing store), and Emmanuelle (muscular therapy). While working for oneself "makes things easier," Emmanuelle said, it does not totally prevent discrimination. Thomas's experience with five banks refusing to provide a loan (for what proved to be a good investment) has already been reported in this chapter. He is not alone. According to Thomas, African banks have been started in France because Blacks have trouble getting loans from French banks.

Amina combined the two strategies by developing objectively verifiable skills and then operating her own one-person business. After working for companies, she became an independent contractor, working with teams of specialists that operate independently of their clients' corporate structures to execute technical tasks. These teams are staffed by people of different backgrounds and have little interaction with the companies' French management. Amina explained why she became an independent contractor:

> It would be different if I worked at a company. At a company, your advancement ends at the point of gaining responsibility. With Maghrebis and people from sub-Saharan Africa, there's always a moment when you realize this, when you need to find another way. You can't dream of a high-level career at a company when you have these handicaps.

The case of Nawab is revealing. The only Black person I spoke with who is largely uneducated and unskilled, Nawab works a menial job at the back of a local restaurant. He lives in a neighborhood with people like him (working-class Blacks, mostly from the Comorian Islands off the southeast coast of Africa), and he accepts his low status and salary. He pays more attention to his family and religious faith. Though Nawab said he knows that millions of French people are "racists," he does not have contact with many French people, and anyway, few would insult him in public. He recalls this happening only once, when an elderly person was abusive on a bus.

If one considers all the Black people I spoke with, a distinct pattern emerges. Only two did not report workplace bias: the one who holds a PhD and works at an international laboratory (Alejandro), and the one with little education who is content with a menial job (Nawab). Virtually all others described career obstacles and workday woes grounded in their *faciès*. Some mitigate their problems by specializing in technical fields (Charles, Amina, Ariel) or by turning to self-employment (Clément, Isabel, Emmanuelle, Lucas, Thomas, Amina, and Marie). Others are mired in positions below their level of training and work history (Philippe, Anna, Abbas, François) or underemployment (Djibril, Jean, Jacques).

Other Types of Discrimination

Black interviewees also spoke of problems involving education, housing, and daily life. Emmanuelle recounted a "major event" in her third year of professional studies. "I had two operations. I was in the hospital for two and a half months and missed three and a half months of classes," she said. Upon her return, Emmanuelle asked her professor for an accommodation for the end-of-year examination. He turned her down, even though he had made such arrangements for two of her classmates, both White, who "hadn't even been hospitalized." Facing the exam as scheduled, Emmanuelle worked furiously to learn the months of material she had missed and passed it.

As already reported, Amina, Caroline, and Charles also experienced bias in schooling. Amina was shunned by her private business school classmates because she came from Africa, where people are thought to be like "monkeys." A native French speaker, Caroline was advised to move from her class with Whites to the "idiots' class," where newly arrived Africans were learning French. Although Caroline was a successful student, the director of her high school told her that a Black person could not represent the school in a national competition. A White math teacher from mainland France told Charles and the other Martinican students, "You'll never succeed; you're a bunch of welfare cases."

Interviewees also reported incidents of housing discrimination. When Clément calls about renting an apartment, everything goes well over the phone, since he speaks French without an accent and his first and last names are European. But when he comes to see the apartment, "there's always a pulling back" by the landlord. And though Clément has a completely middle-class way of dressing and acting, he says, "I have to convince potential landlords that I have a good job, lead a quiet family life, won't break the walls, won't attack the neighbors, will pay the rent on time, et cetera, et cetera." He has had much the same experience when seeking a mortgage. "I always have the sense when I walk in the door to meet with a bank officer that there's a label on my forehead saying 'welfare case.'"

Marie, Philippe, and Thomas also reported problems with housing. Marie has been told over the telephone that an apartment was available and then, when she arrived on site, that it was taken. Philippe was once told that no apartments were available a few minutes before his White girlfriend was told there were. And Thomas spoke about parts of the city that are not for people like him: "These neighborhoods are for the French, the 'true French,' the French with White skin, and not for the French with Black skin."

If a Black person is able to rent an apartment in a majority-White neighborhood, problems often arise with White neighbors.

Many of Caroline's neighbors, she says, are racist and refuse to greet her. Although Amina is a well-dressed and well-spoken professional, one neighbor reminded her that "this building is not a housing project" when she moved into her current apartment, and another told her that the building "must remain clean."

There is also bias in everyday life. Incidents of bias from the childhoods of Clément, Anna, Caroline, Markus, and Jean have already been reported. And while adults are more discreet, some make their feelings known. Isabel once politely asked a woman who lives above her store to stop feeding pigeons from her window, because they dirtied the sidewalk in front of the store. One morning, Isabel recounted, "when I was cleaning the sidewalk outside my store, Bam!," a stone hit her on the top of her forehead. When she spoke up, the woman feigned amazement: "So you speak French?"

Many interviewees recounted problems in public places such as stores and restaurants, and nightclubs are particularly notorious for turning away Blacks. Emmanuelle and her friends were once barred from a club. "The White couple behind us were admitted," she remembered, even though "they were completely sloshed. They were having trouble even walking."

Black people can face apparently biased behavior at any moment. Emmanuelle spoke about the time when two of her brothers, "dressed in suits and ties," ran for a bus. Police officers ran after them, got on the bus, and asked "Why were you running?" Another time, she remembered, "after my little brother left a party, he tossed a pebble in the canal. A police car stopped, they got out and asked what he was up to." A simple pleasure spoiled, her brother felt "diminished."

Finally, one may wonder whether the interviewees' experiences with discrimination are statistically common among people like them. Although such questions fall outside the scope of this ethnography, findings of the monumental Trajectories and Origins study may be summarized.[12] As the study's lead investigators report, "[a]round 10 percent of individuals comprising the mainstream population . . . report experience of discrimination, compared with 24 percent of second generation and 26 percent of immigrants" (Beauchemin, Hamel, Lesné, and Simon 2010: 2). But the latter figures of 24 percent and 26 percent are not distributed equally: "The most visible groups are targeted most frequently. Almost half of immigrants and second generations from sub-Saharan Africa report experience of discrimination" (ibid.). Those originating from the overseas *départements*—overwhelmingly Black—report only slightly lower numbers: 31 percent among immigrants, 40 percent among the second generation (1).

The problem may be more severe among people who, like almost all the interviewees, have higher levels of education. Taking all "visible minorities" together, the investigators found that reported discrimination is "39 percent higher for persons with a degree in higher education" than those who "left school with a lower vocational certificate" (3). This may be due, in part, to a particular obstacle facing this cohort: "a degree in higher education enables members of ethnic minorities to occupy jobs where . . . they are treated with a certain wariness. When seeking promotion, . . . their qualifications are not sufficient to curb the expression of racial prejudice towards minorities" (ibid.).

"Subterranean" Bias and "Intelligent Racism"

Given all the accounts of stereotyping and discrimination recounted in the interviews, surprisingly few interviewees reported overt, confrontational insults from French adults. While it is true that Thomas's parents once had to deal with "direct racism" in the form of slurs like "dirty black" said to their faces, such behavior is "finished today," according to Thomas, because it "will be condemned." The French "code" of behavior that many interviewees described, especially of what is "not done" in public, prohibits such behavior. When an elderly woman insulted Nawab on a bus, other passengers tried to shush her.

This is not to say that Whites do not communicate their biases. Isabel's neighbors let her know their attitudes either anonymously (as with the message in feces on her store window) or with deniability built into their actions (as with her upstairs neighbor). The cruelty of the National Front adherents who invited twelve-year-old Clément to join them for a photo and then laughed at him was done without a harsh word uttered. As an adolescent, Lucas was repeatedly stopped by the police, apparently for being young, male, and dark-skinned.

A recurring problem for the interviewees involves joking, a beloved French pastime that allows a person to say something, as Jean put it, "between humor and racial insult." Jean has been teased about his purported resemblance to a gorilla or monkey. Earlier in life, when he was deeply ashamed of being Black, he did not "show that this was not at all funny." Today, he is unsure how to react.

Emmanuelle is in a similar predicament when she is the object of racially tinged jokes. She said that she either goes along with it by responding with an insincere laugh or "takes it badly" and is made out to be the spoilsport. But Thomas, who is proud of being Black and successful in his career, responds to such jokes with jokes of his own. When a White friend joked about the heightened sexuality of Blacks, he replied, "Well, you can't do anything with your wife because you have a small penis."

The fact that bias no longer takes the form of insults, at least from polite adults, masks its significance. Abbas said that bias is now "a subterranean reality" and that keeping it unexpressed, at least in the form of explicit insults directed at Black people, serves to normalize it. French people, he continued, "don't express their prejudices out loud, but that's the way they live and how they turn the prejudices into something natural." Of course, none of the interviewees could report what Whites say among themselves when Blacks are not around.

While "direct racism" is socially unacceptable, Thomas said, some Whites use "intelligent racism" to create "psychological barriers" within Black people. Thomas provided an example from his own life. When his IT teacher openly doubted his abilities—"You can't do it, it's impossible, it's not for you"—she was trying to "destabilize" him. He believes that she and others who act that way are "conscious" of what they are doing. "Psychological barriers," he thinks, also "come from politicians, from TV, from everywhere. It's incredible."

For Clément, "there's a visual, a connotation of inferiority" that Whites communicate. According to Thomas, such attitudes have been absorbed by many French-born Blacks, who "are submissive and feel inferior" to Whites. Black people may feel self-conscious when they are with Whites. This is the case with François, who felt that "you must always justify yourself."

Bias is communicated in everyday social life in subtle ways. François spoke of having a "subliminal vision" of public places where he is not welcome. Daniel is used to being followed "like a thief" in certain stores. While Emmanuelle has "never experienced frontal racism," she said, "it's always the little remarks." Sometimes, she reported, "I can't tell if I've grasped it all, whether they're racist." Emmanuelle feels a lack of "respect," she said, when Whites "touch my hair" without asking. A White person told a Black friend of Emmanuelle's that her hair was "like a sheep's."

CONCLUSION

Despite their diverse origins, experiences, and temperaments, the interviewees discussed throughout this chapter share certain facts of life. Even those who were born and educated in France, are fully "integrated," and feel themselves to be French are seen as something different: Black. And because they are Black, they are subject to stereotypes that suggest that they are inherently inferior. How do these people deal with this? The first group of interviewees discussed in this chapter focus on fraught issues of identity: Who am I? How do Whites see me? Am I as worthy as them? The second group of interviewees push ahead with life, excelling where possible, and, in so doing, showing that "I'm not what you think I am."

Anti-Black stereotypes and the demeaning behavior of many Whites—what Thomas calls "intelligent racism," and Abbas calls "subterranean" bias—threaten to undermine the self-confidence of the Black interviewees. But despite this disparagement, the profiles in this chapter reveal a striking pattern: while a few of the interviewees who focus on issues of identity expressed self-doubt, the great majority of Black interviewees did not. Instead, they described stereotyping and prejudice as something external that must be dealt with, but not something that is true about themselves. As Emmanuelle put it, "You manage because you don't have a choice. Either you adapt or you're angry all the time about the injustices. If I can change something, I will. But even if I can't, at least I know my own value."

Even the interviewees who think that many people in sub-Saharan Africa live in backward ways do not think that Blacks are inherently inferior. To Daniel's mind, the difference between Europeans and Africans is not one of natural ability, but of knowledge. In France, he said, he learned a lot and "realized that everyone is equal." If he were to teach people back in Africa what he now knows, he feels, they too "would be knowledgeable."

None of this makes prejudice go away, and discrimination in employment is particularly problematic. The interviewees described how this begins when a Black person first looks for a job and continues through the decades of attempting to forge a successful career. While a successful career may also be a goal for Whites, it carries a particular significance for these interviewees. As Caroline said, "in France, if you're Black and don't have a high-level job, you're not worth much."

Another striking pattern in these interviews is a matter of absence. As seen in chapter 1, some Maghrebi interviewees foresee the possibility of one day becoming "French" (as they use the word referentially); that is, as being seen as having a European *faciès*. Whether or not a Maghrebi person seeks this outcome, many recognize that there is a path that makes it possible, at least in later generations. By having children with "French" people, a Maghrebi may have children or grandchildren who are seen as "French." None of the Black interviewees spoke in these terms. Even Lucas said that he is not seen as "French French," but as a different "category" of person. This is true even though his family has been living in mainland France for more than two generations on one side and even longer on the other side, even though he lives like the "French" people around him, and even though one of his parents is *métis* and the other White.

Others described much the same experience. Like Lucas, many Black interviewees grew up in France, behave according to French norms, and consider themselves French, but are not seen that way. As Jean put it, "I'm French, but I'm no fool. I fully understand that in the eyes of many people I'm something else." Anna said, "From my point of view, yes, I'm French. For others, I will never be." Thomas's father told him, all too presciently, "Even though you were born in France, you won't be considered a true French person." And when Emmanuelle says "I'm French," she reports, some people "look at me as if to say, 'ha ha.'"

This brings to mind W.E.B. Du Bois's concept of "double consciousness" among American Blacks. Writing in 1903, he noted:

> It's a peculiar sensation, this double-consciousness, this sense of always looking at one's self through the eyes of others, of measuring one's soul by the tape of a world that looks on in amused contempt and pity. One feels his two-ness,—an American, a Negro; two souls, two thoughts, two unreconciled strivings, two warring ideals in one dark body. . . . He would not Africanize America. . . . He simply wishes to make it possible for a man to be both a Negro and an American, without being cursed and spit upon by his fellows, without having the doors of Opportunity close roughly in his face. (1903: 7–8)

To the vast majority of "French" people, this concept would seem ludicrously foreign to France. Even mentioning it might seem like a projection onto their country of the ugly American experience of slavery and its racist aftermath. But perhaps not. After more than 350 pages of his magisterial study of "the Black condition" in France, Ndiaye begins his conclusion with a discussion of Du Bois. His comments would surprise these "French" people:

> Despite obvious differences between the United States at the beginning of the 20th century and France at the beginning of the 21st century, "double consciousness" still seems current to me. My study of Black France of yesterday and today brings to light a plea . . . It can be stated as follows: we want to be both French and Black without it being seen as suspicious, or strange, or tolerated as a temporary problem while waiting for assimilation to do its work. (Ndiaye 2008: 361–62)

Ndiaye is not alone in considering the relevance of Du Bois's thinking to present-day France. Recalling his contention that "the problem of the twentieth century [in the US] is the problem of the color line," Didier Fassin says that "one could almost wonder if the racial question is not becoming, in France, the new social question of the beginning of the twenty-first century" (D. Fassin 2010: 148).

Although this book is not the place to weigh such broad issues, one can hear echoes of Du Bois's plea to be accepted as "both a Negro and an American"—and of Ndiaye's to be seen as "both French and Black"—in the accounts of many Black interviewees.

This is most striking among the interviewees who have the greatest claim to being accepted as French: those who have always lived in France. Having met the most exacting standards of behavior, Thomas wants to be treated like other French people, and to be seen as both French and Black. Markus and Jean are much the same. So are Caroline, Charles, and Emmanuelle, all French citizens from birth, who came to mainland France from the "overseas" *départements* of France. And then there is Lucas, who has not only lived his entire life in mainland France, but whose parents have also lived their entire lives in mainland France. If Lucas were not made to feel he must put himself "in a caste," he too might assert the right to be seen as both French and Black.

NOTES

1. As Didier and Eric Fassin have noted, only recently have some people "come to realize that the people called 'French' turn out to be 'white.'" See the introduction for a brief discussion of this literature. However true this may be for Whites, it is not true for people they have categorized as Black. At least among the Black interviewees, the terms "French" and "White" are used interchangeably. See introduction, endnote 15.
2. Based on a study conducted by the market research firm TNS Sofres in 2007, Lozès and Lecherbonnier (2009: 11–17) put the number at five million. This estimate includes Blacks in both mainland France and the overseas *départements*.
3. American readers of this book will think of W.E.B. Du Bois's account of the "double consciousness" of Blacks in the US more than a century ago. The relevance of this concept to France is discussed at the end of this chapter.
4. Sub-Saharan Africans, and Blacks generally, have been likened to monkeys (*singes*) or orangutans (*orang-outans*) in France since at least 1790 (see Ruscio 2020: 136–40).
5. Sylvie Durmelat provides some background. Banania was a "breakfast mainstay . . . for generations of French children" that "used to carry the image of a smiling colonial infantry soldier with the slogan 'y' bon Banania' as if spoken in pidgin French" (Durmelat 2015: 116). This phrase, she argued, "conflates the taste of childhood with the alleged cultural inferiority of the colonised soldier, whose smiling face conveys innocent benevolence" (117). This phrase and the image of the smiling Black soldier were retired in 2005 (see Cartographie des mémoires de l'esclavage 2005).

6. Although *métis* people are categorized as Black, their lighter skin apparently affords them a higher status than Blacks with darker skin (see Ndiaye 2008: 71–109; Ndiaye 2006).
7. While Thomas was able to overcome his teacher's presumption that IT studies were "not for" him, others in his position are not so strong. Reviewing the available literature, the French statistician Romain Aeberhardt and others find the following: "Regarding educational outcomes, while some authors focus on the role of cultural mechanisms in the reproduction of poverty" among children of immigrants, there "is stronger evidence for the role of teachers' conscious and unconscious stereotypes" (Aeberhardt et al. 2015: 585).
8. Alejandro is a special case. Since he declined to have his interview recorded (and it was impractical for me to take notes during the interview), I retain few particulars. He is also an outlier by way of origin: as a Black person from Colombia, his status as originating from a former European colony is remote (i.e., from the time Colombia was a Spanish country).
9. Clément's experience brings to mind Nicholas Bancel and Pascal Blanchard's critique of the curriculum in the French national educational system. By neglecting the history of France's former colonies, they say, the curriculum denies the descendants of these colonies "the ability to understand their own history [and thereby denies] them their roots and the genealogy of what they often experience as a double culture" (Bancel and Blanchard 2017b: 161). As noted here, Clément's classes at school left him feeling "a lack of history." He became alienated from school and the students around him. It was only years later, after four months in Senegal, that he became "proud about having regained my history."
10. W.E.B. Du Bois had a similar experience a century and a half ago. As a child, Du Bois felt that he was like his White friends until the day a classmate refused his Valentine's Day card. "Then it dawned upon me with a certain suddenness that I was different from the others . . . shut out from their world by a vast veil." (Du Bois 1903: 2) Faced with this discovery, he wrote, Black boys could well cry out, "Why did God make me an outcast in mine own house?" (3).
11. While Philippe refuses to attribute his inability to secure a job commensurate with his qualifications—refusing to see himself as a victim—he is not blind to general patterns in French society. "Even with years of study," he noted, most Blacks "can't get past certain barriers" in getting a job. Indeed, it's "rare to see a Black in a management position."
12. See pages 62 63 and 64n14 above concerning this study and its de fined terms.

THREE

NEITHER MAGHREBI NOR BLACK

As one of the interviewees said, there are three kinds of people in France with non-European *faciès*: Maghrebis, Blacks, and everyone else. While, as seen in the foregoing chapters, Maghrebi and Black are distinct social classifications, each with a readily discernible *faciès* and each associated with stereotypical behavior, the remaining interviewees seem to be a jumble. True, virtually all of them trace their origin to countries in Asia—Iran, Turkey, Pakistan, India, Vietnam, China, Japan, and South Korea—but these are far-flung countries with cultures, languages, and histories that range widely. The *faciès* of these people also vary considerably.

Considering all this variety, does it make sense to discuss these interviewees together? The answer is yes, and for reasons that go to the heart of identity in France. Grounded in the same socially created equivalence between Nature and Culture by which people are readily recognizable as Maghrebi or Black and "readable" as having an assumed nature, the people discussed in this chapter are also "readable."[1] They are readable first because of what they are not: they are neither Maghrebi nor Black, and thus are free of the harsh stereotyping to which Maghrebi and Black people are subject. As the interviews discussed in this chapter reveal, this is no small matter. Yet they are also readable as not being White, that invisible but pervasive classification in France. Not White, and thus not "French," is similarly no small matter.

Within this residual social category, there is one distinct classification. This is *Asiatique* (equivalent to "Asian" in today's English): a person recognizable by his or her East Asian *faciès*. Like people of the other classifications, *Asiatiques* are associated with a geographical origin and assumed behaviors. All of the remaining interviewees are truly "none of the above." By their appearance, they are not "French," but they are not readily classifiable. This will prove to be significant.

Finally, a note about assumed origins. All of the classifications in this relational system of social classification are linked to certain "origins." *Origines* was a recurring theme among the interviewees. Maghrebis are said to originate from the Maghreb (Northwest Africa); Blacks from sub-Saharan Africa (some more immediately from the Caribbean); Asians from East Asia; and the rest from elsewhere outside Europe. While millions of "French" people originate from other parts of Europe, this distinction fades over time.

It is time to turn to the interviewees. Not seen as "French," the interviewees in this third group express many of the same concerns as the other interviewees. Who am I? How am I treated? Do I feel accepted by "French" people? What practical issues must I confront in French society? Their answers to these questions turn out to be very different from those of the interviewees classified as Maghrebi or Black.

VINCENT

I was scheduled to stay with Vincent on 1 May, a national holiday in France, and he invited me to arrive early and join him and friends for lunch. My prior Airbnb host was kind enough to drive me to Vincent's home in the heart of a well-maintained town.

The scene that greeted me couldn't have been more inviting. Vincent lives in a sun-drenched apartment with enormous windows and double-height ceilings. When I arrived, he and his two guests were wrapping slices of ham around stalks of white asparagus as they sipped wine. Everyone was dressed casually but stylishly; Vincent wore a crisp New York Knicks warm-up jacket. While Vincent appeared to be of South Asian origin, the couple he had invited—the wife is a colleague of his in the IT department of a large French company—was recognizably "French." We moved on to lunch: the asparagus-ham combination served with bread, more wine, salad, and a sumptuous dessert, all accompanied by the fast-paced, spirited conversation typical of such occasions in France. Vincent was particularly outgoing and jovial, serving as the perfect host. Although he readily agreed to participate in my project, I suspected that his interview would be short and unspectacular, illustrating how comfortable life could be for someone who has embraced French norms enthusiastically.

After the lunch dishes were washed and goodbyes said to Vincent's friends, we sat down at his dining room table, and I turned on the recorder. What followed surprised both of us. For more than two hours, Vincent recounted a painful story of unremitting *intégration*—he used the word more than a hundred times—that started with his grandparents and continues today. He burst into tears after the first ten minutes and was often misty-eyed. Throughout the interview he seemed physically deflated, far from the hearty host he had been at lunch.

Vincent's family originates from the former French micro-colony of Pondicherry on the southeast coast of India. Both of his grandfathers were officials in the colonial government and, he believes, considered themselves French. Although both sides of his family were physically similar to others in that region, with dark skin and straight, black hair, they were part of the local colonial elite. "There was the culture, too," he explained. His grandfathers were Catholic and French-speaking, but also French in orientation. According to family stories, they played *pétanque* (a metal ball-throwing game from southern France), "drank aperitifs every Sunday, and enjoyed French cuisine."

This way of life was disrupted in 1947, when India gained independence from Great Britain. When it became clear that Pondicherry would be absorbed by the new nation of India, Vincent's family was given the choice between Indian and French citizenship. They chose French, and Vincent's father, then eighteen, joined the French army. He was stationed in various French military bases in France, where he "worked day and night" to become a nurse and an officer. His father succeeded, Vincent said, "but had to do battle" every day. In the meantime, he entered into an arranged marriage with a young Pondicherry woman who was also French-speaking and Catholic, and they had two children, Vincent and his older sister. Vincent's parents did their best to fit in among the French military personnel and their families. Despite "the advantage of being Catholic," he says, they "had to struggle to be integrated, to be accepted, to be acknowledged, everything." They suffered "a lot of injustices," even "a false charge of misconduct" against his father. He and his sister witnessed some of these incidents and heard about others. This "hurt us, it marked us."

After fifteen years of military service, Vincent's father retired as a major, and the family settled in a French village of 900 people, where they were "the only people of color." Vincent was nine. His parents did their best to integrate themselves into the community, he said,

> inviting neighbors to dinner at least once a year, even if they didn't really like them. It was important to make a good impression, to be respectable and educated, to serve a good meal on attractive dishes. It was always part of that effort to be integrated, to act like the others.

Vincent's father worked as a nurse at a nearby factory and in the village, where he faced discrimination in getting patient referrals.

Turning to his childhood, Vincent recalled that "my parents made a firm decision to integrate us into French society." They imposed "no food restrictions" on their children and, even at home, spoke only French. Vincent felt "100 percent French." Still, he was sometimes mistreated in school, and he had trouble finding a place with the children of the village. Almost forty years later, Vincent remembers the "extreme humiliation" he suffered in French class at the hands of a "xenophobic" teacher.

Vincent's exclusion from basketball games as an adolescent was so painful that, even now, when he is fifty-one and "all the others have stopped" playing basketball because of age, he keeps at it. "Deep inside me, it's a form of revenge." Vincent suddenly began to cry again. Regaining his composure, he pushed on:

> But now I'm the one who coaches, who plays, even if it's physically hard. I'm faster than them. I think it's tied to that period. I'd never made the connection between *intégration* and exclusion, but I think they're linked together as we speak. This is my journey.

At college, Vincent studied information technology. He recalls "very little" bias there, either among the students or with the faculty. It was a "very pleasant" experience. Less than two months after graduation, he was hired by the same large company where he still works more than twenty-five years later. "I was accepted" by the IT team, he recalls, and "had no problem" at the company during the first few years. Getting promoted proved to be more problematic. He was denied promotions, he believes, partly because of his union activities "and partly because of race." But Vincent doesn't want to dwell on this feeling of being "a victim, a victim of the system."

Vincent is only romantically attracted to "European" women—"There's no ambiguity about that"—but has been "timid" with them. "It was a problem of *intégration*." He ultimately married a woman he describes as "*Française de souche*," though they are now divorced. They have a son, now twenty-two, who is *métis*. Vincent and his ex-wife share a "French culture," Vincent says, and they raised their son to be French. They gave him a French first name, though his last name is Vincent's and thus distinctly non-European.

Vincent wanted his son "not to have problems with *intégration*." Over the years, Vincent took part in school-related activities, partly, he says, in the "unconscious" hope that his son wouldn't "be treated differently than the others," and that he'd be "considered normal like them." Vincent thinks that he "largely succeeded" in this effort. And while his son "may have seen injustices involving racism that I've encountered," Vincent says, he hasn't faced "too much" of this himself. Perhaps he "had fewer problems because he looks less Indian" than Vincent, and even today his son "may need to make less of an effort" to be accepted.

Vincent spoke at length about his own behavior. He "constantly" presents "a good image" of himself. "There's a little light that's always on, saying 'be careful about how you behave.'" He feels it's important to be "very respectful" toward others, and though "it's not fair," he lives by this rule. Vincent recounted an interaction from just the day before our interview, when he went to get food for our lunch:

> When I went to the countryside yesterday to buy the asparagus, I knew to make a good impression on the farmer, to be polite. I knew to greet him, ask about how to cook it and then thank him. And this was just asparagus, with a man I'd never see again.

Avoiding conflict protects him from insult:

> Whenever I drive, I don't want others to say, "dirty foreigner," so I never go through intersections when the light is amber. They immediately make the connection with a person's origins, so I know to be careful that people don't have a reason to criticize me. In my mind, I know this.

Despite his difficulties, Vincent says that he has it easier than many other "foreigners on the outside." He works at the management level at his company "rather than as a maintenance worker at city hall. It makes a difference." In sum, "it's easier in my position than for an Indian in a job that's not thought well of." His religion has also helped: "It's easier to be Catholic in France," especially if you "practice it discreetly. It's a matter of *intégration*." Finally, unlike Maghrebis, who "have many problems" and a "very bad reputation," he says, "Indians don't pose any problems in France."

Vincent has also done a substantial amount of community service, like helping unemployed people find jobs. He thinks that his accomplishments "show the others that 'you see my physical difference, but see also that I contribute something to my country, something concrete.' It's my way of responding. I want to be recognized as a counterexample to what others say about foreigners." For Vincent, *intégration* is paramount. He says, you must "make the effort to integrate yourself so you're not put into an ethnic community. For example, I don't spend time with the Indian community." You "have no problem if you're in the mold," if you "blend in." Further:

> Education is an excellent way to be integrated. Sports is another good way. I joined a sports club because I wanted to, but it's also very important for *intégration*. You need to be like the others. This is a form of normality that allows you to be yourself. Because if you are integrated you can say what you think. But if you're not integrated and you start talking, it will be taken badly.

The safest approach is to be careful in your behavior and speech.

Despite Vincent's efforts to "integrate" himself into French society, one obstacle cannot be overcome. "Out on the street, they only see the color of my skin. No one sees what I've done with my life." Indeed, to some people, he's not just "a foreigner on the outside," but a "foreigner." He says, "I must prove to certain people that I'm capable. Foreigners must do more." His fear of being called a "dirty foreigner" and his desire to prove himself different from "what others say about foreigners" remain sensitive issues. He must be especially "discreet," he says, to avoid the "xenophobia" of some people. It's best to be "discreet and still more discreet."

As the interview went on, Vincent thought about parallels between his parents' search for acceptance and his own behavior. Remembering how his parents invited people to their home for a meal, he said, "I wonder whether I'm doing the same thing at my house. It's a pleasure for sure, but I wonder whether, in the back of my mind, it's also a kind of *intégration*." The memory of our lunch hovered in the background.

Finally, Vincent was struck by the experience of being interviewed. He was surprised, though also embarrassed, by the strength of his feelings. He periodically interrupted his own account with asides like "This is the first time I've thought about this" and "It's interesting to talk about these things." He was also struck by the slow progression of the four generations of his family: first his French-speaking, Catholic grandparents who served in the French colonial government and chose French citizenship; then his parents, who were French citizens (his father having served in the French military for fifteen years) and who did everything possible to be "integrated" into the French communities where they lived; then Vincent himself, who has spent his entire life in France among "French" people, and yet feels that he's perceived not a French, but as a "foreigner" who must gain their acceptance; and finally his son, who has a "French" mother and was raised to be French, but still must navigate French society with his tan complexion and non-European last name.

THE OTHER INTERVIEWEES

The great majority of interviewees who are neither Maghrebi nor Black are either Asians (*Asiatiques*) or people who originate from non-Arab countries of Western or South Asia.[2] These interviewees represent a larger population than one might expect: of

France's 63 million inhabitants in 2011, 1.5 million trace their origins to Asia (Tribalat 2015: 21–22).[3]

The Asian Interviewees

Eight of the interviewees reported that they are seen as Asians.[4] Four of them (Henri, Grégoire, Mathieu, and Rémy) originate from the former French colony of Vietnam, while the four others (Yuka, Emily, Paul, and Kana) originate from China, South Korea, or Japan, all countries that have never been French colonies. While these eight people range widely in personality and life experience, virtually all of them pointed to an evolution in French attitudes that has been important to their lives: while Asians used to be disparaged in France, they are now seen positively (see Chuang 2022: 109).[5]

Henri, Grégoire, Mathieu, and Rémy. These men, all of mixed Vietnamese and "French" parentage, trace their origins to Vietnam's time as a French colony. The history is important here. By the 1880s, France had conquered all of present-day Vietnam and incorporated it into a colony known as French Indochina. In 1945, Ho Chi Minh's declaration of independence for Vietnam triggered a war with France, which France lost in 1954. The United States then fought its own Vietnam War against a political and military organization known as the Viet Cong, which the US lost in 1975. Since 1975, Vietnam has been a unified, fully independent country.

When Mathieu invited me to take part in his family's "daily life," as he had written in an Airbnb message, I had no idea of the whirlwind that was in store for me. Mathieu lives with his wife, Kana, and their infant daughter, Madeleine, in a sunny apartment in a well-maintained housing complex for families of different origins. After a quick lunch, Mathieu took me to the local supermarket, which was filled with people of various ethnicities and an enormous array of fresh food, especially fish, fruits, and vegetables. We spent the rest of the afternoon conducting his interview, and the evening relaxing with Kana and Madeleine.

The next morning, Mathieu drove us to a Sunday family cookout in the country, two hours out of town, where I met his relatives and in-laws. Everyone was in high spirits. As soon as

Mathieu's father and uncle heard about my project, they asked—almost demanded—to be interviewed. Back at the apartment that evening, I interviewed Mathieu's father, Grégoire, who joked afterward that he'd "just been to confession." Next, I interviewed Kana (who will be discussed in chapters 4 and 5), followed by Henri, who is Mathieu's uncle and Grégoire's brother. In total, we did four interviews in two days. The rest of my time at Mathieu's home was spent on nonstop socializing and shared meals, like a mix-and-match lunch of cold fish, rice, and sauce, followed by French cheeses. During my few unoccupied hours, I walked around their multiethnic neighborhood, taking in its outdoor market, stores, and cafés.

Henri and Grégoire. Both now retired, Henri and Grégoire were born in Vietnam in 1946 and 1949, respectively, when Vietnam was still a French colony. Their father was a French soldier who was fighting against the Vietnamese in their war for independence, and their mother was a French-speaking and Catholic Vietnamese woman. While they were still toddlers, Henri and Grégoire were sent to live with their father's family in France for security reasons. Their parents followed after France's defeat in 1954, although the family's reunion was brief. Six months later, their father was redeployed to Algeria to fight against Algerians in the Algerian war for independence. The rest of the family remained in France. Henri and Grégoire's father returned upon France's defeat in that war in 1962, but his marriage to their mother did not last.

Henri and Grégoire shared a troubled childhood. Ridiculed as a "*chinetoque*" (an insulting term for Chinese people and, by extension, other Asians),[6] Henri remembers that he "fought all the time." He was expelled shortly after entering high school. Grégoire's experience was essentially the same:

> I don't have good memories from my childhood because I felt different. My mother was Vietnamese, so I had an Asian appearance. I was called *chinetoque*. I didn't like it; it made me aggressive with the other kids. I felt rejected by them. I left school early.

Being called "*chinetoque*" by other kids made Grégoire feel inferior because, as he says, the Chinese were seen as "nearly savages."

Prejudice dogged Henri and Grégoire throughout their childhood. Their father's family never accepted their mother. According to Grégoire, "they treated her very badly because she was Vietnamese" and ridiculed her as a "sorcerer." Their own father was dismissive toward his sons. At least once, Grégoire recalls, his father joked that his favorite aperitif, Ricard, was yellow like Grégoire.

Grégoire recalls watching TV news reports of the American war in Vietnam, when enormous Viet Cong body counts were announced "every day, every day." This "was the time of Rambo," and Grégoire viewed the American soldiers as the "good guys" who "killed the vermin." Thinking back to how he felt as an adolescent watching these news reports, he says, "I was ashamed of the Vietnamese," who were "just peasants in black pajamas. I identified with the Americans," who were like the television cowboys who "I adored."

Both Grégoire and Henri straightened out their lives, they said, first in the French military and then in government jobs. But it was not always easy. When Henri took the examination for a promotion in the post office system, he did extremely well on the written component three times in a row, but he never got the promotion. He finally realized that a member of the selection panel considered his "*faciès asiatique*" a "disqualifying criterion, since the position involved contact with the public." When Henri asked the man why he had given him such a low grade on the in-person component of the promotion exam, the man responded, "You should understand that the administration in France needs to remain White. It's illogical for you to think otherwise, for you to attempt to gain that position."

Henri also faced bias while overseeing children's soccer. Although he was certified to be a trainer, he was repeatedly turned down. "It was always the same thing." He'd be told, "Yes, well, you have the head of a Viet Cong. That will never work with children." And when Henri served as a referee at soccer matches, the kids would call out, "What's with this? Hey, *chinetoque*, what's with this?" After calling a penalty, he'd hear taunts from the sidelines like "Hey, how did your mother make someone like you? Are you sick? Do you have jaundice or what?"

Despite these obstacles, both brothers got married (Henri to a "French" woman, Grégoire to a Vietnamese woman), raised children, and pursued careers in the civil service. While these years generally went well, some problems with bias persisted, even within their families. Henri says that his son has a "European *faciès*"—three of his four grandparents are "French"—as well as a French first and last name. To maintain appearances, his son would not allow Henri to walk him to elementary school because, Henri explained, "he didn't want his friends to see me, with my Chinese face." Only his son's (White) mother would be permitted to do this.

Both Grégoire and Henri reported that attitudes toward Asians in France have improved in recent decades. "When I was a child," Grégoire said, "a Chinese person was someone who hadn't evolved. Now China is a rich country, the Japanese are rich. They are as evolved as us. Now we play on the same court. It's completely different." Similarly, Henri reports that people now think that Asians "don't make noise; they're seen as very intelligent."

At the end of his interview, Grégoire waxed philosophical. He likes to think "positively" and "wants to forget" the insults he may hear even today. Looking back on his nearly seventy years of life, with his happy marriage (he and his wife certainly seemed happy at the Sunday cookout), his children, and his grandchildren, Grégoire said, "I've had a good run in life. I'm very happy."

Mathieu. Mathieu, my Airbnb host and Grégoire's son, has lived a different life from his father and uncle. By the late 1980s and 1990s, when Mathieu was growing up in France, Vietnam's status as a colony was long in the past. So, too, were Vietnam's war of independence with France, and even its war with the United States. In the meantime, the status of East Asian countries, first Japan and then China and Korea, had risen on the global stage, along with their growing economies.

Now thirty-eight, Mathieu was born in the same French city where he lives today. He grew up in a multiethnic neighborhood with Maghrebis, Whites, and a few Blacks, and even though "many people" called him "the Chinese kid" because of his "different *faciès*," he says, it was "just a joke." He experienced no prejudice at the nearby university he attended. Mathieu has "never doubted" that he is completely French.

Having received a degree in physical education, Mathieu now runs his own business, training children in Tae Kwon Do, the

Korean martial arts sport. After dating a Maghrebi woman for a number of years, he married Kana, who had come to France from Japan when she was in her twenties. Mathieu has traveled to Vietnam a number of times, becoming more comfortable there with each visit. Still, his sense of being French "hasn't changed," he says. "In fact, it might have been reinforced."

Almost alone among the interviewees, Mathieu expressed an ideological approach to French identity. As far as he is concerned, if "you see yourself as French, speak French, and adhere to the values that underlie the language, then you're French." Being French is thus entirely distinct from physical appearance, religion, birthplace, or even where one was raised. I asked Mathieu whether the millions of people who subscribe to the National Front party's slogan "France for the French" would agree; indeed, whether they'd even consider him French. "No, they aren't talking about me," he responded, even though he has spent his whole life in France. But Mathieu is not troubled by this since they're "a minority that just shouts."

Rémy. Rémy is unrelated to Mathieu and his family. A friend of an Airbnb host in a city elsewhere in France, he lives in a handsome house near the village where he grew up. As soon as we arrived, his wife ushered us into his study, which is filled with memorabilia and photos from the career I would soon hear about. Rémy looked to be about seventy, but he is extremely vigorous, bursting with energy, and he speaks in a loud, authoritative voice. His wife served us a tray of beverages and left the room. The interview began.

Rémy's father grew up in colonial Vietnam in a well-to-do, French-oriented Vietnamese family. In 1940, his father left for France to work as an interpreter between Vietnamese factory workers and the factory's management in a small French village. There, he met and married the daughter of a local "French" farmer and had three children, including Rémy. His family lived in a tiny house near the factory. (After the interview, Rémy gave me a tour of the village, pointing out his childhood home and the remains of the factory.) His father consciously adopted French values and customs, including Catholicism, and Rémy was raised to be "a true French person."

In 1955, Rémy's father contracted tuberculosis and was placed in a sanatorium, while the rest of the family was put in preventoriums. Rémy was released in 1957, but this was premature: he, too, had contracted tuberculosis, so he was also put in a sanatorium. Both of his parents died. The family had been "smashed apart," he recalls, and "each person had to fend for himself." Rémy was thirteen.

After he was released from the sanatorium, Rémy threw himself into judo, diving, and other sports to demonstrate that he was neither contagious nor a weakling. Still ridiculed as "*chinetoque*," he jumped at the chance to join the military. His "French" grandmother told him, "After you've done your military service, they won't be able to treat you like the little Chinese boy." At his army intake, he recalls, "I hid my malady, I never said I was tubercular." He served as a commando-parachutist in the army.

"I'm completely French," Rémy said more than once during the interview. Even as a teenager, he refused to accept insults: to anyone who might call him "little Chinaman," he stood ready to "break his face." This didn't entirely do away with the "racism" of others. Teachers "intentionally mispronounced" his (rather simple) Vietnamese last name. Later in life, if he was called "Chinese" he responded in his unaccented French, "I served France, I served in the army. Did you serve France?"

After completing his army service, Rémy married a "French" woman from his village and got his career underway. He joined the National Police and moved up, becoming a combat instructor at the National Police training academy. He also became an expert in martial arts, including judo (in which he earned a black belt), Tae Kwon Do, and boxing. During the following years, he was able to gain several promotions because, he said, promotions were based "on exams, not the color of one's skin." Ultimately, Rémy became head of the entire academy's physical training program. In 1979, he had the honor of preparing the National Police for its first-ever participation in the Bastille Day parade along the Champs-Élysées in Paris. By the time I interviewed him, he had retired to the comfortable home where we met for the interview.

Rémy ended the interview with an anecdote. Recently, he and his grandson were watching the Bastille Day parade on television when the national anthem came on. "We stood up and put our hands on our hearts, even though there was no one there to see us. It was just him and me there." Rémy concluded, "That's the message I pass along to my grandson: this is our country; these are our values."

Yuka and Emily. Yuka and Emily, who live in different cities and do not know each other, have nearly identical backgrounds. Each is about thirty. Each grew up in China, then came to France to study engineering, and remained in France. At this point their lives went in different directions. Yuka immersed herself in French life, became fluent in French, married a "French" man, and now lives like the "French" people in her small town. Emily, by contrast, bore down on her engineering studies and, since her graduation, has held a succession of highly technical positions in the corporate world. She has been successful, but in the meantime has had limited contact with French people outside of her studies and her job. Emily is not fully fluent in French.

Yuka grew up in Shanghai. "From early childhood," she says, "I wanted to live abroad." After three years at a Chinese university, she moved to France, where she threw herself into intensive language courses, lived with an older French couple, and socialized with French people. At the university where she studied engineering, Yuka became friends with the French students around her and had French boyfriends, including the man who later became her husband. When she and her husband visited his family for their first Christmas together, Yuka says she "drank a lot of red wine with his grandfather." By the end of the evening, his grandfather declared that though "I have a Chinese face, I was really French."

After she got her first degree, Yuka switched to biology with the goal of becoming a veterinarian—"it was always my dream to work with animals"—but this didn't work out. In the meantime, she and her husband had a son, settled in a quiet town near the university where they had met, and adopted five cats and a dog. In her work, Yuka turned to "something completely different," hand-sewing children's clothing and selling the clothes online. Although heavily accented, her French is excellent.

Continually upbeat—her enthusiasm didn't flag during any of our conversations—Yuka has never felt bias in France. Today, people in town recognize her as she walks the family dog, goes out with her son, and bikes around town. She feels that she fits in this community. "If there's a problem, we talk it over." Being called "the little Chinese girl," although a common occurrence, has never bothered her. Nor does the slogan "France for the French." "It's dumb, that's all." She thinks that the National Front political party uses it to prey on less educated people, many of whom "are having problems or may be out of work." Yuka feels herself to be neither French nor Chinese, but that doesn't matter. "Why should there be any borders?" she asks.[7]

Emily followed a different path in France. On the advice of her introductory French teacher, she took a European name—her Chinese name is Shihan Zhang—but she was more interested in technical studies than in joining the social life around her. Emily quickly earned two master's degrees in engineering and began working at a French infrastructure company. Since then, she has mostly devoted herself to work. Although her French is still limited, she experiences few language problems because her job involves "lots of numbers." Feeling "well-respected" and "well-integrated" at her company, she now leads the technical team of an entire project. She did not report workplace bias. If anything, she said, she feels a "positive discrimination" because "large companies need to hire foreigners to show that they are international" and to "hire women" to rectify the low percentage of female engineers in their workforce. Being Chinese has also helped, she thinks, since people think that Chinese people "work hard."

Emily lives on her own in a high-rise apartment building in the city. During a pizza dinner nearby, she wondered aloud whether she should keep working as an engineer. She has never studied anything else or done anything else. And at the end of her interview, she also wondered about her decision to come to France. Since her arrival in France, China has made such progress in civil engineering that "by now or soon" it "will no longer need France." If she were to return to China in a year or two, she fears she'd be viewed as "incompetent."

Paul. I met Paul at the downtown apartment where he lives on his own. He was eager to be interviewed, so, within minutes of my arrival, we sat down on his living room sofa, and I turned on the recorder.

Paul's life has been marked by the radical split between his East Asian appearance and his French identity. Born in South Korea of Korean parents, he was adopted from an orphanage at the age of four by a highly educated "French" couple who brought him to France. Paul grew up in the Latin Quarter of

Paris, where his parents raised him to be French. He says he felt both "100 percent French" and "White" even as a child. "It was only when I saw my reflection in a shop window that I realized that I was different from the others." He attended an elite Parisian high school, where his "high-quality French" was perfected.

After graduating from high school, Paul joined the French army, where he trained to be a helicopter pilot. He married a "French" woman and had two children with her, though they are now divorced. Now forty-three, Paul remains an army helicopter pilot.

Paul has no doubt about his identity. "When it comes down to it, me, I'm a White in my head. I hang around with Whites. I have very, very few friends who are Asian." And once people hear his name ("I have a French family name and first name") and hear his unaccented French, he thinks they see him as French. In any case, he says, current French attitudes toward Asians are far from critical:

> In French people's minds, Asians are well-integrated. They're more easily accepted than Maghrebis and Africans. They are discreet and respect other people's cultures. Racism against Asians is very, very, very rare. French people have nothing against Asians.

Although he reports "no problems with prejudice," Paul says that there are more "racists" in the military than in other lines of work. Colleagues openly joke that he's a North Korean spy. Paul laughs to show that these jokes don't bother him, believing that "mocking yourself is the best defense." Rather than living in the small town near his army base, he chose a nearby city he described as "cosmopolitan," with people "of foreign ethnicities." This was where we met.

At the end of the interview, Paul summed up his feelings: "My parents adopted me as a young child, but I also adopted French culture, 100 percent. In my soul I'm totally French."

Interviewees of Western or South Asian Origin

While the interviewees who trace their origin to non-Arab countries in Western or South Asia—Iran, Turkey, India, and Pakistan—are diverse in their cultural backgrounds, the perceived commonality of their *faciès* has proven pivotal to their lives in France. All of the interviewees in this group have dark or "bronzed" skin, black hair, and brown eyes, and yet none of them reported being mistaken for Maghrebi or Arab. Thus, while these interviewees share a *faciès* that is immediately recognizable as distinct from the *faciès* of "French" people, it is also recognizably distinct from the *faciès* of the (much disdained) Maghrebis. This physical distinctiveness, which these interviewees consistently pointed out, is central to how they feel they are seen by "French" people.

Vincent, who was profiled earlier in this chapter, falls into this category. The other interviewees in this group are Shayan, Fatih, Usman, and Nima.

Shayan. Although both Shayan and his wife Christine have spent their lives in the same city where I visited them, they have different social identities. Christine comes from a longtime "French" family with, as Shayan put it, a "*Français de souche*" family name. A "brunette with green eyes," Christine grew up Catholic. By contrast, Shayan's parents came to France from Iran when they were young adults, and they have an Iranian family name. Shayan was raised as a Muslim. Describing his own appearance, he told me, "My hair is black, my eyes are brown, and I have a dark complexion."

Now thirty-three, Shayan spent much of his interview describing how he had gained acceptance among "French" people. His story began with a family where the process of *intégration* was underway even before his birth:

> From the time I was born, my parents never spoke Farsi with their children. It was French, French, French all the time. Internally, they thought, "I want my children to succeed in life, and their life will be in France." As a result, I don't speak Farsi and my French has no accent at all. There's never been a moment when I felt anything other than French.

And while people thought he had a non-European origin, he was not tainted by the "negative connotation" of being seen as Maghrebi because he does not have "a Maghrebi *faciès*." (Although Iran is an overwhelmingly Muslim country, only a small percentage of Iranians are Arab.) Instead, he said, "I have an international face." Because French people are unfamiliar with Iranians, Shayan thinks, they couldn't tell what he was. "I seemed like a bit of everything: Spanish, Italian, Indian, Lebanese."

Shayan "dressed like the Maghrebis" and "hung around" with them in junior high school, but this changed in high school. He began to distance himself from the Maghrebi kids because he didn't want "to be associated with a community that was seen badly." He changed the style of his clothing and paid attention to his speech. To his mind, many Maghrebis born in France "aren't French" because they "don't care about" integrating themselves into French society. By contrast, he said, "I'm in France, so I speak French, a French that's rich, that's beautiful, a French that's well-written and well-spoken."

Religion was also an issue. Though Shayan once considered himself both Muslim and French, he began to move away from Islam in high school. French people, he found, "don't distinguish between Muslims and Maghrebis." By the time he finished college and entered the business world, he had abandoned all Muslim dietary rules. Shayan is now a manager at a midsize French company. At business dinners, "it's difficult to integrate yourself if you don't take part." When a client starts talking about what wine to order, "you can't just drink a Perrier." This hasn't posed a problem for him.

Shayan and Christine got married a year before the interview. While they both wish to raise their children as "totally French" and give them French first names, they disagree about the last name to choose. Christine thinks that they should have her French last name. While Shayan recognizes that carrying his Iranian last name could be a "constraint" for them, he feels that having a French last name wouldn't make a big difference. If their son (he took the example of a son) secured a job interview in part because of the French first and last name on his résumé, his "dark complexion, black hair, and brown eyes" would be evident at the interview. A "racist" would still reject him in favor of a less-qualified "blond with blue eyes," Shayan said, or even "a Pole," because that person would be seen as "a true Frenchman."

Shayan's job interview scenario suggests an enduring limit to acceptance. Even after abandoning the Muslim practices of his upbringing, learning to speak and live in completely French ways, marrying a "French" woman from a longtime "French" family, and then raising their children to be "totally French,"

Shayan anticipates that their children could face discrimination because, though *métis*, they would still not have a "French" physical appearance.

Fatih. Fatih and I met in the afternoon at the small but modern apartment he rented out. He was dressed in crisp shorts and a pastel Ralph Lauren polo shirt, appearing athletic and confident, just like the junior corporate manager that he turned out to be. A far more complex person soon emerged.

Fatih's interview went into the evening and continued the next morning. His parents were Muslims from Turkey. Now thirty-three, Fatih was only three years old when he and his mother joined his father to live in a village in France. He valued both Turkish and French ways while growing up—"I didn't need to choose between the two"—even though "French" people could be "cruel" when he declined to eat pork. Fatih also recalls his "frustration and anger" and a "feeling of injustice" when, as a teenager, he was stopped by policemen because, he believed, they saw him a "foreigner."

Academically gifted, Fatih was placed in the science track of a high school in a nearby town, where the great majority of students were "French." "In high school, there were teachers who had a very false image of foreigners and were sometimes very mean." He came to realize "that the world is difficult, that there are barriers," and that he'd need a "passport for leaving." For him, that passport "was a diploma."

Fatih studied mechanical engineering at a regional university that was "very French." Like the few other "foreigners" there, Fatih says, he had problems with faculty members. One extremist whom he had seen with a right-wing political group was assigned as his mentor for a year-long project. Although this professor "validated" the assumptions underlying the project Fatih planned to conduct and approved his progress "at each stage," after almost nine months of work, Fatih discovered that the assumptions were erroneous. When he reported this to the professor, the professor just "laughed."

Fatih finished his engineering program, but then switched to international business management. "I met people and had experiences I'd never have had." This included learning a number of languages, including English, Spanish, and Russian. After getting a master's degree in marketing, Fatih gravitated to the large city where he lives today in order to work in a more "international" environment. But even there he feels limited. A superior suggested that he change his name to something "simpler, something easier to remember."

Fatih believes that he doesn't have a "Maghrebi look," and he consciously cultivates a European physical appearance. Smoothing his hair's natural curliness and keeping his skin less "bronzed" than before, he says, he now looks "Mediterranean," perhaps "Greek, Spanish, Italian." He wears "designer brands for their quality and cut." Still single, he dates a wide range of women.

Religious issues are now complicated in France, Fatih thinks, because "religion has become very politicized." Some people say that "if you're a Muslim, you can't be French." Fortunately for his business career, Fatih drinks alcohol, though he still abstains from pork.

Near the end of the interview, Fatih summed up a life of feeling, at his core, rejected by the people around him. The gulf between how he thinks about himself and how he is treated is deeply discouraging:

> I grew up in France; it's as if I were born here. I have friends here, the culture. It's hurtful that I'm from here, but people don't really accept me. I feel rejected even in my own country. It's frustrating. Sometimes I'm depressed by this, though more often I'm angry.

Still, there's nowhere to go: "I feel French; I belong here. My life is here."

Usman. I visited Usman and his family at their house in a handsome suburb, up a long and winding road with flowers spilling out of every front garden. Now forty-seven, he is a co-owner of a high-tech start-up, and his "French" wife is a historian. They have two energetic and likable sons. My two days with Usman and his family were packed with spirited conversation, meals with him and his wife, trips around town, and, of course, his interview.

Usman grew up a world away from where he is now, in a remote, devoutly Muslim area in northwestern Pakistan. The son of a non-believing professor and personally unreligious, Usman nonetheless maintained appearances by praying at the local mosque on Fridays. He attended college elsewhere in Pakistan, got an engineering degree, and then worked at an international firm in Islamabad, the country's capital. When he was twenty-three, Usman was offered a scholarship for advanced study in France. Although he spoke no French and had never been outside Pakistan, he seized the opportunity. In France, he got a master's degree and doctorate in telecommunications. Since then, Usman's fast-moving career has brought him into contact with high-tech companies and tech specialists in the United States, Israel, and elsewhere in Europe.

Much has also happened socially during the twenty-plus years he has been in France. In the beginning, Usman says he felt "different from, and I'm not afraid to say this now, inferior to Europeans." Pakistanis are inferior to Europeans "at least in our perspective." The European students around him "seemed a lot like each other," particularly in "skin color and habits." They seemed to be at a higher "level of culture." Even though "the Italians and Spaniards" in his French class were "as much foreigners as me," Usman felt like a "true foreigner" and "less legitimate" than the European students.

Usman had to deal with the "massive cultural barrier" he sensed between himself and the European students. He also felt that "it was normal for the others to reject me." When someone is an outsider, Usman explained, "there's the us and there's the them. It's a sort of combat. When you go somewhere, you're not yet legitimate, the others are more at home than you." These feelings continued even though he experienced no outright rejection, either at the university or in town.

For Usman, the goal was "to arrive at being at home in their home." To do this, he "made an extraordinary effort" to "erase all differences" between himself and the European students. While he couldn't change his skin color, he says, he did everything possible "to be like the others," indeed, "to be more French than the French" (literally, *plus royaliste que le roi*, that is, "more royalist than the king"). He learned French, of course, but he also changed his style of clothing and learned how to dance, something he had not done in Pakistan. He drank alcohol and threw himself into romantic relationships with European women. Before long, he had succeeded in integrating himself into French society. Indeed, many of his friends, he recalls, "said I was too much like the Europeans."

In his physical appearance, Usman has been mistaken for an Indian, Brazilian, or Mexican, but never for a Maghrebi. He has also never been turned away from a bar or nightclub, even though, on the two or three occasions he went with Maghrebis, his Maghrebi companions were not allowed in. People don't think of him as a Muslim, either. Usman isn't surprised. Darker than a European, he still doesn't have the *faciès*, accent, or name of a Maghrebi or, more generally, of an Arab. And because he drinks alcohol, eats pork when others do, and never prays, nothing in his behavior suggests that he's Muslim.

Today, Usman doesn't "identify as French," but he doesn't need to. His wife is "French," he says, and "my children are French. People like me don't need to feel different and inferior." Indeed, Usman now feels "a little superior" to most French people. "Over time, I've established myself here, I've integrated myself. I've succeeded in certain ways. I'm more accomplished." Economically, at least, France is a "tired" country. Perhaps one day, Usman says, he and his family will move to a country where his technical and entrepreneurial skills can be put to better use.

Nima. Nima and I got to know each other at his favorite restaurant a couple of days before my stay at his Airbnb apartment. We spoke about his life, his politics, and my project for more than two hours. Later that week, we conducted his interview at the apartment, digging more deeply into his life.

By his own account, Nima has always charted his own course. Born in 1949, he grew up in a middle-class family in Tehran, Iran, when oil exports were making the country wealthy. After getting his college degree, he worked as a journalist at the country's progressive, high-circulation newspaper, and, as a Marxist, he was active in left-wing causes. "It was a good life." Nima never thought of leaving Iran until he won a scholarship for graduate education in France. At twenty-seven, he moved to a small city in France, where he studied sociology.

Although Nima had planned to return to Iran after getting his doctorate, the 1979 Iranian revolution forced a change. He couldn't return because he had been a journalist and left-wing political activist in Iran. Having already received the two levels of a French master's degree and started work on his doctoral dissertation, Nima decided to keep the dissertation unfinished in order to maintain his student visa. Meanwhile, the Iranian embassy in France refused to renew his passport because he was "a non-believer, a revolutionary, an undesirable person."

Nima had to forge a life in France. By the time of our interview, he had been living in the same French city for more than forty years. He had married an Iranian woman there, had two children, and gotten divorced. Since giving up his studies, he has run various small businesses, including a garage, a butcher shop, a food store, and a bakery. "I've always worked. I've had employees and trained apprentices. That's my contribution."

Nima has almost never encountered overt bias. Early on, when a small shopkeeper brusquely told him, "You're no longer in the jungle," he thought that the shopkeeper must be having a bad day. "It didn't hurt me." There he was, in a rather small French city that was more like a "village," and the "jungle" he'd come from was the large, cosmopolitan capital of an oil-rich country. As a Marxist, he doesn't feel racism as a hurtful rejection, but rather as a tool used by the dominant class to maintain fissures among those they dominate.

Over the years, Nima learned to speak the French "of someone educated." He has also found it easy to conform to French behavioral norms—a style of dressing, a way of interacting with others—because they don't substantially differ from the norms of educated people in Tehran. He's done all this to avoid being "marginalized," but not to be integrated:

> I don't like this term "*intégration*," since it always has "assimilation" as a hidden agenda. I don't want anyone to assimilate into the dominant social environment. Each person should have his own personality, his own character, his own historical, cultural, and familial bonds. Thus, for me, *intégration* is a bad way of talking, with dominance as a hidden agenda.

Having always been, in his words, a "producer" rather than a "user," Nima doesn't feel beholden to France. Recently, when he was criticizing the political situation in the country, the person with whom he was talking said "Don't spit on the hand that feeds you." Nima rejected this outright: "France has not fed me. I have fed France."

Those who declare "France for the French," who speak "ideologically" of "the White race, the country of the Gauls, blah, blah," only make Nima angry. These are "inhumane ways of thinking" that some people use to "justify their rejection of others" and to assert their "rights" over them.

NEITHER MAGHREBI NOR BLACK: RECURRING ISSUES

While the people discussed in this chapter come from a variety of cultural backgrounds and have pursued different lives in France, their interviews show that they deal with many of the same issues relating to acceptance and discrimination.

Acceptance in French Society

As seen in chapters 1 and 2, Maghrebi and Black interviewees reported stereotypes among "French" people regarding their purported inferiority, antisocial behavior, and backwardness. They are thought to live profoundly non-French lives in rundown housing projects in the poor *banlieues*. Even though none of the Maghrebi and Black people I interviewed conform to these stereotypes, many reported a lack of acceptance among "French" people.

The people belonging to the third category of interviewees spoke of a different experience, in large part because they are not seen as Maghrebi or Black. Interviewees of Western or South Asian origin made a point of saying that, despite their dark or "bronzed" skin, black hair, and brown eyes, they are not mistaken for Maghrebis or, more generally, Arabs. In Fatih's words, he is "fortunate not to look Arab or African, since people are meaner toward them." Similarly, the Asians are not mistaken for Maghrebis, and no one in this third group is mistaken for being Black. There are enormous advantages to not being seen as Maghrebi or Black in France. The demeaning stereotypes of these groups are inapplicable.

Then there is the issue of religion. As was the case with the Maghrebis, almost all (four out of five) of the interviewees of Western or South Asian background trace their roots to countries that are overwhelmingly Muslim. Indeed, their countries of origin—Iran (Shayan and Nima), Pakistan (Usman), and Turkey (Fatih)—are known for a politicized, often anti-Western strain of

Islam. But despite this, these interviewees reported that Islam plays little or no role in their interactions with "French" people. And while their behavior in social settings does not suggest that they are practicing Muslims (though Fatih declines pork even as he drinks wine), this does not explain why they feel little or no discomfort among "French" people. After all, Maghrebis who are completely secular find that the very assumption that they are Muslim is unsettling for "French" people. Ayoub, a completely non-religious Maghrebi, feels that he is being "tested" each time he is offered alcohol or pork.

The Asian interviewees reported that Asians have a generally positive reputation in French society today. To be sure, they fall within a distinct classification, hence the label "Asian." And those who are old enough to have experienced the France of the 1950s through the 1970s were ridiculed at the time as "*chinetoques*," a term for Chinese people, who were thought to be "nearly savages" by the French at the time. But the same interviewees report an extraordinary evolution in the stereotype of Asians in France. According to them, Asians are now seen as well-behaved, smart, and hard-working. They are also viewed "very positively," Grégoire said, because they "don't make noise and are seen as very intelligent." The younger generation of Asian interviewees (Mathieu, Paul, Yuka, and Emily) have only known this positive image.

The emotional advantages of not being Maghrebi or Black are considerable. Speaking of Maghrebis, Grégoire said, "People mock their parents, their families. They suffer. I put myself in the place of a young Maghrebi. He doesn't feel pride, he doesn't feel positive." Blacks may also feel badly about themselves. Grégoire recalled seeing billboard and television appeals to feed the starving children of Africa: "There were these campaigns against hunger in Africa. The children there were emaciated. Automatically, a Black is someone who's hungry. It must be very hard for Blacks in France."

Although now seen positively, the interviewees of this third category are thought to be similar to Maghrebis and Blacks in other ways. They are seen as having a non-European *faciès* and, with that, non-European origins and associated behavioral traits. Many of them also have non-European last names, and some have non-European first names. Virtually all recognize that many "French" people do not see them as truly French. Some of them go further. Although Vincent and Fatih grew up in France, they both feel they are seen as "foreigners."

Discrimination

Just as the interviewees of this third category feel a greater degree of acceptance among "French" people, they reported less discrimination than the Maghrebi and Black interviewees.[8] But discrimination is not absent from their lives. Vincent and Fatih both experienced such incidents during their education. Fatih spoke of the fate of other so-called "foreigners" at school: though some of these students were "very strong, very gifted," they were undermined by "teachers or administrators who did what they shouldn't have done." And those who made it to university found that "certain professors intentionally put a stick in the wheel" of their efforts. Many dropped out.[9]

A few interviewees also spoke about mistreatment by government employees. Frequent police stops—a major issue among young Maghrebi and Black men—were also a problem for Fatih. Even Usman, a well-dressed professional, has been treated differently at passport control. Arriving at a French airport with a British colleague, he alone was drawn aside and questioned. The lesson for him was plain: "I have a French passport, but not a French face."

As with Maghrebis and Blacks, the most frequently cited type of discrimination involves employment. While Vincent's Indian last name did not stand in the way of getting a job, it was apparently a problem when he sought a promotion. As he put it, there's "the facade and then there's what people really think." Henri feels that his *faciès* blocked his path to promotion three times in a row. But despite the milder employment discrimination reported by people of this third category of interviewees, all of them have gravitated to the same occupational niches as the Maghrebis and Blacks: information technology (Vincent, Shayan) or other marketable fields (Usman, Emily, Fatih); running their own businesses (Nima, Mathieu, Yuka); or a career in the government civil service (Grégoire, Henri, Rémy, Paul).

Fatih saw how discrimination works from the inside when he served on a hiring committee at his company. "There's a lot of prejudice," he said. "Recruiting depends a lot on appearances. There's always a barrier, especially for positions with direct contact with clients." And even if someone who is not "French" is hired, he added, "it takes a long time for others to accept you."

Henri—who, decades ago, was told point-blank that he could not be promoted to a customer-contact position because of his appearance—provided an overview of today's situation for Asians:

> If I were looking for a job now, I'd still have problems, but fewer, perhaps because Asians are seen better in France these days. It's easier for Asians, not like for a Black or someone with an Arab *faciès*. Even one with a French name, it would be hard for him.

To Be Seen as "French"

As with Maghrebis, people of this third category can start being seen as "French" after a generation or two, if they wish to, as long as later generations look European, have European names, and, for people of Muslim origin, put aside dietary restrictions. Henri's son exemplifies this process. Henri grew up in France, and because of his "French" father, is *métis* and has a French family name. He married a "French" woman, and so his son is three-quarters "French" in physical appearance. This allowed Henri's son to present himself as "French" like the other students at his elementary school—but only if he was not seen with his father, who has, in Henri's own words, a "Chinese face."[10]

Similarly, Vincent spoke about his son, who has Vincent's non-European last name and is a mixture between Vincent and his "*Française de souche*" ex-wife in his appearance. As far as Vincent can tell, this has brought his son only part of the way to acceptance. Vincent's son needs to make "less of an effort" than he does. Although his son is the fourth generation in the family to be French citizens, Vincent said, "it takes time" to be accepted.

Finally, Shayan spoke about his future children with his "French" wife. Even if they raise their children to be completely French and give their children his wife's last name, they will have a discernible non-European physical appearance. Shayan fears that discrimination may result. In sum, the transformation process of becoming French—not French in your own mind, but French in the eyes of "French" people—is incremental.

This said, at least three of the Asian interviewees feel that they have won the right to be seen as French. With half of his physical appearance being "French," Rémy points to his life history in support of this claim: he was born in France and raised to be purely French, served as a commando in the French army, and had a distinguished career in the National Police. He will confront anyone who suggests he's not French. Paul, who has a fully French name and was raised by his "French" adoptive parents to be exclusively French, feels that he is "100 percent French," even "White." People on the street may not see him as French, but he believes that they would change their mind once they learn his name and hear his unaccented language. Finally, there is Mathieu, who has spent his entire life in France, is *métis*, has a fully French name, and proudly adheres to French values. But even for these interviewees—Rémy, Paul, and Mathieu—a broader social reality remains. Each one of them knows that they are not French in the eyes of millions of French people simply because they do not have a European *faciès*.

THE IMPORTANCE OF PERSONALITY—VINCENT VS. USMAN

Comparing the profiles of Vincent and Usman in this chapter can be confounding. On the surface, the two men seem similar. Both are well established in their communities and professions, live in handsome homes, and fully participate in French society. The Vincent known to his "French" guests at our holiday lunch must be the same person whom I saw then: an expansive host serving characteristically French food and wine, full of good cheer and ready to banter about any topic. During my stay at his home, Usman was much the same.

Still, their backgrounds differ markedly. Vincent's grandparents were part of the French-oriented colonial elite, and his father was an officer in the French army. A third-generation French citizen, Vincent has always lived in France among "French" people, and he has worked with the same major French company in the same French town for the last twenty-five years.

By contrast, Usman grew up in Pakistan, a relatively poor country that was once a British colony. He did not arrive in France until early adulthood, and then only with rudimentary French and a feeling of cultural inferiority. Usman promptly abandoned everything from his own world, remaking himself as quickly as possible to be "more French than the French." While this was successful, he still speaks with an accent.

And yet, of the two, Vincent is the one who is so unsure of his place in French society that he stops at amber lights to avoid being called a "dirty foreigner." Vincent is the one who is always trying to make a "good impression" on "French" people, the one who feels he must show that, unlike what "they say about foreigners," he contributes to France. Meanwhile, Usman has no doubt that he fits into French society. Confident, even brash, Usman feels "a little superior" to most French people.[11]

This book's review of issues faced by each of the three groups of interviewees, spanning chapters 1–3, is now complete. It is time to shift focus to issues that cut across these groups. First, among all types of interviewees, how pervasive are feelings of inferiority? How deep are the fears of rejection? Second, what kinds of people have the interviewees of all categories pursued for romantic relationships, marriage, or long-term partnerships? Does a characteristically "French" person hold a particular allure for the interviewees? Finally, among interviewees of all categories of people, what is it like to be a Muslim in France? These broad-based issues will be discussed in the chapters that follow.

NOTES

1. See the introduction to this book for more on "readability."
2. The one exception is Florence, who came from Colombia as a young adult. She is not discussed in this ethnography for two reasons: because she chose to speak about painful family and gender issues throughout her life rather than the issues central to this book, and because many people assume she is from elsewhere in Europe (specifically Spain or Portugal). At one of the few moments when she spoke about her place in French society, Florence said that people "don't have prejudices toward me like they have with Arabs."

3. The actual number is higher because, in keeping with French legal constraints, data collection went back no further than the generation of immigrants' children (see Tribalat 2015).
4. Just as Black is a social construct, as noted in chapter 2—"[b]eing black is neither an essence nor a culture, but the outcome of a social relationship" (Ndiaye 2008: 69)—there is no Asian essence or unified culture. The family origins of people seen as Asian span a swath of East Asian countries with more than two billion inhabitants and a vast array of cultural traditions.
5. Chuang (2021: 9) points to the relative paucity of studies about Asians in France. While there have been many studies of racism and discrimination, he says, relating to people "from the overseas territories or from postcolonial immigration (Maghreb, sub-Saharan Africa)," few have focused on people originating from South and East Asia.
6. While "*chinetoque*" initially referred to someone from China, the term has been applied to anyone with an Asian physical appearance. It "is often used in an abusive way for people who have slanted eyes" (Chine informations. n.d.).
7. The morning after our interview, Yuka and her husband asked about my project. As we spoke, it appeared that her husband hadn't thought much about issues confronted by people of non-European origin in France. He also had little sense of France's colonial history; as previously noted, the history of French colonialism is "patently neglected" in France's national school curriculum (Bancel and Blanchard 2017b: 161). He did not know that Vietnam had once been a French colony or that Vietnamese people had fought a war of independence against the French. He had only a vague sense of France's history in Algeria or its war of independence.
8. The interviewees' experiences are consistent with the statistics generated by the monumental Trajectories and Origins study (see Beauchemin et al. 2010: 2 and Figures 1 and 2).
9. See Aeberhardt et al. 2015: 585, as discussed in chapter 2, concerning the economic consequences of "teachers' conscious and unconscious stereotypes" about such students.
10. Three French social scientists argue that the concept of "passing," so familiar to Americans, could be usefully employed to describe this process in France (Bosa, Pagis, and Trépied 2019).
11. A comparison between Shayan and Fatih, men with similar life histories who are both profiled in this chapter, also illustrates the importance of personality. Why is Shayan sure that the more he lives like a French person, the more he'll be accepted, while Fatih is equally sure that, no matter how much he conforms to French norms, he will always be seen as fundamentally different?

PART II

FOUR

FEELING INFERIOR, FEARING REJECTION

As interviewees recounted throughout this book, simply having a non-European *faciès* subjects a person to stereotypes, bias, and discrimination from many "French" people. But how do the interviewees feel about themselves? Have they internalized these demeaning attitudes and behaviors? Do they feel inferior to "French" people? Do they fear being rejected by them? While these issues have already been discussed on an individual level, they have not been considered across the range of people interviewed for this book.

There is much to say. The first section of this chapter is an extended profile of Karim, showing the complexity and pain of one person's experience. This is followed by a discussion of a phenomenon that an interviewee called "colonialism in the head." The next section discusses the broader feelings of inferiority among many people who trace their origins to former colonies, together with the corresponding feelings of superiority they perceive on the part of many "French" people. The scope then broadens further. Among all the interviewees who originate from former colonies, how prevalent are feelings of inferiority or a fear of rejection? Who suffers from these emotions throughout their lives, and who grows out of them? The same questions are then asked about the handful of interviewees who originate from countries that had not been colonies. A striking contrast emerges between those with a colonial background and those without that history.[1]

This chapter concludes with a section about the interviewees who spoke about the stereotypes, bias, and discrimination they face, but who have not internalized those experiences; that is, people who do not feel inferior or fear rejection. How do these people maintain their self-respect and navigate their way in France? How do they forge productive and mostly happy lives?

KARIM

Karim met me at the end of his workday and drove us to the small village where he lives on his own in an old farmer's cottage. Made of wooden logs and beams, his house is snug and homey. We turned to making dinner, with Karim manning the stovetop while I chopped vegetables at the kitchen table. The outcome, thanks to him, was the classic French beef stew *boeuf bourguignon*, the perfect dish for a cool fall evening.

We started the interview right after dinner. Now fifty, Karim began with an anecdote from his early childhood, when his family still lived in a Moroccan village. One day, a "small French construction entrepreneur who needed workmen" appeared and, after explaining his proposition, returned to France with the men who agreed to go, including Karim's father. His father was placed in a village in the middle of France. This worked out well—"he was the best mason in the area"— and his family joined him four years later. This included Karim, who was then seven, and his siblings. As time went on, other children were born in France.

As he thought back on those early years in France, Karim recalled, "We were the first foreigners in this little village. I learned later that there'd been a meeting to decide whether they'd accept us—this astonished me—and the village elder opened the door." Although "some of the neighbors weren't happy," they "didn't show it openly." At the Catholic school where the family's children were placed, the nuns "took special care of us" and permitted "no racist insults. It was a very good period."

"During my childhood," Karim continued, "I was lucky never to have had problems with direct, frontal racism." This might have been because he was tall, but a bigger factor was the nature of the community. "It was a small village, so there couldn't be any confrontation. That wasn't possible." Karim's family was "well integrated" into village life—"not just integrated, but assimilated," even "swallowed up." The children fit in (today, one of his brothers is a volunteer firefighter in the village), and they left behind many of their parents' ways. Karim abandoned the Ramadan fast and other Muslim practices.

Unlike now, "when thirty or forty percent of the village votes for the National Front," Karim reports, and "people express insults openly, back then it was shameful to be racist." Still, he felt a condescending attitude from the people of the village: "We were inferior beings." It was as if these people thought, "They're pleasant, the little Moroccans, the little chihuahuas. They're like a nice pet who's inferior but not mean." He felt this attitude "in their looks, their words, their intonations, all that. We were marked by this."

During these years, Karim recalls being "polite, nice, and docile," and careful "always to make a good impression." This was not just an act. He was "timid" and, he says, "stayed in my corner, risking less and less." Most of all—here, Karim hesitated and cleared his throat—he "lacked confidence." I asked what he thought of himself at the time. "That I was less intelligent than the others, that I wasn't capable. This really sank in."

Karim was struck by the importance of these early years. "I've never thought about how that period marked the rest of my existence." Holding back tears, he pushed on: "I've always wondered whether I'm intelligent. I've had that doubt for a very long time." When he was growing up, apart from "my family and the nuns at school," the people around him, Karim recalls, "didn't give me confidence. It's for sure that this brought about a lot of the things that I am, that my brothers and sisters are."

Perhaps because his mother pushed her children to succeed—"All the time she'd say, 'You must work at school, you must be good at school to have a profession, to have a good life.'"—Karim went to middle school in a nearby village, then high school in a nearby town. This went well, though he felt a void at times: "Was there a moment when they taught my history to me? No, not one. Not at school. They only spoke of the history of France, of the French people, a lot of the lies that schools continue to perpetuate." The reality of France's "colonial history, of the countrics, thc people who were there" was never mentioned.

Karim completed some college courses, followed by technical studies. He financed his education with part-time and summer jobs, where he encountered attitudes far from the inhibiting norms of the village in which he grew up. "In the world of manual work," he said, recalling the jobs he had at the time, "the racism was visible." His coworkers occasionally called him "the *bougnoule*,"[2] even "the *nègre*." His supervisors were "overtly racist."

At twenty-four, Karim got a diploma in information technology and was hired as a technician at a governmental research center. He has worked there ever since. He said little about this experience during the interview, even though it has occupied the past twenty-five years of his life, except to note the demographics of the research center: "I look around. There are loads of *Français de souche*, but not many people like me." This is especially the case in "very high positions." Still, Karim received a rarely awarded promotion four years ago, and he feels that bias did not enter into the process. "There was a panel of six people who didn't know each other. Racist stuff wouldn't have been accepted."

Turning to his love life, Karim said, "I'm attracted to women who are different from me." This started with "blondes." Over the years, he has dated a variety of women, but none of these women have been Maghrebi. His two long-term relationships, he made clear, were with "*Françaises de souche.*" He had children with each of these women, though he is now single again.

During the interview, Karim kept coming back to his efforts to fit in. He had done everything, he said: "I think in French ways, I have European values, I defend French causes." Karim is a French citizen, and, though he was born into a Muslim family, he has never been religious. He became, he said, "more French than the French," but even this wasn't enough:

> One day, you wake up and realize there's been a deception, you realize that French people won't ever truly accept you. It's a terrible thing to realize. It's unjust. It's unjust to have thought you had to be like that to belong, but in the end you realize that you'll never, ever belong. You remain forever different in the eyes of others.

And so, even though Karim says he has fully "assimilated" himself into French society, it has been a "false assimilation."

When all is said and done, "I know I'll never be accepted by the French."

This realization has eaten into his sense of identity. "If the question is whether I feel French, the answer is no. I feel like I have no country." He likened his place in France to someone who's been caught shoplifting at a store and knows that whenever he returns to the store he'll be under suspicion. And though Karim has never done anything wrong, he said, "I feel this way myself. It's necessary; it's normal. It's a feeling coming from other people. You feel it, you feel it inside. And so, you must always show that you are someone, that you have some value." Recently, he decided to focus less on trying to fit in:

> I'm becoming less French than the French; it's a waste of time and energy. I'm letting that fall away. Little by little, I'm paying attention to myself and other people. I'm involved in organizations that help migrants and at work with defending people like me who aren't researchers. A lot of things.

I asked Karim whether he thinks that he's seen as French. No, he responded, "I'm a foreigner. That's on my face." And because his physical appearance will never change, his place in France won't either: "A foreigner remains a foreigner forever." I asked whether it would be different for someone who, unlike him, was born in France. Not at all. Even though his younger brother was born in France, Karim said, "he's a foreigner." Indeed, even "my children are foreigners."

Struck by that last statement, I pointed to the photograph of a cheerful-looking boy on his mantelpiece. The boy is the youngest of his children, he explained. Like all of Karim's children, the oldest of whom is twenty-seven, the boy has spent his entire life in France, has a French first name and, he says, a "*Française de souche*" mother. Indeed, his son is "mostly White." So, I asked, isn't he French? Aren't all his children French? No, they can't be, because they "have kinky hair and are *métis*." They're all "foreigners." It's "impossible" to be French, he said, if you're not White.

Exhausted, we finished the interview at about midnight. When I asked Karim for a final comment, he said, "It's good, what you're doing. It's very, very interesting." The next morning, he drove me back to town and went to work.

"COLONIALISM IN THE HEAD"

An early interviewee, Tsiory, told me that he suffered from "colonialism in the head." While the psychosocial effects of colonialism have been extensively discussed since at least Frantz Fanon's 1952 book *Black Skin, White Masks*, Tsiory spoke about it as an experience that arose directly from his years growing up in Madagascar. As it turned out, Tsiory was far from alone: although only one interviewee mentioned Fanon or any of this literature,[3] quite a few spoke about their own experiences in similar terms.

I met Tsiory at his small but carefully maintained apartment in the *banlieue* of a city. Tsiory, who is physically slight, lives on his own. When we sat down at his dining room table, he was so quiet and uncomfortable that I thought that the interview would go nowhere. I was wrong. As soon as I turned on the recorder, a lifetime of emotionally raw experiences started pouring out. His account continued through the late evening and resumed after breakfast the next morning. When the interview was over, he returned to near-total silence.

Tsiory grew up in the capital of Madagascar, a former French colony off the southeast coast of Africa where some people, like him, are of Malayo-Indonesian rather than African origin. Now twenty-nine, he moved to France eight years ago to study information technology. After finishing both an undergraduate and a master's degree in IT, he sent out hundreds of résumés, but received few responses. He finally accepted a job far beneath his credentials as a desktop computer technician. He would not let himself wonder whether his foreign name and appearance hampered his job search, he explained, since "this wouldn't be good. I might start hating people and I don't want to be like that."

Working at the same job today, Tsiory follows a strategy of putting himself in an "inferior position" relative to his French coworkers: "Even if I know a subject better than someone else, I make him think I'm less than him. I never contradict him. My strategy is to make him feel superior to me, to feel that he's already beaten me. That's my goal." Tsiory lowered his head and shoulders to demonstrate how he acts "to disarm them."

We turned to his life in Madagascar. Though the country has been independent since 1960, he said that people

> are still colonized in the head. You see, when a White person comes to Madagascar, he's seen as something altogether different, like a god. We say "Yes, yes, yes" to whatever he says. In Africa, at least in Madagascar, we're independent, but we're still colonized.

Laughing uncomfortably, Tsiory added, "even I'm colonized in the head." When he came to France, he "considered Whites superior to us," and, even now, "when I see a French person, I consider him superior to me."

Although he will become a citizen in a year, Tsiory will never be French, he says, because French people are "White, White, White." He wonders how people from Madagascar with children born in France "explain to them that the French will never, ever consider them French." If he ever has children, he said, "I'll explain this, that they're not French for the French, that they're only French legally."

Other interviewees also spoke about colonialism. François (profiled in chapter 2), who grew up in Gabon, was candid about his opinion of colonialism: "I don't have a negative opinion of it." France, he said, brought "television, the Industrial Revolution, the automobile, et cetera" to Gabon. But the French also brought their skin color: "France is the White man." The Gabonese ethnic group that first encountered the French, the Myenes, "wanted to be like the Whites," and they succeeded. "People say the Myenes are the Whites" of Gabon. They see themselves as "superior," treating people farther inland "as savages." François is Myene.

Like those around him, he says, François thought that Whites were "superior," and he wanted to absorb "the culture that came with colonialism." He wanted to "act like the Whites and speak like the Whites, to belong among them." François's profile shows how this desire still eats at him, more than twenty-five years after his arrival in France.

When Daniel (also profiled in chapter 2) was growing up in the Ivory Coast in the 1990s and 2000s, he knew that "it was France that had colonized us." This wasn't all bad, he believes, since French people "brought what Africans didn't know" and "taught us so much." But even decades after the Ivory Coast had gained independence in 1960, "we were submissive, we always felt inferior." Ivorians thought that French people are "more intelligent because they know a lot. "When they spoke," he recalls, "everyone listened, everyone was quiet, because this was a French person speaking." People felt they should be "submissive" to French people to "receive things"; they thought that "if you behaved properly," you might "gain their benediction and be blessed by them." But Daniel grew out of this way of thinking after he came to France, where he realized that "everyone is equal." Remembering how people felt back in the Ivory Coast made him laugh.

Abbas has a decidedly negative view of colonialism and its aftereffects. Although the colonial era was hardly mentioned during his childhood in Senegal, he said that some people knew that "the French had come to colonize us, to reduce us to slavery and to pillage our wealth. At base, we knew that they were our invaders." He believes that the colonial experience also resulted in people having "an inferiority complex" toward the French. Even relations among Senegalese people reflected this. "French was the language of those who dominated us," so people who spoke it well had "an air of superiority." Dressing in the French style—"in a suit and tie and all"—had the same effect.

For Djibril, who also grew up in Senegal, the fact that the Senegalese "were colonized by France plays a big role psychologically between the two peoples." Complicating this, he believes, is the fact that "France is still very much tied to its former colonies." Djibril calls the resulting feeling of "inferiority" among many Senegalese people "the African complex."

Tsiory and Black interviewees like François, Daniel, Abbas, and Djibril were not the only ones who traced feelings of inferiority to colonialism. Mohamed described his native Morocco as "a country that had been colonized by France." And while Morocco had been "colonized under very difficult conditions, with many victims and much exploitation," Mohamed said, Moroccans "idealized" France and were "fascinated" by it. "Unconsciously, we felt inferior to the West, which was stronger, more intelligent, and better organized. It was a collective mindset. We didn't have a good opinion of ourselves. We had a feeling of being a nothing, of mediocrity."

I asked Mohamed how he felt about the differences between Europeans and Moroccans while growing up in Morocco. Thinking back, he spoke of the cowboys-and-Indians movies he loved as a child: "I didn't ask why they were one way and we were another, but I was fascinated." Laughing at the memory, he continued, "Me, I hated the Indians and loved the cowboys. The cowboys never did wrong. I thought the Indians were savages, barbarians. I was always happy when the cowboys exterminated those cruel Apaches, those savages. I wanted to be like the cowboys." Such feelings weren't limited to cowboys. "We wanted to be like them, to have White friends, Europeans, et cetera." When Mohamed later saw White tourists, "there was a fascination with their physical appearance. Also, they spoke another language, the language of civilization. It was everything."

Finally, Usman (profiled in chapter 3), who came from the former British colony of Pakistan, talked about the psychological effects of colonialism. "It's always tied to the colonial connection. Even though we weren't a colony when I was born, there was always a connection with the distant Europeans, the people who are strong, of our recent history, the inaccessible people." He lowered his hands to illustrate Pakistani feelings of "civilizational inferiority." Although he came to France feeling this way, Usman outgrew it as he excelled academically and then professionally.

After coming to France, Usman dated only European women. He explained why. "If you look at history, we were formerly colonized by European people, so the fact of being close to them, to be one with them is a kind of success." The wall that colonialism had created between him and Europeans was breached in the act of sexual intercourse: "I was able to go beyond that barrier to become one with . . ." Usman stopped himself there, but he returned to the memory a minute later. Sighing, he said: "To cross that barrier, ahhh."

It is hard to report Usman's account without recalling the beginning of the chapter "The Man of Color and the White Woman" in Frantz Fanon's *Black Skin, White Masks* (1986 [1952]). Having grown up in the French colony of Martinique, Fanon describes the experience of sexual intercourse with a French woman: "By loving me she proves that I am worthy of white love. I am loved like a white man" (63). As will be seen in chapter 5, Usman was not alone among male interviewees in his desire for "French" women.

THE COLONIAL MENTALITY IN FRANCE

Since the interviewees who explicitly attributed feelings of inferiority to colonialism—Tsiory, François, Daniel, Abbas, Djibril, Mohamed, and Usman—spoke about the former colonies in which they grew up, one might assume that "colonialism in the head" is limited to life in former colonies. Not so, according to many interviewees. As Tsiory's and François's experiences make clear, this feeling can live on among people from former colonies who have moved to France. But it is not limited to such people. According to a number of interviewees, this attitude is also common both among people who trace their origin to former colonies but who grew up in France and among "French" people, who feel superior to such people.

Before turning to what these interviewees reported, it is worth recalling that the colonial experience is still fresh in the family histories (if not the conscious awareness) of people in France today. Most French colonies did not become independent until the 1950s or early 1960s. Three of the interviewees (Grégoire, Henri, and Rémy) were born when their country of origin (Vietnam) was still a French colony. And all of the other interviewees who trace their origin to former French colonies have parents or grandparents who lived there when their countries were still colonies. They would thus have been among the "natives" of so-called French Indochina, French Antilles, French West Africa, French Equatorial Africa, and the French Maghreb. Some of the interviewees' grandparents would have lived their entire lives in those French colonies, under the control of France.

Much the same is true for today's "French" people, except that they were on the flip side of the colonial experience. Although many "French" people benefited from colonialism without leaving France, others lived in France's colonies for years. These included soldiers, administrators, settlers, missionaries, businesspeople, and many of their family members. Nearly a million *pieds-noirs* (French citizens of European origin) were living in Algeria when it won its independence in 1962. The vast majority fled to France. In sum, millions of "French" people today grew up with parents or grandparents who had participated in the French colonial enterprise. And even those who were not personally involved in colonialism would have learned of France's "civilizing mission" among "inferior" peoples through newsreels, magazines, exhibitions, and other media.

It is not surprising, then, that a number of interviewees pointed to the role of colonialism in their relations with "French" people. At least two identify as Maghrebi. Lina believes that the disdain she experiences in France "goes back many years to colonialism." Karim thinks that "there was always the position of inferior-superior" between his family from Morocco and the French villagers around them "because we had been a protectorate."

Interviewees seen as Black also spoke about the influence of colonial attitudes on "French" people today. Jean, who has spent his entire life in France, traces French images of Blacks to "the colonial past of France. All the things they did." And Abbas thinks that the sense of superiority he sees among many White people "comes from the history they're taught." This history is like the history "told by the winners of a war," he says, and "the winners of a war never tell a history that doesn't suit them." French people are told that France "went to Africa to civilize Africans because they were savages."

According to Abbas, it is neither innocent nor accidental that this colonial-era attitude persists today. "French" people, he said, "hold on to a good memory of colonialism to avoid being ashamed. They think the actions they took in Africa were to help us. They don't see colonialism as a way for one people to enslave another people, to impose their will upon another people." Not being "French," Abbas cannot know exactly what such people think of Blacks, but he offers a guess: "Maybe between their history of French colonialism in Africa and what they see in the media and newspapers, they imagine that they're superior to Africans, psychologically, intellectually, and in ability."

Djibril spoke in much the same way. "French" people, he said, have a "vision of Blacks, a vision they have from colonialism." For them, "there's a connection between the fact that we were colonized by France" and the feeling that "Europeans are superior." He thinks that this is significant for how Blacks are treated in France today. "There are people who still have a vision of slavery, of colonialism. They don't want to leave this behind. They don't want to give up this domination. That's why they try to keep us on a very low level."

If French assumptions of superiority may be grounded in the colonial experience, Thomas thinks, assumptions of inferiority among some people of colonial origin in France may likewise derive from colonialism. Thomas reported that many French-born Blacks "feel inferior" to Whites and "are submissive" toward them. He gave an example: "If a young Black man who was born in France, who grew up here, comes into contact with a young White man of the same age, he'll feel inferior. You'll see it in the way he speaks, how he speaks in a very formal and polite way." To explain where these feelings came from, Thomas turned to the experience of prior generations in sub-Saharan Africa, when Black people were subjugated to French colonial control:

> In France that continues to play a role in people's minds. Why do Blacks feel inferior? This is automatic. It's very hard to find the source. Maybe it's historical. The grandparent lived this way. He transmitted it to his child, who retransmitted it to his grandson. That's how it follows down the generations.[4]

France's involvement in the slave trade for more than two centuries and its enslavement of Black people in its Caribbean colonies through 1848 was discussed at the beginning of chapter 2. Just as this history may underlie feelings of superiority among "French" people today, it may underlie feelings of inferiority among Black people. Blacks in mainland France whose families came from Martinique, Guadeloupe, or Haiti are the direct descendants of people who were owned and worked by "French" people. As noted in chapter 2, Jean was "ashamed when they talked about slavery" in history class: "Ow! It really weighed me down." Similarly, Black people whose families came from Africa may see themselves in accounts of slavery. In history class, Clément recalled, "I identified with the Blacks in chains. People of my origin were the ones who'd been enslaved" by people like the White students around him.

While these accounts suggest that all types of people in France experience "colonialism in the head," one thing is certain: feelings of inferiority and a fear of rejection were important concerns for many interviewees. But how many? Among these people, do these feelings last a lifetime, or do they change over time? And how many of the interviewees do not experience these feelings? How do such people handle the stereotyping, bias, and discrimination that they experience? These questions must still be answered.

FEELING INFERIOR, FEARING REJECTION—WHAT THE INTERVIEWEES REPORTED

Although each interviewee is unique, their accounts can be clustered into four groups. Among those who trace their origin to countries that had been colonized by European powers—the great majority of interviewees—many feel deeply inferior to "French" people, fear rejection from "French" people, or both. These interviewees are discussed in section (a) below. A few other interviewees, discussed in section (b), were beset by these feelings when they were young, but have since grown out of them. Section (c) switches the focus to the interviewees who originate from countries that had not been subject to European colonization. Finally, in section (d), all of the interviewees are reviewed to determine how many do not harbor feelings of inferiority or fear rejection, and to understand the methods they use to maintain their equanimity.

In reviewing the interviewees' accounts, it is important to remember that the feeling of inferiority and the fear of rejection are closely intertwined. Some of the interviewees, like Jean and Tsiory, dwelled on their feelings of inferiority, though they also reported fearing rejection because of their perceived inferiority. Others, like Samuel and Asma, spoke more about fearing rejection, though their fear is grounded in the perceived superiority or greater social power of those who would reject them.

(a) *Those Who Feel Inferior or Fear Rejection*

Both Karim and Tsiory, who were profiled early in this chapter, experience intense feelings of inferiority or fear of rejection. They are hardly alone.

Ibrahim, who has not yet been profiled, came to France from Algeria when he was eighteen. Since then, he says, "I've done everything to integrate myself" into French society. At the ceremony where he and others received their French ID cards, they were told, "You are now French. You are no different from other French people." This thrilled him, but he discovered that it wasn't true. He continued to face bias, discrimination, and demeaning scrutiny in stores, bars, and nightclubs. Following the 2015–16 terrorist attacks in France, he felt "stigmatized" and pressured to "justify" himself. By the time of our interview, the misery of feeling rejected was complete. "It's as if I had a lover who left me." Today, Ibrahim lectures his five-year-old son, who speaks only French and has never been outside the country, that he is not French but Algerian.

Many of the interviewees profiled in chapters 1–3 also suffer from feelings of inferiority or a fear of rejection. Three of them are Blacks, all profiled in chapter 2, who grew up in France:

- Throughout his childhood, Jean had an intense desire "to be White" or at least "succeed like the Whites succeed," and experienced an equally intense shame that he could do neither. While he has recently (and only tentatively) shaken off this feeling of inferiority, a fear of rejection remains keen.
- Since childhood, Lucas has felt that he's "not in the category" of White people. Concerned that they will put him "into a caste," he has decided that "I'll be the one to put myself into a caste." Although both he and his parents have always lived in mainland France, he identifies as Guadeloupean.
- Clément spent his adolescence in a largely White neighborhood, where he often felt "different in the eyes of others." He sensed "a lack of belonging" and sometimes felt "rejected," "ashamed," or "angry." Although less intense today, these feelings have not disappeared.

At least five other interviewees profiled in chapters 1–3 report problems with self-respect or fear of rejection:

- Samuel has sought acceptance from "French" people since childhood, but, despite his professional success and life in a well-off, downtown community, he still feels excluded because of his Maghrebi appearance.

- Although François lives "like French people" and has had a series of "French" romantic partners, he still feels excluded because Blacks are "always foreigners."
- Olivier has adopted the "clothes, accent, way of speaking" of "French" people, speaks "perfect French without any accent," and has only "French" friends, but he can do nothing about his Maghrebi *faciès*. As a result, he feels, "people consider me inferior to a French person."
- Asma, who is of Maghrebi origin, has always had "only French friends" and a "French mindset," lives according to French norms, and married a "French" man, but has never been able to "live as an equal" in France. This, she says, is because "people here are idiots, they're completely racist."
- Finally, Vincent has feared rejection his whole life, even though he is a third-generation French citizen and an IT professional in a French company. At each turn, he says, "I must prove to certain people that I am capable. Foreigners must do more."

While all these people have successfully integrated themselves into the norms of the "French" people around them, the process has been emotionally fraught. Olivier explained what it's been like for him: "To have to integrate yourself is submission. *Intégration* lets me survive," he says, but it's an act of "submission, absolutely."

(b) *Outgrowing Feeling Inferior and Fearing Rejection*

Four of the interviewees felt inferior or feared rejection when they were young but have grown out of these feelings over time.

Ariel, a Black woman who has not been profiled yet, grew up in Madagascar. When she first saw a White person, she thought that he was a "superior being." She continued to feel this way because on TV Whites lived in a "technologically superior" world. Their "technological superiority was a sign of an intellectual superiority." But her sense of French superiority started to erode when she learned of strikes and dysfunction in France from the TV news. And when she came into contact with French high school students, she was struck by how unimpressive many were. She began to think, she says, that "I could be their equal."

Ariel went to France for college, where she studied information technology. She soon discovered that the French students were "far from perfect," both personally and academically, and began to wonder how she could have "idealized White French people." But even after getting both undergraduate and master's degrees in IT, she was unable to get a professional-level job. Since, she said, "it was out of the question that I'd take a job as a technician with my master's," she worked at a pizzeria until she found an appropriate position in another city. She has worked as a tech professional ever since.

Ariel married Charles (another tech specialist, profiled in chapter 2) and has a three-year-old son. Now a French citizen, she considers herself French, though more a "citizen of the world." The fact that followers of the right-wing National Front party might think that she isn't French doesn't bother her, because "their France doesn't really exist." Today, "France belongs to the world." She is also unbothered by bias: whatever others may think, she says, "I don't attach any importance to racism." Throughout her interview—indeed, throughout my two-day stay with her and Charles—Ariel was the soul of confidence, laughing at whatever she found absurd.

While listening to Ariel, I thought of Tsiory. They are about the same age (Ariel is thirty-four; Tsiory is twenty-nine), they both grew up in Madagascar, they both went to France to study information technology, they both got undergraduate and master's degrees in IT, and they were both unable to get a professional-level position. But the similarity ends there. While Tsiory is reclusive, meek, and always deferential to "French" people, Ariel is outgoing and confident. Tsiory took a job as a desktop computer technician, while Ariel bided her time until securing a professional-level position. Today, Tsiory is still a laptop computer technician, pursuing a "strategy" of extreme deference, while Ariel made a career in IT among other IT specialists, unfazed by French bias.

Struck by how these near-identical backgrounds led to completely different adult lives and attitudes toward "French" people, I told Ariel about Tsiory's feeling of "colonialism in the head."[5] Ariel was incredulous: "He thinks that? What a shame."

The other interviewees who have outgrown childhood feelings of inferiority or fearfulness of rejection have already been profiled. Henri and Grégoire (profiled in chapter 3), the sons of a "French" father and Vietnamese mother, grew up feeling deeply inferior in France during the 1950s through the 1970s. The decades since have brought major changes. Beginning in the 1980s, each got married, had children, settled into civil service jobs, and ultimately retired. During the same period, they say, the image of people seen as Asians improved significantly. Although bias by some "French" people continues, today neither Henri nor Grégoire feels inferior or fears rejection.

Growing up in France feeling shunned as a "foreigner," Nassim (also profiled in chapter 3) worked at becoming "more French." He ultimately "passed the exam" of becoming "more French than the French," but even this didn't bring true acceptance. He then turned back to his Maghrebi and Muslim origins. Although, he says, "this made me socially less acceptable in France," he is no longer afraid of being rejected.

Four interviewees remain. Although different from each other in original culture, personality, and career, Daniel (profiled in chapter 2), Philippe (chapter 2), Mohamed (chapter 1), and Usman (chapter 3) experienced a similar evolution in their feelings about themselves. Each grew up in a former colony feeling inferior to Europeans, each moved to France as a young adult, and each discarded the feeling of inferiority within a few years of arriving in France. Daniel, a factory team leader from the Ivory Coast, discovered that he could learn whatever French people know and work harder than most of them. As far as Daniel is concerned, he is their equal. Philippe, a law graduate from Guinea, shook off his feeling of inferiority after studying the writings of Frantz Fanon. Mohamed, a social worker from Morocco, spoke of a growing "intellectual and psychological maturity" during his years in France: "I now see people as they are, not as French or the like." Asked whether he feels inferior today, Mohamed responded with a flat "no." Usman, who felt "inferior" to Europeans when he arrived in France from Pakistan twenty-five years ago, put his mind to fitting into France and advancing in the world, ultimately getting a PhD in telecommunications and achieving professional success. Now a high-tech entrepreneur, he admits to feeling "superior" to most French people.

(c) *Interviewees of Non-Colonial Origin*

While the great majority of interviewees, including all of the Blacks and all of the Maghrebis, trace their origin to countries that were once European colonies, eight other interviewees trace their origins to countries that had never been colonies, even if they went through periods of yielding to European economic, political, or military power. Since these people are also of non-European origin, studying their experiences presents an opportunity to eliminate the factor of outright colonialism. Do they feel inferior to "French" people? Do they fear being rejected by them? Each interviewee must be reviewed to find out.

Three of these interviewees trace their origins to non-Arab, yet predominantly Muslim, countries in Western Asia. These are Fatih (Turkey), Shayan (Iran), and Nima (also Iran). Though all were profiled in chapter 3, each had more to say on the issues of inferiority and rejection. Fatih has never felt inferior because of his background. Even as a child in a French village, he says, "I felt proud" because of the "education from my parents." Today he remains proud of Turkish values, such as care for family "and the right way to behave."

Although Fatih has never felt inferior, he has feared rejection much of his life. When he was young, he needed to decline pork at French friends' homes even though it was "poorly seen." He recalled, "moments of discomfort, that's for sure. It was frustrating when people rejected me." Although milder today, Fatih's fear of rejection remains a part of his life. "In my heart, it remains complicated. It's hard to explain." Fatih recounted incidents at work when his foreign name or his avoidance of pork came to the fore. "I was frightened that people would be insulted. They could have taken it badly." When he declines pork at business meals, people's reactions can be "hurtful." Still, fear can turn to indignation: "Sometimes it was depressing, but it was more anger than depression."

In Shayan's profile, he described a lifelong effort to participate in the "French" community around him. Born and raised in France, he made sure to act like the French people around him, so that "no one ever said anything like that about me." During his interview and our time together, Shayan never spoke about feeling inferior, but a fear of rejection hovered in the background: "I wanted never to be among those they pointed a finger at."

When Nima left Iran forty years ago to attend graduate school in France, Iran was so oil-rich that "it was lending money to France." From the start, he says, "I had a pride in myself, a self-confidence." Nor has he feared rejection. When French people "acted in a dismissive way toward me, I didn't feel it. I mastered their rejection of me. It created a feeling of pity toward them. It didn't touch me at all." Their behavior "made me angry, but it never hurt me."

The remaining five interviewees, all Asians, originate from countries that had never been European colonies. They are Emily (China), Yuka (China), Eric (China), Paul (South Korea), and Kana (Japan). Since all are now in their thirties or early forties, they have only known the time (as recounted in chapter 3) when these countries were growing economically and French attitudes toward Asians were improving.

All three of the interviewees from China came to France in their early twenties for advanced engineering studies. Emily (profiled in chapter 3) spoke about feelings of inferiority when growing up. "Chinese people were dominated by kings for thousands of years." In Chinese culture, she said, there's this feeling "that government officials, or the state, or the king are superior." In France, her success at elite engineering schools and then at large civil engineering companies, she says, made her feel "more confidence in myself." At no point did Emily speak about fearing rejection.

Yuka and Eric, the two other interviewees from China, had less to say on these issues. As her profile (also in chapter 3) reports, Yuka has been comfortable with French people from the start. Nothing she said suggested a feeling of inferiority or a fear of rejection. Eric, who has not been profiled, has kept to himself since coming to France. His graduate studies were conducted in English rather than French, and he rarely went into town. After gaining a research doctorate in engineering, which he said failed to prepare him for a real-world job, he has been unable to find regular employment. He reported no feelings of inferiority, and though there have been times he felt that French people acted rudely toward him, he has been annoyed rather than fearful.

The remaining interviewees can also be discussed briefly. Kana, who has not been profiled, came to France from Japan to do graduate studies in museum studies. After getting a master's degree, she worked briefly and married Mathieu (who was profiled in chapter 3). Kana is now a full-time mother in the multiethnic neighborhood where the family lives. At no time during the interview or the two days I stayed at her home did Kana say anything suggesting a feeling of inferiority or fear of rejection. Finally, there is Paul (profiled in chapter 3), who was adopted from a South Korean orphanage by a French couple when he was four, brought back to France, and raised to be French. He reported no feelings of inferiority, and despite jokes concerning his Korean appearance, he does not fear rejection.

This overview of the eight interviewees who trace their origin to countries that had not been European colonies reveals a distinct pattern: unlike many of the interviewees who trace their origins to countries that had been colonies, not one feels inferior to French people. The difference between them and the interviewees with colonial origins largely disappears when it comes to rejection: a quarter of them spoke of fearing rejection, although in less intense terms. These are Fatih and Shayan, who have a particular concern: each wants to avoid alienating "French" people by flagging his Muslim background.

(d) *"I Know My Own Value"*

Despite the number of people who experience continuing and, for some, debilitating feelings of inferiority or fear of rejection, a striking fact arises when one surveys the interviewees as a whole: the great majority of interviewees who reported demeaning stereotypes, bias, and discrimination directed at people like them did not report having internalized these experiences. They do not feel inferior or fear rejection from "French" people.[6] Thus, despite the low regard shown by people who are unquestionably French—behavior that seems intended to keep them at a lower social level and, some would say, intended to undermine their sense of worth—most interviewees do not feel inferior to such people. Similarly, despite behavior that seems intended to keep people like the interviewees from being fully accepted—including the refusal to treat even French-born, fully integrated people with non-European *faciès* as truly French—most do not fear rejection.

This absence of, or refusal to harbor, feelings of inferiority or a fear of rejection is found among all types of interviewees: among men and women; among the young and old; among those who grew up in France and those who grew up in their countries of origin; among those who originate from former colonies and those who originate from countries that had not been colonized; among Blacks, Maghrebis, Asians, and others. Many interviewees were categorical about their own sense of value. Although Thomas has experienced what he calls "intelligent racism," or behavior he thinks is intended to make him feel inferior as a Black, he says, "I was hurt, but I was never, ever, ever ashamed." Similarly, Djibril, whose efforts to succeed in France have been sidelined and who remains underemployed, says, "I don't feel inferior to anyone. Everyone is equal. It's for you to decide what you're worth."

The disjunction between experiencing acts that signal rejection and the internal fear of rejection is illustrated by Youssef, an interviewee who has not been profiled yet. Now forty-six, Youssef grew up in a village in Morocco. Although his mother was nonliterate, she was "preoccupied with her children getting a good education." Youssef ultimately went to a Moroccan university, where his courses were taught in Arabic. Although he spoke only "a little French" by the time he graduated, he decided to move to France to do postgraduate studies. He hoped to realize his "intellectual dreams" and to pursue "a life of research."

In France, Youssef "made an enormous effort to learn French, to learn, learn, learn all the time." He only socialized with French people. As he recalls, "my ambition was to integrate into the intellectual world in France, to understand the thinking and philosophy of France, which for me was also universal." By living with French people, he also hoped to "feel French" and absorb "the heritage, particularly the culture, of this country." Although born into a Muslim family, he says, "I wasn't religious. This helped me to integrate quickly into French society, and one day to become a French citizen with the same values as a native-born French person." As the years passed, Youssef got both a master's degree and doctorate in sociology, married a French woman (from whom he is now divorced), had children with her, and became a French citizen. He became not merely a citizen, he says, but one "who's at ease as a citizen."

But many French people are not at ease with Youssef. Laughing uncomfortably, he described how his "Arab mug" makes women pull in their handbags and telephones and keeps him from entering certain restaurants. He feels "tension" in the public transportation system, and some people change seats to get away from him. In cafes, some people stare at him "bizarrely." But despite all this—despite knowing that he can be rejected "at any time"—Youssef's sense of belonging is unshaken. The people who snub him, he says, "don't know that I'm as French as they are, that I'm in my own country."

How do the dozens of interviewees who do not feel inferior and do not fear rejection deal with the frequent disparagement they report experiencing from "French" people and the French media? How do they maintain their feelings of equality and belonging? While the profiles in this book provide answers on an individual level, recurring patterns appear when these interviewees as a whole are considered. The most frequently cited strategies can be briefly summarized:

Maintaining high-prestige levels of language, behavior, and lifestyle. As reported throughout this book, the interviewees live like the "French" people around them. For some, like Elise, Anna, and Mathieu, this has come naturally; for others, like Youssef, Olivier, and Shayan, it has required years of effort. But however this is achieved, many interviewees become, as Nassim, Usman, and Karim all described themselves, "more French than the French."

Working harder, advancing educationally, and excelling in a field that rewards marketable skills. Chapters 1–3 are filled with accounts of sustained work, university degrees, and the pursuit of excellence in fields that reward demonstrable skills. One need only think of Salma, Rania, Isabel, Marie, Amina, Ariel, Charles, Usman, and Emily. Some interviewees even use bias to their advantage. A teacher's "disdain" for Thomas's abilities because he is Black "gave me motivation," he said. "It made me work two times, three times harder than the others." He succeeded in getting the IT diploma that the teacher said was out of reach, and then two more. Later, when a company supervisor failed to give him a promised promotion, Thomas threw himself into mastering a new field, real estate investment and management, where he could make his own success.

Going against the stereotypes. Interviewees defy stereotypes in various ways. Amina said, "I always have a classic appearance, always super-well-coiffed, super-well-dressed," rather than a look "that fits into the prejudices." Disgusted by such insults as "dirty Arab" and "dirty race," Lina maintains an impeccably clean home and dresses elegantly. Ridiculed "as a little Chinese boy," Rémy became an army commando-parachutist, a martial arts expert, and a combat instructor at the national police training academy. Daniel has shown French people "that we Africans are not what they think" by "getting the job done" as a factory team captain. Abdel spoke politely with a "neo-Nazi" at a bar to convince him that some "Arabs" don't act badly. Isabel excelled academically and professionally, proving—as her father said Blacks must—that "I'm intelligent. I'm not what you think I am." Charles has repeatedly done the same, from the time a White math teacher disparaged the Black students in his high school class through his years as an IT consultant.

Being firm in the face of bias. As their profiles make clear, Lina, Rémy, and Amina will not tolerate behavior suggesting that people like them are not equal to everyone else. Zhora's life shows how challenging this can be. She began defending herself in the workplace when she was cleaning offices to support her education—she went to her boss for redress for being called *bougnoule*—and, decades later, she still defends herself, as she did recently at a conference. She has been equally firm in her personal life. When her mother-in-law disparaged Maghrebis as "*bougnoules*," Zhora told her, "Mother, don't ever say that in front of me."

Refusing to accept the role of "victim." As reported in their profiles, Amina, Philippe, and Thomas each refuse to accept the role of "victim." Anna feels much the same way. While a friend of hers complains that "being Black is always a handicap," she won't dwell on bias. "I refuse to see this as a fact of life, since you can't live in a country if you think that everyone sees you poorly." And while Emmanuelle believes that "racism will always exist in France," she insists on maintaining an "open spirit." She has "learned to live" with racism, she said, "because you don't have a choice. If you're always angry at these injustices, it hurts the most."

Not dwelling on the possibility of bias in everyday life. Although he is convinced that "French society is very racist," Charles refuses to see racism in daily events, like "the silly example of being served second at a Starbucks, after a White," to focus on the more pressing obstacles in life. Thomas provided a detailed explanation of why he refuses to think much about bias. After being denied a bank loan five times despite a solid business plan, he thought that "perhaps if I were White, they would have given me the loan," but he refused to dwell on this possibility, because "in the end, who'd pay the price for this?" Thomas thinks that "holding on to your hatred, your anger, won't help you advance," and you'll miss out on the "people who'll put out their hand to help you."

Abdel takes this attitude one step further:

> If I greet someone and he doesn't respond, it never crosses my mind that it's because I'm an Arab or I'm a Muslim. It's automatic for me. Each time something like this happens, I say to myself that the person is grumpy, that he's having a bad day, or that he's just mean by nature.

Although Abdel said that bias "never crosses my mind" on such occasions, the phrasing of his account ("I say to myself") suggests a coping mechanism. He continued, "I don't even hate him, since that would be unhealthy for me."

Accepting reality while making your way in life. The French-born daughter of Arabic-speaking parents, Fouzia learned French in school and set about integrating herself into the community around her. She finished high school, trained and worked as a nurse, and raised a daughter. Although there was always "an atmosphere, an ambiance" of anti-Arab bias, she did not let it derail her. Eleven years ago, a household accident left her a quadriplegic. Now, when Fouzia leaves her apartment, "it's the same. There are the looks at you, it happens with a handicapped person as with an Arab. There are schemas in people's heads. There are prejudices against handicapped people as with Blacks and others. You can feel different." But with her quadriplegia as with anti-Arab bias, Fouzia accepts reality and gets on with life.

Not letting right-wing politics undermine your identity. The National Front party long used the slogan "France for the French." Markus, a young Black man who has spent his entire life in

France, is untroubled by people who subscribe to this way of thinking. "Their vision is limited to a category of French people," he said, those "of the 1940s" who were in France before the wave of immigration that came later. But "the true French people" of today, Markus feels, includes people like him. Sami, meanwhile, has pity for people who have a narrow view of who belongs in France. They must be saddled with "a feeling of inferiority, maybe because other people succeed." Although Fouzia finds the National Front slogan "hurtful to hear" because its supporters really mean "France for the *Français de souche*," she feels that people with a different "physical appearance" like her can also be French.

Growing up feeling worthy. This is not a conscious method of dealing with prejudice, but an aspect of certain people's personality and life circumstances. It is evident when one compares the many interviewees who grew up in France and have faced the same stereotypes, biases, and discrimination. While some (like Samuel, Karim, Jean, Clément, and Vincent) have felt inferior to "French" people since childhood, others (like Thomas, Markus, Elise, Anna, Nour, Abdel, Paul, and Mathieu) have always felt good about themselves. Differences in economic and social class must also play a role—life has been easier for Elise and Paul than for Samuel and Jean—but this alone does not explain the difference. One need only compare Thomas, who grew up poor, with Clément, who grew up in more comfortable circumstances.

Fortified by these ways of protecting themselves from hurt and self-doubt, many of the interviewees would agree with Emmanuelle's declaration that, despite the prejudices she faces, "I know my own worth."

CONCLUSION

According to various interviewees, feelings of inferiority and the fear of rejection can be traced to the history of European subjugation of non-Europeans in Africa, Asia, and the Caribbean. Those who grew up in the former colonies say this explicitly—thus, "colonialism in the head"—but much the same is reported by those who grew up in France. They see the history of colonial domination at work both among people of colonial origin and among many "French" people, who apparently feel superior to them. That none of the interviewees of non-colonial origin feels inferior suggests that the tie to colonialism is not imagined. Even Fatih, who originates from a poor country (Turkey), who grew up poor in France, and who fears rejection by "French" people, does not feel inferior to them.

Given the interviewees' many reports of ugly stereotypes, biased behavior, and discrimination, it is remarkable that the majority have not internalized these attitudes, and that they are not beset by feelings of inferiority or fears of rejection. This may have much to do with who the interviewees are: people who have been successful enough to offer a room in their home or a separate apartment for rent through Airbnb. Most are university educated and have been able to secure work well above the menial level often thought appropriate for them.

The issues discussed in this chapter are complicated and nuanced. Still to be discussed is the deeply personal world of romantic desire and choice of spouse or long-term partner.

NOTES

1. As noted in the introduction, the terms "colony" and "colonialism" are used in this book to encompass various forms of control. In the case of France, these included colonies, protectorates, territories, and the onetime *départements* of Algeria.
2. This highly insulting term for "Arab" or "Maghrebi" was discussed in chapter 1.
3. This was Philippe, as discussed in chapter 2.
4. Pap Ndiaye (2008: 363) provides the historical context for this point: Africans who come to France from former French colonies have "national and familial memories [that] have been marked by colonization."
5. In keeping with my interview protocol, I did not identify Tsiory by name or city.
6. While there is no simple binary dividing line at play here, the following interviewees reported stereotypes, bias, or discrimination against people like themselves, but did not report ongoing feelings of inferiority or fears of rejection: Mohamed, Philippe, Emmanuelle, Sami, Youssef, Abbas, Isabel, Anna, Mathieu, Salma, Khira, Nour, Zhora, Charles, Daniel, Marie, Markus, Amina, Abdel, Ariel, Fouzia, Achraf, Djibril, Aya, Lina, Thomas, and Hiba. Many of these interviewees nonethe-

less sense a feeling of superiority among "French" people and/or a readiness on the part of "French" people to disparage and marginalize people like them.

FIVE

ROMANTIC ATTRACTION AND MARRIAGE

When this project began, I had no intention of delving into the interviewees' romantic lives. But I soon discovered that many men wanted to talk about this subject, particularly about their sexual desires, and that some women were interested in sharing their own romantic preferences. Along with attraction came talk of romantic relationships, spouses, and long-term partners. And in all these domains, interviewees dwelled on the identity of the people they chose, particularly whether he or she was "French" or something else.[1]

This chapter begins with a theme expressed by many of the male interviewees: their intense attraction to "French" or "European" women, particularly "blondes with blue eyes," and their pursuit of such women. This is followed by what women said about their own romantic attractions and relationships, which was altogether different. The final section focuses on the choice of spouse or long-term partner among the dozens of interviewees who have taken that step. Romantic attraction, relationships, long-term-partnerships, marriage: for many of the interviewees, this aspect of life is, in the words of one, "a cradle of *intégration*."

While most of the interviewees discussed in this chapter have already been profiled—see the Appendix for page references for each interviewee—details relating to these subjects have been largely deferred until now. Readers are advised that some of the interviewee statements quoted here, especially relating to men's sexual desires, are extremely candid, even raw.

"BLONDES WITH BLUE EYES"

"I think that, like all men, I have a fantasy of blondes with blue eyes." That is what Shayan said, and, as it turned out, many of the male interviewees expressed a strong attraction to such women.[2] That relatively few "French" women fit this image—only about ten percent are natural blondes,[3] and fewer still are also blue-eyed—did not put them off. Indeed, many have had relationships with precisely this kind of woman. Even those whose interest was somewhat broader sought women they described as "French" or "European." They focused on hair color (blonde or light brown, but not black, like theirs) and hair texture ("smooth," rather than "curly" or "kinky"). The desired eye color was blue or another light color (not brown, like theirs), and the desired skin color, perhaps most important, was "fair" or "white" (not "tan," "swarthy," "dark," or "black," like theirs).

Where does the desire for a "blonde with blue eyes" come from? What is its connection to the feeling of acceptance by "French" people? A number of male interviewees offered answers to these questions, at least for themselves. Samuel's account is the most detailed.

Samuel. Now forty-three, Samuel was born and raised in the same French city where he still lives. His mother was "French," and his father was Maghrebi. By his own account, Samuel's life has been marked by the conflict between how he views himself and how others see him. "I felt French," he said, but French people "didn't see me as French. They catalogued me as Maghrebi." He felt their "contempt." It was worse:

> I always had the impression that they considered me subhuman. They made me feel that I didn't belong to their world, with their insults, with how they looked at me. I wanted to prove that I was French like them. I wanted to find a door to enter into their world. I am French! I am like you! You must accept me!

For much of Samuel's life, "French" women would play a big role in this effort. A "blonde with blue eyes" was the kind of woman that, Samuel says, "I dreamed of, the one I searched for." It started with Monique, when he was only ten. Monique was blonde. "I was in love with her like a crazy person." When he was fifteen, he fell "madly in love" with Elena, who was "French, but of Ukrainian origin." He recalls, "I was very, very proud. I'd entered, a bit, into the world that had kept me out." But Elena's mother was "incredibly racist. She called me *le crouille,*" the "very worst insult for Arabs back then." It was "worse than shit."[4]

Samuel's first long-term relationship was with Julie. Although of mixed "French" and Algerian origin, Julie didn't look "very Arab." Unlike Samuel, Julie had light skin and a "purely French name." One could see that she "had some foreign origin, but nothing more." Although Samuel and Julie stayed together for six years and had two daughters, he didn't really love her. "Julie was too similar to me. We were more like brother and sister."

One day, when he was twenty-six, Samuel passed a woman as he entered a local café. "I fell in love the moment I saw her, this magnificent blonde with blue eyes. She was beautiful, everything I'd always dreamed of in a woman. I was crazy, crazy in love." When she reappeared at that cafe two months later, "she said she'd come back for me because I'd been in her head the whole time." Her name was Céline.

Samuel left Julie to live with Céline. During the years that followed, Samuel says he saw his daughters regularly but was otherwise swept up with Céline. While his relationship with her was troubled from the start, it was also thrilling. Samuel loved her—"At the time, I would have given my life for her"—and she loved him. He was thrilled. "Finally, someone of that world found me important, found me handsome, and loved me. Her love transported me; it was incredible." While "the most important thing was how she looked at me," Samuel recalls, he was also proud "when we went out together. French men didn't like it at all, a beautiful blonde with blue eyes to be with a foreigner."

Not merely a "blonde with blue eyes," Céline "had no foreign origin at all. Physically, she represented the French woman." Being loved by, in his words, "*une Française de pure souche*" was

> something that had never happened in my life, to me, the Maghrebi. I had a blonde with blue eyes! It allowed me to enter into the world that didn't want me, to prove that I am French, like them. When she accepted me into her life, I felt I had almost acquired a new social status, pushing away my status as a foreigner. Finally, I had succeeded in life.

While thrilling, the relationship with Céline was, he says, "the most brutal time of my life." Céline behaved bizarrely and often lied; she disappeared for weeks at a time and told far-fetched stories about where she had been. Though they had a son together, Samuel had no contact with her "racist" parents after they told

Céline they would never even see the child once he was born, "since he'll be the son of a *bougnoule*."

After fifteen years together, Céline put an end to their relationship. Since then, Samuel says, "I've begged her a thousand times to come back. Today, I suffer." But losing Céline meant something more for Samuel. Toward the end of the interview, he summed this up: "I had sought to enter into that world through a woman, a woman who is purely French. I'm sure I knew this unconsciously at the time, but this is the first time that I've realized it consciously." That's over now. "The blonde with blue eyes, the one who had accepted me into this world, now rejected me. It was like that whole society had rejected me." Céline "put me back in my place as a Maghrebi."

Other male interviewees. Before turning to the accounts of other interviewees, it is important to place the image of a "blonde with blue eyes" into context. Various people used this term as the archetype of a "French" person in completely non-romantic circumstances. When Zhora was insulted during an argument over a parking space with a "French" couple, she thought, "Oh, so that's the problem. It's not that I was already waiting for the parking spot, but that since I'm a *bougnoule*, I don't deserve it. But if I'd been a blonde with blue eyes, the space would have been for me." Shayan spoke about the future, when his son, who would have a "dark complexion, black hair, and brown eyes," will apply for a job. A less-qualified "blond with blue eyes" might be chosen instead because he would be "a true Frenchman." Olivier says that when a Maghrebi like him passes "a blond with blue eyes" on the street, the Maghrebi is "seen badly."

Other interviewees spoke in the same vein. Looking back on her early childhood, Caroline says, "I wanted dolls that were White, blonde with blue eyes." When speaking of his adolescence, Clément spoke of how a friend was treated differently wherever they went, repeatedly noting that the friend was a "blond with blue eyes." Indeed, the interviewees are not alone in using this term for the archetypal French person. According to anthropologist Didier Fassin, French employers of the recent past used various "codes" when hiring,

> the most classic of which was "BBR" for "Blue-white-red" [*Bleu-blanc-rouge*], but not meaning "French national," as one

> might be tempted to think, but rather "of the white race." . . . More explicitly, some resorted to the formula "BYB" for "blonds with blue eyes" [*blonds aux yeux bleus*]. (D. Fassin 2006a: 150)

Like Shayan (who spoke of his "fantasy" attraction to blondes with blue eyes) and Samuel, many male interviewees were clear about the kind of woman they sought for romantic relationships. Paul, who has a Korean *faciès*, grew up in France after being adopted by a French couple. They raised him to be purely French and he has always seen himself that way; indeed, he says, "I'm White in my head." And so "the type of woman who appeals to me is European. I'm not at all attracted to Asian women." Like Samuel and Shayan, Paul has followed through on this preference. His first wife was a "blonde with blue eyes" and, now divorced, he is engaged to a woman who is "blonde with light brown eyes."

Usman felt "inferior" when he came from Pakistan for advanced university studies. Trying to fit in as quickly and thoroughly as possible, Usman only dated European women. "Those of other ethnicities didn't appeal to me," he explained. While the relationship between this preference in women and colonialism has already been noted, Usman had far more to say about his feelings:

> I always liked, I was always very lucky to be with someone of European origin, blondes with blue eyes. That always pleased me. It was very important. I was very happy about that. I'm not afraid to admit that to be with a woman from here was, for me, a kind of success.

This feeling was not limited to dating. "If you marry such a woman and you have children here, it brings a sort of satisfaction." Usman's wife is blonde, and he has two sons with her. Usman added, "I'll now say something that's not very correct. I'm happy in comparison with my friends, even those who live abroad, men who accepted the weight of family tradition, who went back to Pakistan to marry a girl there. I made my own choice."

Saying that "there's something of our parents in us, something of their history, because we follow them," Usman contrasted his experience with his father's a generation ago. His father had been a student in Scotland shortly after Pakistan won its independence from the United Kingdom in 1947. A Scottish woman, he said, "was apparently in love with my father, and my father had a certain sentiment for her." This "shocked" people back in Pakistan and, chastened, "my father married my mother. The story ended there," he said, "though my father always had a certain regret."

Youssef threw himself into mastering all things French as soon as he came to France from Morocco for advanced university studies. He has only been attracted to "*Françaises de souche*," he said, and married a woman who is "White with very blue eyes." Through the present (he is now divorced), he has "always been with French women, certainly."

Perhaps because Youssef has a doctorate in the social sciences, he explained his attraction analytically. According to him, "the psychological unconscious is very important." What one desires may be formed early in life, but "you only discover it at the moment when the person is there and those characteristics manifest themselves, a beautiful White woman and all, you seize on it." With such a woman, Youssef feels a "desire for cultural and linguistic conquest." He says that this "crossing"—he grew up in a small village in Morocco—makes "me richer than I am myself." French women "teach me things. That's important to me."

Of South Asian origin, Vincent has spent his entire life in France. His profile details how thoroughly he integrated himself among the "French" people around him, but also how fearful he remains of being rejected. Vincent said that he is attracted to only one type of woman: "clearly White, a European type." He has "no interest" in women of his own "origin." Early girlfriends were "of German origin" or "purely French" and blonde. He married a woman who is not only French, but also, he points out, a "*Française de souche*."

Growing up in Gabon in Central Africa, François had a strong, positive feeling toward Whites. Even before coming to France for university studies, he was attracted only to women with "light, white skin." He says that

> there are beautiful Black women, but I've never felt the attraction. Much to the contrary. I ask myself why. I once told a

> friend about this. She asked, "Do you realize what you said?" I responded, "Yes, but it's real. I feel this. I can't hide it."

Continuing, François said that "all the women I've gone out with in France are White." When he got married, a friend from his childhood remarked to him, "We always knew you'd marry a White woman." They had a child, but the marriage did not last. He has since had two children with other women, both "White, pure French, White."

While all of these men—Shayan, Samuel, Paul, Usman, Youssef, Vincent, and François—share an unchanging interest in a certain type of woman (whom they describe as "White" or "French," some specifying a "blonde with blue eyes"), a few other male interviewees voiced more nuanced preferences. They include Thomas, Nassim, Jean, Mohamed, Mathieu, and Charles.

Thomas, a twenty-nine-year-old who has spent his entire life in France, is proud of being Black but is also proficient in making his way in an overwhelmingly White world. When the topic of his romantic interests first came up in his interview, Thomas was emphatic. "There are men who need to 100 percent integrate themselves into French society and, to do so, feel they have to be with a White woman. That's not me." He has never been attracted to Whites, he said, and, though his wife is a *métis*, "I'm not especially attracted to *métis* women."

Thomas then reported that "mixed couples are all the rage these days," and that six men in his group of ten Black friends are with White women. Thinking about this, he said, "Maybe that's what attracted me to my wife. It's possible. Unconsciously." He left the thought unexplained, but he returned to it at the end of his interview. Out of the blue, he told me, "If you saw my wife, she's *métis*, but she's White like you."

Of Algerian origin, Nassim also grew up in France. As his profile shows, he worked at mastering French styles of dress, speech, and behavior and at being accepted by "French" people for most of his life. His romantic interests followed the same pattern. He said, "I was attracted to European women, not Arab women"; indeed, he sought "the most European woman possible. I preferred blondes with blue eyes." His first girlfriend had "very big, blue eyes, smooth hair, and a slim physique." She "was everything that was most European." But this was "an impossible love," since her parents were "extremely racist."

After that relationship ended, Nassim continued to date only "European" women, he says, until a couple of years ago, when he returned to his Maghrebi and Muslim roots. He broke up with his "European" girlfriend at the time and began dating a deeply religious Maghrebi woman. This was significant, he explained. "She was my first Arab, my first Muslim girlfriend." And unlike all his romantic relationships over the prior fifteen years (he is thirty now), this one is

> chaste, as Islam requires. That was also new for me, to have a relationship with someone with whom there's no fornication, not even kissing. It's been a spiritual battle. It intrigues me enormously to get past the act, even past desire. I've found a meaning, even a pleasure, in working within myself.

After a year and a half together, he says, "I asked her father in the traditional way for her hand in marriage." The couple is now engaged.

Jean grew up in France feeling ashamed of being Black, although he is now moving toward acceptance, even pride, in this identity. A longtime artist, Jean used to depict only White people in his work—even rendering himself as White when including an artist in a design—but now mostly draws Black people. He portrays Black struggles in much of his current work. Jean's feelings about women have followed the same evolution, though he says that the change has been slow. When he was growing up, his image of beauty was a "White woman." He says, "I was never attracted to Black women" and "didn't want Black girlfriends. A Black woman had a way of talking that was too Haitian for me, too African, very close to their culture, which isn't mine. I was nearly assimilated. They smelled of Haiti, they smelled of Africa, they smelled of it all. I was just a French person at that time."

Jean's only serious relationship was with a White woman, and even today, he says, "I prefer a White woman." But as with his more recent drawings, Jean is nurturing a new interest in Black women:

> Since I accepted myself for what I am, there's been a discovery of Black women, who I appreciate a bit more as I begin to know them. I don't think I'm attracted to them, but I take them for who they are. And I think that they can understand

> me better than a White woman can, that they can understand me internally.

Jean's sense of beauty is shifting, too, though this has not been easy. He needs to "unblock" his attraction to White women, he says, "but it's a process. Before I didn't see the beauty of Black women. Now I'm trying to destroy the Western view of beauty to build a beauty that's more universal." Jean would also like to be more "universal" when thinking about himself. "There could be people like me who'd be seen as handsome."[5]

A devout Muslim, Mohamed grew up in Morocco. He reported that, "like most Moroccan men," he was drawn to "European women, blonde or not. It was a dream." After moving to France at age twenty-five, he first married a Maghrebi woman whose family had come from Morocco. After this marriage ended, he married his current wife, Clara, who conforms to his early feelings of attraction. Clara is a French-born woman who is "blonde with blue eyes and very pale skin." But Islam is still important to Mohamed: of Albanian and Montenegrin origin, Clara is also a devout Muslim.

Mathieu, who is of mostly Vietnamese origin, has spent his entire life in France. He feels that everyone who subscribes to French values should be considered French, regardless of a person's origin or length of time spent in France. His romantic preferences do not focus on native-born French women either:

> Since adolescence, I've always been attracted to Mediterranean women. With big eyes, maybe accentuated by kohl. And black hair that's a little curly. A bit dark-skinned. Italian or Spanish, Algerian, Turkish; for me, all Mediterraneans are the same. But any type of woman is ok, except an Asian.

Mathieu dated a woman he described as "Algerian" for five years, as well as "another Algerian, a Russian, a Bulgarian, and a French woman." Then, counter to his preferences, he dated an Asian woman. "At first," he says, "I was curious." This girlfriend was Kana, who had come from Japan as a young adult. Mathieu and Kana are now married.

Finally, there is Charles, who is from Martinique. He said, "I don't have an ethnic ideal" among possible romantic partners. "It's very simple. There are two things that are very important in a woman. She can't be skinny, and she must have a strong personality. The rest are accessories: white, black, yellow, green, or red, long hair or short. All accessories." Charles explained further. A woman he's with can't be a "skeleton" or "mannequin," and she must not be "submissive" or "crumble" in the face of his strong views. "Above all else, she must be accomplished professionally and intellectually." Of his major relationships, "first there was a White, second a Maghrebi, and then a Malagasy woman. Between them were a Japanese woman and a Martinican." The last girlfriend, the Malagasy woman, was Ariel, who's now his wife.

Among the male interviewees who are attracted to "French" or "European" women, some avoid women of their own origin. One of the Maghrebis spoke about the importance of cleanliness in his love life. Explaining why he has only been interested in "*Françaises de souche*," he said, "there's hygiene, for example." Although he has evidently never had a sexual relationship with a Maghrebi woman, it has been French women who have taught him "important things on a hygiene level" and made him see things differently in "matters of hygiene."

A Black interviewee reported similar feelings:

> I've always had trouble establishing a relationship with a Black woman. It goes further. It's on the order of repulsion. I can't go out with a Black woman. It's repulsion. It's very strong. It's terrible. It's always been like that. I find that they are dirty, that they stink. Even if that's not been confirmed, that's how I feel.

In sum, the great majority of male interviewers who spoke about their romantic preferences focused on a particular aspect of the woman they sought: a specific physical appearance. Most sought "blondes with blue eyes," or, more generally, what they called "French" or "European" women. But what about the female interviewees? What were their preferences?

WOMEN'S ROMANTIC PREFERENCES

As it turned out, the few women who talked about their romantic preferences spoke very differently from the men. While it is impossible to know how much that difference arose from the dynamics of these interviews, particularly the fact that the interviewer was a male, it is still worth reporting what these interviewees said.

Born and raised in France, Nour grew up in an urban neighborhood that was overwhelmingly "French." Although her parents had come from Algeria, she and her siblings fit into this community from the start. Their friends were Catholic. "I never felt judged," Nour explained. "There was a great tolerance. I didn't sense racism at that time. Not at all." She felt French and has been adamantly "non-Muslim" since childhood.

By the time Nour's older siblings started dating, they "always went out with French people," she said, the kind of people who "could be called 'the true French.'" At first, Nour did not follow their lead. She was "very tolerant about appearance" and "dated many Maghrebi men." The problem was that she "didn't want a Muslim," and all the Maghrebi men she dated "had religion in their heads." They criticized her for drinking alcohol and "because I ate pork and ignored Ramadan. It was very difficult," she recalled. As time went on, she turned to "French" men, and her two long-term partnerships have been with such men.

Fouzia, whose parents came to France from Algeria, has spent her entire life in the same city in France. Now in her mid-fifties, she graduated from high school and a nursing program and then, as an accredited nurse, had a career working in a hospital. She went out with "French" men, she explained, "because in my social, cultural milieu there weren't any Algerians. By my senior year in high school, there weren't any. And after that, in the professional milieu there were fewer and fewer. There were a lot more Europeans, French." I asked whether she had a preferred type of man. No, "it was a matter of encounter. When you meet someone, it's not a question of origins. It's a story of emotions, of feelings." As it turned out, Fouzia's first boyfriend was "half-Arab and half-French," but "after that they were only French." This includes the father of her daughter.

Zhora, who grew up in a poor *banlieue* in France, left home to finish high school and attend college in the city center. Although Zhora was romantically attracted to Maghrebi men, with their "olive skin and black eyes," relationships with them didn't work out. "I was very free," she said, and Maghrebi men "of that generation weren't as free as me." And so "I realized that it had to be a

European." When she was twenty-two, Zhora married a "French" student at her university. Laughing at the memory, she said, "I didn't intend to marry a person like him. He didn't fit any of my criteria. It was a shock."

Anna, who is Black, was raised in France by her White stepmother and a father who had rejected his West African origins. "I was raised as a European," she said. "I was very White; I was very French." Anna's romantic interests have matched this sense of herself:

> I've always dated only Westerners. I've never felt any attraction for Black men. I can't explain it. It's always been like that. I can see that some Black men are handsome, but I don't feel an attraction toward them. It's something I reproach myself for, that I'm only interested in Whites. It's not normal. Poof. Well, that's the way it is. Sorry. I'm not going to force it.

Caroline, who is also Black and grew up in France, reports a similar experience, though a shift may now be underway. Romantically, she says, "I'm more attracted to Whites. I'm not particularly attracted to Africans." She described her longtime boyfriend, who became her husband and now ex-husband, as "French," by which she means "White." Her current boyfriend, with whom we had dinner, is too. Perhaps, she says, "I'm like my mother" who is Black but married a White man, Caroline's stepfather. Unlike Anna, Caroline thinks that she might change in the future. "For a long time, I couldn't see myself with an African or a Black, but now it wouldn't bother me."

When Yuka arrived from China to attend college, she set about integrating herself into the community of "French" students. She had no romantic preferences, and when she began to date, "everything happened naturally." Yuka went out with "French" men, she said, because "in the final analysis, they were the ones in my classes." I asked Yuka whether she might have dated a fellow student who happened to be Chinese. She laughed. "Chinese, clearly not. I don't know why, but I wasn't at all attracted to Chinese men. And then Western men," she laughed again, "they might have brown or blond hair and be tall." The man she chose to marry, "just a classmate who'd become a friend," is a tall, brown-haired man from a longtime "French" family. But his being "French" didn't matter, she said, "not at all."

Amina is an IT consultant who came from Cameroon in sub-Saharan Africa almost twenty years ago. A forceful personality, she is clear about the kind of man she likes:

> I'm attracted more by a mindset than a skin color. I'm attracted to someone who's like me, with a strong personality and a way of life that's neither completely European nor completely African. Someone who'll understand my desires and needs. Someone who accepts me as I am, who doesn't seek to dominate me.

But that's not all. "I'm attracted to a certain type of man, okay. He has to be tall, strong, handsome, and intelligent. Because I want someone to talk with. But no, I'm not attracted to a skin color."

Finally, there is Aya, a thirty-one-year-old Maghrebi woman who came to France a few years ago. She explained her attraction to Black men in detail:

> I go out with men from sub-Saharan Africa for a number of reasons. There's the mindset and the physical side. In mindset they're close to me. They have similar origins, the colonial history, all that, plus the food, which is spicy. Then there's the physical side. There's a precise type for me.

Laughing, she continued:

> I'm little and I go out with big men, always a meter eighty-five [six feet. one inch] or taller. It's bizarre, but it's like that. In general, they're hefty, either heavy or muscle-bound. Attractions are like that, you can't explain them. I like dark-skinned men and no body hair. I've never seen a Black person with body hair, so that avoids the problem. I detest body hair, especially on men. I can't tolerate it.

Since only eight women spoke about their romantic preferences, sweeping generalizations must be avoided. A few observations are still possible. Unlike the men, none of these women mentioned or sought "blonds with blue eyes." None of the women used images like "cultural conquest" or "entering into" the world of "French" people, and none focused on the sense of being an outsider who wants in. Finally, while physical characteristics were important to some of the women, many spoke about the personal characteristics they sought in a man. These women sought a man who is like them (temperamentally, professionally, religiously), who is a member of the same community, or who would accept them as they are.

THE CHOICE OF A SPOUSE OR LONG-TERM PARTNER

While only about two dozen interviewees spoke about their romantic preferences and experiences, all of the interviewees who had been married or had taken a long-term partner[6] readily spoke about the person they had chosen. Each person's choice of spouse or long-term partner (for some, more than one spouse or partner over time) might be viewed from the outside as a choice between someone whom the interviewees typically described as "French" and someone of non-European origin. This would generate some simple numbers: 60 percent of those who married or lived in a long-term partnership did so with a "French" person, 30 percent with someone of their own non-European origin, and 10 percent with someone of a different non-European origin. But this breakdown does not capture the interviewees' own ways of thinking.[7]

Interviewees instead chose spouses or long-term partners in accordance with how they felt about themselves. Their choices fall into four general types:

(a) a person like you, i.e., a person with whom the interviewee shares an identity;
(b) among interviewees who want to feel French, a "French" person;
(c) someone who helps the interviewee recapture their origin while still feeling French; and
(d) a person of any origin or *faciès*, since the interviewee is indifferent to such matters.

(a) *A Person Like You*

A number of interviewees spoke about having an identity that has remained stable over the years. While it is not surprising that many of these people married or partnered with people of the same identity, it may be surprising that fewer than half chose people of the same origin as themselves.

Some, of course, married or partnered with people of the same origin. Two of the Maghrebi women who grew up in France, Hiba and Khira, entered into arranged marriages with men from their countries of origin. Sami, who remains proudly "Tunisian" despite his decades in France, first married a woman of Algerian origin and then a Tunisian woman who still lives in Tunisia. Nima, a political exile from Iran, married a woman from Iran. And Eric, who is from China, married a Chinese woman.

But other interviewees married or partnered with "French" people, seeing no difference between themselves and the person they chose. The fact that millions of "French" people would disagree, or even find it ludicrous in light of the interviewees' non-European *faciès*, is immaterial to them.

Rémy, the son of a "French" mother and a father from Vietnam, is now in his seventies. Growing up in France, he was raised to be totally French, even while he was mocked by other children as "the little Chinaman." At twenty-one, he married the seventeen-year-old daughter of a local "French" farmer. "We got married. It's now been more than fifty years that we're married," he said. Rémy will not tolerate anyone suggesting that he is Chinese. Rémy's intense feeling of being French motivated him to join the army and then pursue a career in the National Police. Now retired, he still stands and puts his hand on his heart when the French national anthem comes on television.

A similar experience was reported by Henri, whose father was "French" and mother was Vietnamese, and who is also retired. Although he was ridiculed for his Asian appearance and subjected to discrimination for much of his life, Henri's sense of identity is clear: "I've always thought of myself as French. Always." He married a "French" woman and pursued a career with the postal service. As he explained, "I worked for France. I always worked harder to prove that I'm French."

Isabel grew up in the Republic of the Congo, a former French colony in sub-Saharan Africa. From a Western-educated, super-elite family, she heard only French "since the cradle," and French was the sole language at school. Throughout her childhood, she said, she did not learn a word in any African language. Isabel came to France at sixteen and became a citizen at twenty.

She married a man from a longtime "French" family and, though now divorced, has retained his distinctively French last name. She is a lifelong Catholic. Her sense of identity is clear: "I am, before anything else, French. I am French."

Other interviewees who consider themselves French and chose "French" spouses or partners have already been discussed in the context of romantic attraction. Shayan has spent his entire life in the same French city and has always thought of himself as French. He married a woman who is from a longtime "French" family. Nour, who has also spent her entire life in the same French city and has always felt French, partnered with two "French" men. Paul and Caroline have felt French their whole lives and have chosen "French" people as spouses. Although Paul's *faciès* is entirely Korean and Caroline is Black, they both say they feel White.

For Rémy, Henri, Isabel, Shayan, Nour, Paul, and Caroline, the choice of spouse or partner was obvious: feeling French, each chose a "French" person.

(b) *"French"—The Kind of Person You Would Like to Be*

While the interviewees just discussed have always felt French, many others started life not feeling French, but have spent decades mastering French norms while fitting in, or trying to fit in, among "French" people. Since this experience was reported in their profiles, each interviewee in this group requires only a brief mention.

For some of these interviewees, their efforts to fit in have had the desired result: a feeling of acceptance. Usman, who came to France from Pakistan for advanced studies, avidly learned to behave like the "French" people around him, married a "French" woman, and forged a successful career in high-tech business. Yuka, another interviewee who came to France for university education, cast aside her Chinese background and enthusiastically participated in the life of the "French" students around her. Now married to one of these fellow students, Yuka feels comfortable in the community where she lives. Achraf grew up in a successful business family in Tunisia and came to France for college. After partying his way through college (he had never been religious and had no discomfort with drinking alcohol), Achraf married a woman who was "pure French" and launched his own business career in France. Successful from the start, he was accepted by the elite of the French town where he and his wife settled.

A far larger number of interviewees have worked to integrate themselves among "French" people—and married or partnered with a "French" person—but still do not feel accepted. Although Vincent has always lived in France, has had a long career at a large French company, and married, he said, a *Française de souche* woman, he is still afraid of being rejected. Samuel, another lifelong resident of France, became successful in the entertainment business and gained acceptance through the love of a "French" woman, but he felt cast back to his original Maghrebi status when she ended the relationship. Yet another interviewee who has spent her entire life in France, Zhora worked hard to advance her education, married a "French" man, and pursued a career in the French civil service, but she feels that she is still seen as a *bougnoule*.

This list continues. Karim said that he made himself "more French than the French" and partnered with "*Française de souche*" women, but he feels that his *faciès* precludes true acceptance. Asma values all things French and married a "French" man, but she feels spurned as a Maghrebi. Youssef mastered French social norms, earned advanced degrees at French universities, married a "French" woman, and feels French, but sees people pulling away because of his "Arab mug." Finally, François has thrown himself into life among "French" people and married or partnered with three "French" women, but he still feels excluded because he is Black.

A striking pattern emerges when these people are considered as a group. True, all are integrated into norms of the "French" people around them, and all married or partnered with "French" people, but there is a sharp divide between those who feel that they are accepted by "French" people (Usman, Yuka, and Achraf) and those who feel at risk of being rejected (Vincent, Samuel, Zhora, Karim, Asma, Youssef, and François). While all of the marriages or long-term partnerships of the people who feel accepted remain in place, all of the marriages or partnerships of the people who feel rejected (or subject to rejection at any time) have broken apart.

(c) *Someone Who Helps You Recapture Your Origin While Still Feeling French*

Such distress is not inevitable. Of the many interviewees who felt rejected by "French" people while growing up in France, two made trips to their country of origin that changed their lives. These are Clément and Grégoire. After taking these trips as young adults, each returned to France feeling proud of the culture and values of his country of origin, and each married a woman from that country. During the years since, each has combined a strong appreciation of his non-European heritage with an equally strong feeling of being French. Their experiences are worth reporting at length.

Clément. Clément's family came to France from Senegal, West Africa, when he was six. Growing up, he did his best to fit into his largely "French" neighborhood but was repeatedly humiliated. He felt that "France didn't accept me. There was never a moment when I felt I belonged; the color of my skin reminded me of this." Clément's experience with girls followed the same pattern. "I never succeeded in going out with a French girl even though I tried many times. It wasn't possible," he said, because of "my category."

Even after five years of military service in France, Clément didn't feel "fully a part of France." He "needed to break with the rhythm of French life," he said, to "go back to where there are people like me, to know the community, the ethnic group I belonged to." Clément decided to spend "three or four months in Senegal to rejuvenate myself," he said, "and track down my roots, to know who I am, to regain a bit of my origins. I had to know. I was like the adoptive child who needed to see his biological parents, even if they didn't want to see him."

Although his time in Senegal began as "a true shock," Clément gradually adjusted to the life there. With time, he went further. "I began to see deeper. It was interesting and refreshing. I learned to live as people there do," and finally "I felt at home. The four months restructured how I saw things, my values." Clément also fell in love with a Senegalese woman. The trip, he reported, "was truly an upheaval for me. I came back to France completely transformed. I was proud because I had recovered some of my background, because I'd enriched myself culturally. I felt I'd gained new powers, that I'd grown."

Clément visited Senegal again to court the woman he had met there. Overcoming obstacles that will be discussed in chapter 6, he married her, and they settled in France. Now, Clément says,

> I know who I am. I know that my origins are in Senegal. So, even though they don't let me fit in completely into France, it's not terrible. I can let it go a bit; I can be less affected by that. And so today I'm lucky to be immersed in a double culture. While I can't fully lay claim to my French identity, I can draw upon that other part of me. It's a great advantage.

Clément, his wife, and their daughter have made a life in France. And even though Clément still "can't gain the same respect as others in France," the connection he forged with Senegalese culture has made him more "confident."

Grégoire. The son of a Vietnamese mother and "French" father, Grégoire was mocked for his Asian appearance while growing up in France in the 1950s and 1960s. He felt "ugly, truly ugly." Then came an experience that, he said, "completely changed me": he accompanied his mother on a two-month trip to Vietnam in 1974. He was twenty-five.

Grégoire's mother's family gave him a bed with a mosquito net while "they slept on the ground." He still marvels at this. "They didn't know me, but they gave me the best they had. Why did they do that? Because we're family, it's my family. I found this extraordinary. These were worthy people." As the visit progressed, "I realized that I had a family. I had a strong feeling for them. It was overwhelming." His time in Vietnam made him "enormously" prouder of himself.

Although Grégoire had only been attracted to "White, European" women before his trip to Vietnam, he started courting a young Vietnamese woman, Thanh, while he was there. It was an "unimaginable," an "impossible" romance. After returning to France, he corresponded with Thanh, proposed to her in a letter, and then returned to Vietnam to marry her. During our interview, Grégoire wondered aloud what had motivated him. "Why? Why her? To discover my roots, maybe." The couple settled in France and now, after "forty-two years of marriage," he said, "it's been good. It's worked out well."

Although Grégoire still feels intensely French, he has been active in his city's Vietnamese-French friendship association since his trips to Vietnam. In the media, he says, "things are said about Vietnam that are false. We must speak the truth." He attends conferences and writes to journalists "to reestablish the truth." Insults about his Asian appearance no longer bother him: "It's me who decides about myself. I changed during my trip to Vietnam."

Clément and Grégoire are exceptional cases, of course, and Grégoire's brother Henri presents a striking counterexample. Although the brothers' joint profile reports virtually identical lives, they differed in one respect: only Grégoire returned to Vietnam and underwent a change in his romantic interests. Henri did not. As a young man, Henri liked European girls (especially Polish girls, "because they were blonde") and then married a "French" woman. Apart from Clément and Grégoire, few of the interviewees who grew up in France have spent time in their countries of origin, and none have seen their attitudes change so radically.

(d) *A Person of Any Faciès Since You Are Indifferent to Such Issues*

While the great majority of interviewees who have gotten married or entered into a long-term partnership cared about whether their spouse or long-term partner was "French" or someone of the same origin as themselves, this was not universal. Four interviewees were completely indifferent to this issue. These are the members of two married couples: Mathieu and Kana, and Ariel and Charles. While the romantic preferences of Mathieu and Charles have been reported earlier in this chapter, the choice of spouse for all four requires further discussion. As seen below, these people are outliers, either because their concept of who is French is unrelated to *faciès* or because they are indifferent to whether their spouse or partner is French.

Mathieu and Kana. I met Mathieu and Kana at their apartment in an ethnically diverse housing complex where they live with their infant daughter. Mathieu has always lived in France and has always felt French. For Mathieu, being French has had nothing to do with a person's *faciès*, and, unlike his father Grégoire and uncle Henri, his mostly Vietnamese *faciès* has never made him uncomfortable. He socializes with people of all origins. This began in the neighborhood in which he grew up and the multiethnic schools he attended, and it continues today. As a former Maghrebi girlfriend once remarked when she looked at the "twenty or so Whites, Blacks, and Arabs" he had invited for a social occasion, the group looked like "Benetton." Mathieu, he said, "hadn't even noticed it." Although being French is important to Mathieu, he has an expansive view of what that means: everyone is French so long as they see themselves as French, speak the language, and adhere to basic French values. This could include his wife Kana, even though she came from Japan just five years ago. When he decided to marry her, he was indifferent to whether she was "French" or something else.

When Kana was growing up in Japan, she recalls, "I always dreamed of living abroad. For me, the Japanese—and I'm Japanese—aren't free. There's always something unstated that they hide." They are also "programmed." It's always "you mustn't do this, you mustn't do that." After college, Kana "fled" Japan. She chose France by happenstance, because it was the only European country that offered her admission to a master's program, but she has made a life there.

Kana's view of French identity, like Mathieu's, has nothing to do with origin or *faciès*. For her, "the French are descendants of immigrants," and are "not only White." And so, she said, "when I think of who's French, I don't differentiate among black, white, yellow skin color. For me, France is a mixture. Just because I was born in Japan doesn't mean I'm Japanese. If I feel French, then I'm French." Like Mathieu, Kana did not consider the *faciès* of the person she chose to marry.

Ariel and Charles. Ariel and Charles are IT specialists who work and live in a tech hub among engineers and other IT specialists from a wide range of countries. Although cognizant of bias among "French" people, they are unbowed by it, focusing instead on their own lives and the protection and satisfaction afforded by their technical expertise.

Originally from the former French colony of Madagascar, an island nation off the southeast coast of Africa, Ariel came to France for university studies. The issue of who is or isn't French does not interest her:

> If someone says he's French, then he's French. I don't distinguish between White French people of ancient French origin and more recent French people who originate from immigration. They have different ways of behaving and different cultures, but I see them all as French.

Ariel's interest in a partner or spouse was unrelated to whether he was "French." Her former partner of eleven years was from Martinique, an overseas *département* of France in the Caribbean. While he was "very pale" with only a bit of "charcoal" in his skin, she says that his skin color didn't matter "at all." And though Madagascar and Martinique are thousands of miles apart, "I felt close to him culturally because he too had left his island." They had both "cut an invisible rope to live in France." Ariel later met Charles, who is also from Martinique—she chuckled at the coincidence—and they got married. She is dismissive of racism in any form. "Racism is totally unimportant to me," she declared; it's nothing but "intellectual pollution." Indifferent to such issues, Ariel said nothing about Charles's *faciès*.

Charles, who grew up in Martinique and has lived in mainland France since his college years, has always felt French. While some French people can speak of "our ancestors, the Gauls," he says, that's of no consequence for him. Indeed, Charles finds the subject of who counts as French so unimportant that he didn't mention it when discussing his romantic partners or his marriage with Ariel. As reported above, for Charles, a woman's *faciès* matters not at all.

Patterns in the Fate of Marriages and Long-Term Partnerships

Although the interviewees present a small, non-scientifically selected sample of people of non-European origins in France, it is worth looking at the fate of their marriages and long-term partnerships:

Section a. Much like the overall population of France, where about half of all marriages end in divorce (Statista 2019; INED n.d.), approximately half of the interviewees of this group—people who forged relationships with people they consider like themselves—saw these relationships break apart.

Section b. Among the interviewees of this group—people who have worked at becoming more French and entered into relationships with a "French" person—a sharp divide emerged. The marriages or partnerships of virtually everyone who did not report feeling inferior to "French" people or subject to rejection at any time remain intact, while the marriages or partnerships of everyone who reported such feelings have broken apart.

Section c. These two men, each of whom became proud of his heritage during a trip to his country of origin and married a woman he met there, remain in their relationships.

Section d. All of these people—who were indifferent to the *faciès* of the people they chose—remain in their relationships.

CONCLUSION

Even though this chapter addressed issues that are personal to each individual, some overall patterns are evident among the interviewees.

First, there is a marked difference between men and women with regard to romantic attraction. Among the men, those who have been focused on fitting in among "French" people (notably, Samuel, Shayan, Usman, Youssef, Vincent, François, and, for most of their lives, Nassim and Jean) feel an intense desire for women who embody their image of the supremely "French" woman. For each of these men, this means a *faciès* that is altogether different from his own. The women who spoke about their romantic interests described a very different orientation. Most who feel themselves to be French (notably, Nour, Anna, and Caroline) were drawn to "French" men. Most of the other women are interested in a man of any *faciès* who values her for such things as her values, strength of character, and professional career.

The fates of marriages and long-term partnerships among all the interviewees suggest two broader patterns. First, a secure sense of one's worth and place in France is typical among those whose marriages or long-term partnerships remain intact. Second, an abiding feeling of inferiority to "French" people and fear of rejection appears to be particularly problematic for any marriage or partnership with a "French" person. Literally all of these relationships have broken apart.

NOTES

1. Although two or three of the interviewees were apparently gay, none of them chose to discuss the topics covered in this chapter.
2. This attraction is hardly new. In Fanon's "little tale" of sexual intercourse immediately following the account described in chapter 4 of this book, the French woman is a "'maddening' blonde" (*Black Skins, White Masks* (1986 [1952]: 63).
3. See Ladepeche.fr 2007.
4. Derived from Arabic, "*crouille*" or "*crouillat*" became a stinging insult for Arab people during the twentieth century but has "progressively disappeared from the vocabulary of racist insults" (Ruscio 2020: 69).
5. That Jean could be seen as handsome—which he has only begun to consider—stands in sharp contrast with his feelings as a child. He no longer needs to do such "ridiculous" things as pinch his nostrils in the hope of looking like a White person.
6. Since 1999, the French legal code has recognized a contractually-based civil union known as PACS. In their accounts, the interviewees did not limit themselves to such government-recognized relationships.
7. These percentages also cannot be compared with broader demographic studies, since French law prohibits the collection of data relating to race or ethnicity —leaving statisticians with the inexact proxy of country of origin—and even this identity stops at the first French-born generation. Someone like Lucas, who is Black but was born in France of French-born parents, would be counted as a member of the "mainstream population" (see, e.g., Beauchemin, et al. 2010: 2).

SIX

TO BE MUSLIM, OR ASSUMED TO BE MUSLIM

Even before my formal interviews began, an Airbnb host introduced me to a predicament faced by people in France who are either Muslim or assumed to be Muslim. Ayoub, a young Maghrebi man with no religious feelings, talked about a test he feels that "French" people impose upon him. Whenever he socializes with someone new, it seems that there's a charged moment: Will Ayoub join him in a glass of wine? Will Ayoub have some charcuterie? If he does (which doesn't raise an issue for him), there's a palpable sense of relief: he's okay. But if he doesn't—or if a practicing Muslim friend doesn't—there's a tensing up. The guy's not like us; he could be trouble. It was even worse following the 2015–16 terrorist attacks in France.[1] At work the day after each attack, Ayoub's boss wanted him to swear his loyalty to France.

During the interviews that followed, I spoke with many people for whom some sort of Muslim identity is an integral part of life. Some are practicing Muslims;[2] others are former Muslims or non-Muslims from Muslim families. Apart from their own religious identities, some are assumed by "French" people to be Muslim, while others are not. Further, even individuals who have similar backgrounds—for instance, practicing Maghrebi Muslims or former Muslims of Iranian origin—have fashioned very different lives in France. But despite all this variety, these interviewees have something in common: they must deal with the stereotypes of Muslims in France.

The experience of being Muslim—or just being assumed to be Muslim—is the focus of this chapter. The first section surveys the wide variety among interviewees who have some sort of Muslim identity, whether felt subjectively or perceived by others. The second section reviews pivotal issues of French identity—*laïcité*, *intégration*, and the shared pleasures of French life—and how the interviewees deal with these issues. The next section involves a discussion of the stereotypes and assumptions that interviewees feel "French" people have about Muslims. Finally, there is the question at the heart of it all: can a Muslim be French?

THE INTERVIEWEES

Throughout this book a sharp division has emerged between how a person feels internally (for example, "Am I French?") and how others see that person ("Is she French?"). The same duality applies to being Muslim. As various interviewees explained in chapters 1–3, while anyone can be Muslim, since it is an internal matter decided by the person alone, to be seen as Muslim hinges on social signals. The most obvious signal is physical: those who are seen as Maghrebi (or, more generally, Arab) are assumed to be Muslim, while others—even interviewees who originate from such predominantly Muslim countries as Iran, Turkey, and Pakistan—are not. "French" people assume, according to Samuel, "You're Arab, so you're certainly Muslim; you're Muslim, so you're certainly Arab." The other social signal of identity is behavioral. Among the interviewees, this involves dietary restrictions: those who abstain from alcohol, pork, and meat[3] are suspected of being Muslim.

In the following accounts, the interviewees speak about both their own religious identities and how they are seen by others. While these people have already been profiled in previous chapters, where the focus was on other aspects of their lives, each had much to say about these issues. (For what has already been reported about these interviewees, see the page references for each interviewee in the Appendix.) The interviewees are grouped according to the way they are initially seen by others, either as Maghrebi (and thus assumed to be Muslim) or as something else (and thus not assumed to be Muslim). But this is just the beginning. As the headings that follow indicate, each interviewee has a distinctive perspective on what it is like, in one way or another, to have a Muslim identity in France.[4]

Interviewees Who Are Seen as Maghrebi

Although "French" people apparently assume that Maghrebi people are Muslim, the Maghrebi interviewees have pursued a wide array of approaches to religious identity and practices.

Samuel: "Forgetting God," then rejoining the "detested" religion. Although Samuel's life and romantic interests have been extensively reported, the history and depth of his religious faith have hardly been mentioned. Samuel was born into a Muslim family in France, given a Muslim name for use within the family, and raised as a Muslim. But by his early twenties, he was desperate to escape "the rejection of French society." He abandoned what he says "French" people consider Muslims' "funny customs, like Ramadan, the prayers, the food." He began to drink alcohol—"I drank so I could fit in"—and, he said, "little by little, I stopped praying." As time went on, he made his way among "French" people, falling in love with a "French" woman and pursuing a career in the French entertainment industry.

"I forgot God for ten years," Samuel recalled. Even though his relationship with the "French" woman continued and he became professionally successful, Samuel was full of "suffering." Samuel teared up as he spoke about this time of life. He remembered that it "was a very long process to accept my life as it is. It was very hard." He finally realized that "the only way" to escape this distress was, in his words, "to give myself over to God." And so, he said, "I was recaptured by God" and "became a new man."

While Samuel thinks that his return to Islam "was a blessing," it has complicated his interactions with non-Muslims. He now hides his religion with everyone until he has "sounded them out." He did this with previous Airbnb guests, he said, who "might have wondered if I had an exploding belt." He also did it with me: "When you arrived, I paid attention to how you looked at me. I do that all the time. All my life is like that with everyone, to sound out others before revealing who I am. That's the way of life here in France." But Samuel cannot always control whether people learn that he is Muslim. When he declines wine on social occasions, he "senses a look" from "French" people "trying to find out" if he does this because he's a Muslim.

The 2015–16 terrorist attacks in France further complicated Samuel's life. Though Islam is "a religion of peace," he said, and the perpetrators of the attacks "don't belong to my religion," the media and many people turned against Muslims. "It works well to make the Muslim the criminal. Today people like to detest Muslims." Once, upon hearing that Samuel is Muslim, a man blurted out, "Ah, you are Muslim, a terrorist." The attacks have even warped Samuel's own way of thinking. One day in the subway, when he "saw a Muslim, a brother, bearded, with a sack on the floor," Samuel found himself "terrified."

Samuel tries to show "French" people that Muslims are not terrorists. "I often help people on the street who can't carry bags or the like. It's my nature. But when they look at me, astonished, I want to say, 'It's a Muslim who helps you.'" This is not enough to do away with the association. In the eyes of many, he thinks, if he's Muslim, he might be a terrorist. Miserable at the thought of this, he said, "We Maghrebi Muslims are the first victims" of terrorism.

Nour: a "non-Muslim." Although her parents were devout Muslims from Algeria, Nour was born in France and grew up in a "French" neighborhood. From the start, she felt no affinity for Islam. Nour "secretly" ate pork and, she said, during Ramadan "never fasted, not even one day." She took part in the world around her. "My friends were very Catholic. I attended catechism school with them and loved the beautiful catechism stories. I was invited to all my friends' first communions. Everyone was very well dressed, there were loads of gifts, an enormous buffet. It fascinated me."

Nour's siblings also had no interest in being Muslim. It was the 1970s, she said, and "my older brothers were great hippies. It was all 'Peace and Love,' long hair and guitars. It was very Woodstock." She laughed at the memory. One weekend, when her parents were out of town, Nour's older brothers hosted a party. "There was alcohol everywhere. My brothers were completely soused." When her parents came home unexpectedly and saw this scene, their father "went crazy." Despite the beatings that followed, her siblings persisted in living like their Catholic friends, with little regard for Islam.

Nour says she's a "non-Muslim" because "I'm neither practicing nor a believer. I'm completely agnostic." She is not an "ex-Muslim," as some people think, since she never was a Muslim. Neither is she "of Muslim origin," she says, because Islam "isn't an origin, but a religion." While her being a non-Muslim has never been a problem with colleagues at work, Nour is still stung by a memory from the 1990s, when she worked as a supervisor at a local high school. "By this time, the problems with religion had begun." One day in the lunchroom, she said, when "I had a tray with sausages on my plate, some Maghrebi students" challenged her for eating pork, saying, "You're Algerian." Furious at this "lack of respect," Nour told them, "First, I'm not Algerian but French, and second, I'm not Muslim."

Another incident occurred when Nour was only seventeen. The father of "one of my best friends was extremely racist," she recalls. "He voted for the National Front, he told me all this." One day "he explained why." During the Algerian war, when the man was still living in Algeria, he said that he "had another daughter who was tortured" by Algerians. Nour asked him whether this experience made her a problem in his eyes. He told her, "No, you're not like them. You follow all the rules, you're not a believing Muslim, you eat pork, et cetera." For him, Nour believes, "my face showed my origins, but behind that I was as French as his daughter."

Rania: "I show them what they want to see." Rania grew up in Tunisia. Although her mother was "a free thinker" who cut her hair "like a boy" and sometimes wore pants or applied makeup, Rania decided to veil herself when she was twelve. While many Muslims do not consider veiling a religious obligation, it was important for her, she explained. "The veil became a part of my identity, it was me. It became a part of my body." She'd have felt "completely naked" without it.

After receiving undergraduate and master's degrees at a French university, Rania went to work for an IT firm in a major city. She was still veiled. Soon, her supervisor spoke to her privately:

> I know that the veil is extremely important to you. The concern is not the veil itself—it's not you who are the concern, we know you, you are very congenial and open—but there are people who have prejudices. You may be at a meeting with a client who's prejudiced, and, because he sees you veiled, he'll cut ties with our company. It's not against you, but how people see you.

Rania decided to take his advice. "I took it off." Indeed, she transformed her entire workday appearance, dressing and grooming herself like a young French professional. Her reasoning was practical. "A person's appearance changes the attitude of the people around her. It's very important."

Rania is hardworking and talented, but she recognizes that more is needed to succeed. She is against presenting herself as different from her true self but does it anyway. Why? "I don't do this for others, I do it for myself. I do it because if I do it, I'll win. And why not? I need a promotion, I need opportunities, I need people to say 'very good' at work, so I do it. It's not an obligation, but an adaptation. In my environment, I adapt."

Although she dresses and acts like her French colleagues, Rania is open about being Muslim. "At work, I'm not ashamed to say that I'm Muslim. Everyone knows I don't drink; everyone knows I don't eat pork, that I eat fish." And while she faces prejudice from some colleagues, including anti-Muslim jokes and resentment that "a Muslim" is getting the good assignments, she is not put off. Other colleagues have been "very sympathetic and generous," and her supervisor has taught her "so much."

Each evening, Rania catches up on the mandated daytime prayers (a sanctioned practice known as *qadaa*). "Every Saturday and Sunday, no make-up, not a drop. I live for myself," she explained. Gone are her stylish clothes. Rania also "transforms" herself when she visits her parents five times a year: "When I return to Tunisia, I toss that appearance in the trash. I put on a veil that goes down to my chest. I wear an enormously ample dress. I become another person. The true me is when I'm at my parents' home, when I'm with my family. I feel myself."

Rania grounds this double life in her view of *intégration*. There's the "inside," who she really is, and the "outside," how she presents herself. *Intégration* exists only on the outside, as people are only "interested in appearances." She explained, "You've got to change your skin to be well integrated. If I hold onto my identity, who I am, and change the outside, they'll all come toward me. They'll all like me. They'll say, 'she's like us.' They'll accept me." But this does not change her inside. The outside, Rania said, "doesn't matter to me. None of it counts, none of it has value, none of it is real. None of it represents my identity. It's not me."

Rania's inside/outside dichotomy is nuanced. Because she maintains a reassuring "outside" whenever she is with French people, she does not need to hide her "inside" from them. Her colleagues and friends know she's Muslim. Indeed, she reports, "When I return from Tunisia, I show my photos." Seeing her fully veiled, "they say, 'You're like that?' and I say, 'Yes, I returned to my origins. Take a look!'" They think that the photos show how much Rania has changed in France. They see it as "evolution, as *intégration*. They take it positively."

Rania summed up her approach to the work world in France. "Professional life is a theatrical play for me," she said. "I have one colleague, Stéphanie, who knows everything, who accepts me as I am. Those who don't accept me as I am, I show them what they want to see. And so, they accept me. That's *intégration*."

Nassim: "almost French," then "transformed." Nassim, the son of religious Muslims from Algeria, grew up in a small French city. Often the only Muslim in his class, he said, "I had trouble finding my place." He wanted to change "my appearance in the eyes of others," he said, so "when I was sixteen, I started distancing myself from religion." Seeing a lack of "coherence" in Islam, Nassim stopped following its practices, such as fasting during Ramadan and praying. Discontinuing Islam's food and drink restrictions was particularly important:

> I said to myself, if I no longer made myself eat halal, if I no longer kept myself from drinking alcohol or eating pork, well, when we went on an outing or to the movies or a restaurant, I could eat like everyone else, drink like everyone, and feel myself integrated like everyone else. I'd have a different appearance. All this was a motivation for moving away from Muslim practices.

Nassim's abandonment of Muslim dietary restrictions had an immediate effect. "People would say, 'You're almost French' and things like that." His "French" girlfriend's parents, he said, noticed that "I drank alcohol, I ate pork, and I didn't eat halal." They thought, "He's fine by us." This type of reaction continued into adult life. "I noticed something in business. When I drank wine and had no food restrictions, everything went smoothly."

A couple of years ago, when Nassim was almost thirty, he turned away from this way of life. "I had to transform myself." He broke up with his "French" girlfriend, learned to read and write Arabic, and, he said, "returned to my religion." While deeply gratifying, this transformation complicated his interactions with "French" people. "When I returned to Islam, I started to follow the rules, eating halal. When I ordered fish at restaurants and said I don't drink alcohol, that always raised questions, always."

Although ordering fish is a seemingly unobtrusive way to avoid non-halal meat, a colleague once told him, "That makes two times that you ordered fish. I noticed that." Nassim said "Wow!" just recalling this incident. "By contrast, if my European colleagues order fish or don't drink wine, they're never asked questions."[5]

Hiba: "If I weren't Muslim, I'd be 200 percent French." Hiba's family came to France from Morocco when she was seven. She loved France from the start—"I adopted France or France adopted me—but even today, at forty-seven, she doesn't feel accepted. Though "I behave like a French person," she says, Hiba has to "explain all the time" why she doesn't drink alcohol or eat pork. "I'm of this country, but people are bothered that I'm Muslim. That's it. If I weren't Muslim, I'd be 200 percent French."

Being Muslim in France was not always so problematic. But after the 2001 terrorist attack in New York City, Hiba recalls, "it was Muslims all the time on TV." All anyone heard was "religion, religion, religion," and that the perpetrators were "Muslim extremists." People "pointed fingers, you felt it." This attitude became more intense after each of the 2015–16 attacks because they were "in France, not America."

Hiba has always worked for "French" families. It hurt her, she says, in 2015–16, when her clients talked about how the attackers were Muslim, since "it's not true about Muslims. Muslims search for peace." The problem has not gone away. She says that "all my clients accept that I'm Maghrebi, even if they think they're superior to us. But when they hear that I'm Muslim, that stresses them." In their minds, "it's the Muslims who cry 'Allahu Akbar' and kill."

Sami: "No problem" being Muslim. Now fifty-five, Sami grew up in Tunisia, where his whole family was religious. For the last twenty-eight years, he has lived in a town near a large French city, where there are 5,000 Muslims, but many more non-Muslims. The Muslim congregation just built a large mosque at a cost of five million euros (at the time, about $7 million). He has had "no problem" practicing his religion.

Sami also has "had no problem with French people." He runs his own electronics repair shop, where, he says, "I see French customers every day." They're "friendly" and "appreciative"; "even the Christians, the Catholics are fine. There are no issues." Sami does not have to interact with "French" people outside his community because he rarely travels elsewhere in France.

Sami says that "even if I see prejudice, it has no importance." Slurs "don't interest me," and prejudiced people "wouldn't dare" take action "against men. Those who are sick will remain sick, that's all." And though "people have changed a little" since the terrorist attacks of 2015–16, Sami dismisses the attacks from a religious perspective. "No one has the right in our religion to take a life that God has given. All Muslims agree with this. The beasts who don't understand anything, they kill people. They are manipulated."

Interviewees Who Are Not Seen as Maghrebi

Just as the Maghrebi interviewees are assumed to be Muslim, interviewees who are not seen as Maghrebi are not assumed to be Muslim. From what these interviewees can tell, many "French" people do not even consider the possibility. But some of these people are Muslim or at least come from Muslim families. Each person had a distinctive story to tell.

Amina: "I'm a woman and I'm Black. On top of that, I'm Muslim." Amina grew up in a Muslim family in Cameroon, West Africa, and has remained "profoundly Muslim" throughout her time in France. This hasn't been a major problem for her, though not because of open-mindedness on the part of "French" people.

Amina carved out a professional niche that helps her sidestep bias. She is a highly trained consultant in the field of business intelligence, where the only thing that matters, she says, is "being technically solid." Her appearance also limits the bias she might otherwise face as a Muslim. "Me, I'm not veiled. I dress normally, so I'm not rejected for this reason. There are times when people distrust women who are veiled. It's a matter of what one fears." She dresses "like Oprah Winfrey," she says, with tailored black dresses and stylish hair. With "no religious sign" in her clothing, she's "Mrs. Like-Everyone-Else." And because she is Black rather than Maghrebi, her religion "isn't visible."

Still, Amina doesn't hide the fact that she's Muslim. She abstains from pork and non-halal meat, fasts during Ramadan, and has a Muslim first name. She doesn't keep her religion a secret either. "When the subject comes up, I always say I'm Muslim." But even people who know she's Muslim aren't put off; when they see how she dresses and acts, they assume that she's "moderate."

I asked Amina whether she ever feels the sting of anti-Muslim bias. She laughed aloud. "Sure," she replied, but "in my case, already I'm a woman and I'm Black. On top of that, I'm Muslim. I have everything going against me."

Fatih: "It's frustrating." Turkish by origin, Fatih grew up in a small village in France, where he followed his family's Muslim practices. He says that "it was complicated at the beginning because I wanted to be like the others. People would point their finger, saying 'He doesn't eat pork.' The experience wasn't good." In particular,

> I had problems at family dinners at the home of French friends. I had to justify why I didn't eat pork or even chicken, since it wasn't halal. They didn't understand and I was uncomfortable. To refuse is impolite. This gave me problems with frustration and confidence. It was frustrating when someone rejected me.

Now thirty-three, Fatih has pursued a career in business. Keeping his skin pale and smoothing his hair, he says that he's never mistaken for a Maghrebi. It's still hard for him. When "French" people interact with any "foreigner"—by which he means someone who doesn't look "French" —there's "always a blockage in the beginning. But with people of a different religion, for Muslims," he continued, "it's an enormous blockage." At one job, "there were small remarks in the beginning." When this didn't let up, he said, "I realized that I didn't have to work with such people, so I left." He now lives in a large city. "It's good, even if there are still intolerant people. There will always be some imbeciles." Food continues to trigger discomfort for him. Even though Fatih now drinks alcohol, he says, "when I go to restaurants with colleagues, they remark, 'Ah, you don't eat pork. Is that a matter of religion?'"

Shayan: Leaving behind the "constraints" of Islam. Now thirty-three, Shayan has spent his entire life in France. Originally from Iran, his parents followed Islam's dietary restrictions, and Shayan did the same until junior high school, when he noticed that many people found Muslims "troublesome." Then came the 2001 World Trade Center attack, which, he said, "spoiled the image of Muslims, just like that." Uncomfortable with "this cap, this label of being Muslim," he said, "little by little I detached myself from Islam. I asked myself whether it makes sense to continue following the prohibitions for a system of religion I don't particularly believe in." He stopped fasting during Ramadan in high school, began drinking wine at twenty-two, and began eating pork at twenty-five or twenty-six. Ultimately, he became a "non-Muslim."

During the same period, Shayan says, he "gravitated toward the Catholics." He began "speaking in the same way as the French Catholics," which brought him "closer, indirectly, to them." He also "identified with" them, though this was "more as a social category than a religion." A year before our interview, Shayan married Christine, a "French" woman of Catholic background, though neither of them practices Catholicism or any religion. And that, he says, "is how I am today."

Usman: Seizing the "opportunity not to classify myself as Muslim." Now forty-seven, Usman grew up in northwestern Pakistan. His family did not follow Muslim practices at home. Still, he said, "the society around us was very religious and you had to at least show yourself at the mosque. I showed myself there every Friday." But even in Pakistan, "I wasn't convinced. I already had a critical attitude."

Coming to France for graduate studies, Usman said, "was an opportunity to not classify myself as Muslim." Religion was not an issue among the people at his university. "I came to understand"—he chuckled here—"that if you're going to be someone sophisticated and intellectual in this society, you won't believe in God." He fit right in. "I felt free. It was good." Though "I wasn't used to eating pork," Usman said, he'd have some when it was served. "For me it was a question of respect. I always made an effort to be like the others." He readily drank alcohol.

Usman said that he hasn't had a religious identity for the entire twenty years he's been in France. He's not mistaken for a

Maghrebi, and, he says, "no one has ever asked me, 'Are you Muslim?'" Even during the tense days following each of the 2015–16 terrorist attacks in France, "Never did anyone ask a question like 'What do you think of it as a Muslim?' No one asked whether I'm a Muslim."

Clément: "Cut off from Catholic society" after converting to Islam. Although Clément was ashamed of being Black during his childhood in France, he was, at least, Catholic. But even this social advantage, as he sees it, was lost in his mid-twenties, when he fell in love with a Senegalese woman who agreed to marry him, he says, "only if I converted to Islam." Clément became Muslim, finding the experience "super-enriching," but he has paid a high price. While a Black who's "a good Christian isn't completely integrated into White, Christian society"—he laughed at his own understatement—"being Muslim is to be cut off from it. That's certain."

When someone learns that he is Muslim, Clément senses "a different look, a completely different look. A coldness sets in." He has decided to keep his new religion "behind closed doors," but this has exacted a high price, he says. "To my regret, to my very great regret, I can't express this side of my identity." Although "it has great value," he feels "forced" to keep it hidden.

Elise: "It's not easy to be a Muslim in France." Elise presents a special case among the interviewees. Born in France of a mixed couple (her mother comes from Morocco, while her father is "French"), she grew up in a well-off French neighborhood in the center of town. She attended private schools and then universities in France and England. Now twenty-eight and "very well integrated," Elise is an investment banker. Her sense of self is unqualified. "I was born in France, I grew up in France, I am, before all else, French."

But how is she seen by others? Using a striking turn of phrase, Elise said that people usually take her for "a normal French woman." Her name is completely French (since she also has her father's last name), she has long, smooth hair, and her complexion is relatively light. Because she lacks the manner, name, or appearance associated with Maghrebis, she doesn't have "the stain on one's forehead that you can't wash off." And since she is not seen as Maghrebi, she is not assumed to be Muslim. But she is Muslim, and she has adhered to Muslim practices her whole life.

This first became a problem when Elise was only ten or twelve. She was the sole Muslim at her private school, and each time another student realized that she was Muslim (as they would when she declined pork or, in later years, fasted during Ramadan), she says, "I had to justify myself." Because other children saw being Muslim "as bizarre" or "as an error, a defect," Elise decided to "show it less." She thought, "If they didn't see it, they wouldn't criticize it. I didn't hide that I was Muslim, but I avoided saying it because it would trigger questions, remarks, judgments, and so on." Whenever it was discovered, she recalls, "I always got the same questions, always the same looks."

The problem became worse when Elise grew up. Although she makes sure to practice her religion privately, social life doesn't allow her to keep it private. At meals, she must explain why she doesn't eat pork, and alcoholic beverages are a particular sticking point. "I'm asked every day, 'Why don't you drink alcohol? Is it religious?' People ask me directly, 'Are you Muslim?'" For her, it's "a battle every day."

Ever since Elise left home for college, "it's been difficult during Ramadan." She remembers the early years well. "When I was a student in my studio apartment and came home from a day of fasting to eat pasta all alone, the feeling of Ramadan—ah, there was none at all." Even today, "I have no one with whom to share the breaking-fast meal in the evening." Instead of the warmth of spending Ramadan evenings with family and friends, she feels that "social life is on hold."

Elise's profession adds another level of stress. "It's worse in my line of work, in finance, since I work with clients, meaning we go to a restaurant, share a glass of wine." This is all part of "business culture." People often "push" her, she says. "It's like a mission in their lives to make me drink. It's almost an insult that I don't drink alcohol." When she still declines, some people "get annoyed," insisting that they know "other Muslims who drink alcohol."

To sidestep these interactions, Elise sometimes speaks vaguely of special diets. She also makes excuses during Ramadan, when, she says, "I can't have lunch with clients. This is difficult professionally." Such ploys are painful for her since "avoiding saying that I'm Muslim is almost a denial of myself. It's as if I'd made a mistake. But I haven't made a mistake. I'm Muslim. There's nothing reprehensible about that."

The 2015–16 terrorist attacks in France made life for Muslims even more problematic. Elise is furious with the perpetrators. "These are not Muslims. In the Qur'an, it doesn't say, 'Go ahead, kill people.' The moment you kill someone you are not Muslim." But many people don't realize this; they think that "Islam is a religion of war." And so, even though "it's easier for me because I'm a girl," she says, after each attack "I have to justify myself." She has to tell people who know she's Muslim that "I haven't done anything at all. No, I will not set off an explosion. I promise not to launch an attack tomorrow."

In sum, Elise says, "It's not easy to be a Muslim in France." And since she cannot avoid having her religion discovered—and having people make so much of it—she finds herself typecast: "I'm a Muslim before I'm Elise." There's nothing she can do about this. "In the end, one must make peace with oneself."

LAÏCITÉ, *INTÉGRATION*, AND THE SHARED PLEASURES OF FRENCH LIFE

Muslim interviewees repeatedly complained about how Muslims are stereotyped as rejecting core French values, particularly *laïcité* and *intégration*. They also spoke of how Muslims are criticized for declining alcoholic beverages, pork, and non-halal meat at social occasions. Their positions on these issues say much about how they see themselves in French society.

Laïcité. Generally speaking, *laïcité* is the principle of French law and values by which the public sphere is kept neutral with regard to religion. Although freedom of religion is guaranteed, religiously based behavior is limited to private spaces, such as places of worship or homes. In theory, the principle ensures that neither the government nor French society favors a particular religion or lack of religion. (See introduction; Bowen 2007: 29.)

While the interviewees agree that some Muslims in France reject the principle of *laïcité*, all of the interviewees embrace it. Elise spoke at length about her adherence to *laïcité*. "Everyone has the right to practice her religion," she said, "but only in private places." For Elise, *laïcité* extends to everything that reflects a religion in the public sphere. She insists that the *burkini* (a modest type of swimwear associated with the Muslim *burka* body covering) "must not be worn at the beach." She applies that same principle to other religions. While Muslim veils shouldn't be permitted in public, she said, "nuns are veiled too. It's exactly the same. Why doesn't this bother anyone?"

All of the Muslim interviewees evidently keep their religious practices out of the public sphere. This includes praying, even for those who adhere to the five-times-a-day rule. Where necessary, they postpone the daytime prayers until they have returned home in the evening. None of the interviewees mentioned praying in public, and none of them wear clothing in public that expresses or even reveals their Muslim faith. Rania was the only one who once veiled herself, but even she put this aside once she entered the work world. As their profiles show, all of the practicing Muslim women—Lina, Amina, Khira, Hiba, Rania, and Elise—present themselves in public as the opposite of the stereotypical Muslim woman. Amina said that she is "super well-coiffed" and dresses "classically" in "tailored" dresses and "pumps." None of the men mentioned wearing a skullcap in public. When Sami and I went to the local mosque for evening prayers, he put his skullcap on upon entering the mosque.

Intégration. Because *intégration* is such an important concept in France—and vital to the interviewees—it has been discussed throughout this book. A few still-unreported comments illustrate the role of *intégration* in being Muslim in France, at least in the lives of the interviewees. Even when Shayan and his family were practicing Muslims, his parents wanted him to "fully integrate" into French society, and he feels that he has succeeded. "In my childhood, I never felt non-French as a matter of *intégration*. No one said otherwise."

Always a devout Muslim, Rania delights in fitting in with French people: "To live here in France, well-integrated and well-dressed, to put on make-up, speak well, et cetera, is to be integrated, it's to take part." In France, she added, "*intégration* is very important to live. To survive."

"If you're in a country," Elise insists, "you behave according to that country's code of conduct." You must "integrate yourself into that country's practices." Her entire family—including her mother Lina, who is also deeply religious—has done this. "I'd like the French to see people like us, who've embraced France as their country, who've integrated themselves here, as Muslims in France."

While they readily acknowledge that some Muslims do not try to fit into the broader French society, Muslim interviewees were offended by the belief that Muslims as a group resist *intégration*. This stereotype is nevertheless common among "French" people. As Mohamed put it, debates in France "go in a single direction: Islam is a problem, Muslims are incapable of integrating themselves into French society." But the interviewees, including those who are active Muslims, are altogether different. As seen throughout this book, they pride themselves in having French values, including a firm adherence to *laïcité*, and in speaking high-quality French as they live, work, and socialize in French society.

Joining in the social pleasures of French life. This is a complicated issue. Almost everyone discussed thus far in this chapter—Nassim, Samuel, Nour, Shayan, Rania, Elise, Usman, and Fatih—spoke about social occasions that French people delight in. In business and personal life, in restaurants and in homes, people in France come together to drink aperitifs, share a bottle of wine, snack on appetizers (often pork-based charcuterie), and dine together. Scholarly literature supports this perception. According to Mathilde Cohen, food is "central to French identity," and "the French meal is represented as a national ritual to which every citizen can partake on the same footing" (Cohen 2021: 26, 27).

This presents a problem for practicing Muslims. As Shayan explained, "In France, you have all the ritual of aperitifs and good wine. People say such things as 'This wine is a little fruity' or 'This wine is a little tannic.' They ask, 'What charcuterie would you prefer?' 'What would you like to eat? Maybe a pork chop?'" A person cannot just opt out, Shayan said, because "if you do, it's difficult to fit in." While this is no longer an issue for Shayan, who has given up the dietary restrictions of Islam, it is a major problem for practicing Muslims like Samuel and Elise. When Elise declines a glass of wine, she said, people insist: "But it's French. Wine is a part of French culture, so you have to drink."

The problem goes beyond alcohol and pork. Because many practicing Muslims abstain from any non-halal meat, they cannot eat the meat dishes served in the great majority of French restaurants and homes. This may leave them ordering fish or hard-boiled eggs and salad at every meal, as Amina does, but it is not a social problem until non-Muslims make it one. Some do just that, as Nassim and Fatih repeatedly discovered. Practicing Muslims also fast from sunrise to sunset each day during the month of Ramadan. When someone says to Elise during Ramadan, "Let's have lunch next week," she has to decline. "People don't understand."

These dietary restrictions present a conundrum for practicing Muslims. The problem bubbled to the surface during my interview with Elise, who had just spoken emphatically about the necessity of "integrating" oneself. When I wondered aloud whether her practice of declining wine could be seen as a refusal to fit into French social life, she answered, "I've had such thoughts myself. I'm in France and it's part of French culture. It's almost denying your culture not to drink."

STEREOTYPES AND ASSUMPTIONS

Many interviewees who are Muslim or of Muslim origin complained about the stereotypes and assumptions that many French people have about Muslims. Their comments bring home how they feel they're seen by others.

"Muslims are backward." Mohamed is incensed by the portrayal of Muslims as backward. "It's incredible," this "permanent humiliation in the media." The media, he reported, "always talk about the veiled women, saying that they're forced" to veil themselves. Veiled women, who are never given "the opportunity to speak" for themselves, are assumed to be subjugated by the men in their families. Mohamed thinks that "politicians add to these prejudices. There was even a government minister who said that Muslims sacrifice, that they slit the throat of sheep in their bathtubs." He doesn't "understand why there's this obsession, this bad faith" in depicting Muslims. It's "very stigmatizing for us." As already discussed, Samuel and others reported how "French" people show disdain for even routine Muslim practices, like daily prayers, dietary restrictions, and the Ramadan fast.

Whatever practices might be followed by other Muslims in France, the interviewees feel that modernity is not inconsistent with Islam. As their profiles make clear, all of the practicing Muslim interviewees – Amina, Clément, Elise, Hiba, Khira, Lina, Mohamed, Nassim, Rania, Sami, and Samuel – are full participants in the economic and social life of France. They live and work like others in France. Many are highly educated professionals. And on the issue of female subjugation, one need only consider the lives and forceful personalities of Amina, Rania, Elise, Hiba, and Lina.

"Muslim equals terrorist." Many interviewees—practicing Muslims, former Muslims, and non-Muslims alike—complained that the terrorist attacks of 2015–16 in France were blamed, immediately and unthinkingly, on "the Maghrebis" or "the Muslims." This attitude started even earlier, Shayan believes. Following the 2001 attack at the World Trade Center in New York, he said, a simple equivalence set in: "Muslim equals terrorist." While the effect of these attacks on Shayan, Samuel, Hiba, Nassim, Elise, and Sami has already been discussed, Mohamed's and Ibrahim's experiences should also be reported.

Mohamed described life following the terrorist attacks. As soon as they began, "a tensed-up mood took hold." People felt that "all the Muslims are guilty, all are responsible," and "demanded that individual Muslims disagree" with each attack. Mohamed finds this grossly unfair. "Muslims have been denied the right to be individuals. We became the people who always have to justify themselves, always. No one ever asked Christians about an act done by a White, to say that it's not in the Bible, that it's not Christianity." Mohamed believes that it doesn't stop with terrorism. Some people think that "the lack of safety" they feel in France "is the fault of Muslims."

Ibrahim feels hurt that "French" people blame the terrorist attacks on Muslims. He says, "the only thing they have in their mouths is 'Muslim.'" But the man who committed the 2016 attack in Nice "didn't pray, he took drugs, he smoked hashish, he frequented homosexuals, all things that Islam prohibits." The perpetrator said "'I killed the people because I don't like immigrants,'" even though he had come from Tunisia. "He was crazy," Ibrahim said. In spite of all this, the media portrayed the perpetrator in religious terms, as a "Muslim who'd been radicalized, a fundamentalist."

Ibrahim believes that such attitudes fuel violence against Muslims in France. "Every day there are Islamophobic acts," but "people don't respond." He reported that, ten days before our interview, a man insulted a "bearded Muslim man on a bus" and "stabbed him in the back," and, five days later, "a man on a motorbike ran over two veiled women with a small child." But "this wasn't reported on TV."

"French means Catholic." Although France is officially a *"laïque"* nation—the First Article of its Constitution defines it as such—interviewees report a different social reality. Abbas described France as "a country with Christian origins." This can be "camouflaged," he said, "but society is permeated with this way of thinking." It's part of French "culture, of their heritage."

Even though French people are less religious today—according to Sami, "the churches are empty"—the association of France with Catholicism complicates the interviewees' lives. Shayan said that "even though I felt French, French means Catholic." At least in part to be seen as French, Shayan gradually abandoned Muslim practices and began identifying with the Catholics around him. Elise said that France is a "country with a Catholic history" and that it's difficult "to be Muslim in a Catholic country, a dominant Catholic country."

Vincent is on the other side of the religious divide, coming from a devout Catholic family that originates from South Asia. He believes that life is simpler for him than for Muslims. "It's easy to be Catholic in France," he said. "There's not the same look from French people as with Muslims. For them there's a blockage." Clément, the Black interviewee who converted from Catholicism to Islam, feels much the same way. When he was Catholic, he shared something with "French" people, but now he finds himself "forced to avoid the subject of religion." He believes that "there's a great hostility toward Muslims in France'" The very subject "is taboo."

Maghrebis are assumed to be Muslim until they prove they are not; non-Maghrebis are not assumed to be Muslim until they reveal they are. As seen in their profiles and the accounts in this chapter, the Maghrebi interviewees are assumed to be Muslim, while the non-Maghrebi interviewees are not. The first of these assumptions is not surprising. After all, the vast majority of people in the Maghreb, as in the rest of North Africa, are Muslim.[6] Even Nour, who has always been a "non-Muslim," is assumed to be Muslim. Vincent, a non-Muslim of South Asian origin, captured this Maghrebi-Muslim equation when he (unselfconsciously) said that "Maghrebis and Catholics are not seen in the same way."

It is the opposite for the interviewees who are not seen as Maghrebi: they are not assumed to be Muslim. Samuel thinks that this reflects a blind spot among many French people, because only a small percentage of Muslims worldwide are Arab.[7] As it turns out, many of the interviewees who are not seen as Maghrebi are Muslim or have Muslim backgrounds. Fatih originates from Turkey, Nima and Shayan from Iran, and Usman from Pakistan—all non-Arab countries that are overwhelmingly Muslim—and each comes from a Muslim family. Amina, Abbas, Djibril, and Clément, who originate from sub-Saharan Africa, are all Muslim. Then there is Elise, whose mother is Maghrebi but who is usually taken for "a normal French woman," she says. When she reveals that she's Muslim by declining alcohol or pork, it's often a surprise to the people around her.[8]

These assumptions put both Maghrebis and non-Maghrebis in a peculiar position. Although assumed to be Muslim, Maghrebis can show "French" people that they are not Muslim—at least not practicing Muslims—by drinking alcohol and eating pork or non-halal meat on social occasions. For some of the Maghrebi interviewees (like Nour, Zhora, Achraf, Abdel, Youssef, and Karim) this is not a problem. Indeed, they are happy to participate in these shared pleasures. But some other Maghrebis, even non-practicing Muslims, are made uneasy at social occasions, feeling that they are forced to make a public statement, either by joining the "French" people around them or setting themselves apart. Ayoub's predicament was reported at the beginning of this chapter. The test he reported is simple: does he drink and eat like the others, showing that he's a good guy, or does he decline and align himself with those troublesome Maghrebis who hold fast to their Muslim ways? Similarly, Nassim "noticed something in business" before he became a practicing Muslim. He felt accepted by colleagues and clients. "It was almost like being tested: 'Good, he eats meat, he drinks alcohol.'"

Non-Maghrebis of Muslim background have the opposite experience. Although they are not assumed to be Muslim (because they are not Maghrebi), they reveal that they are Muslim if they decline alcohol, pork, or non-halal meat at a social occasion. This is not an issue for people like Nima and Usman, who feel no affinity for Islam, or for non-Maghrebi Muslims who have abandoned these dietary prohibitions, like Shayan. Today, no one wonders whether Shayan is Muslim. But the non-Maghrebis who are practicing Muslims do not have this luxury: when they decline such food or drink, they reveal their faith. While this doesn't pose a problem for Amina, who is openly Muslim, others are uncomfortable. Fatih said that people notice whenever he declines a pork dish and ask if it's a matter of religion. Elise, whose half-Maghrebi parentage is not evident, tries to keep her faith private, but when she declines alcohol or pork dishes, people "systematically" ask if she's Muslim and then insist that she justify herself.

CONCLUSION: CAN A MUSLIM BE FRENCH?

In his 2010 book, John Bowen asks, "Can Islam be French?" by which he means, "can Islam become a generally accepted part of the French social landscape?" (Bowen 2010: 3). To answer this question, Bowen listened to Muslim "scholars and educators and public figures who are trying to configure a set of teachings and norms and institutions that will anchor Islam in France" (5). After careful study of their "public reasoning," Bowen offered a cautious answer to his question: yes, Islam can be French, but only if "makers of public opinion" in France can shift "toward an ideal of shared respect for a common legal and political framework" (198).

A similar question—can a Muslim be French?—is at the heart of this chapter, although the focus here is on non-experts (the interviewees) and the answer is particular to each person. Further, the question is answered for each person on two levels: the personal (Do I believe that a person can be both Muslim and French? Am I?) and the social (Do others believe that a Muslim can be French? If they know that I'm Muslim, will they think I'm less French?).

Shayan's evolution illustrates how these two levels coexist and potentially interact. As an adolescent, when he still saw himself as Muslim, Shayan said that he was both Muslim and French "in my head." But when he discovered that many people found Muslims "troublesome," he thought, "Wow, it's complicated to say, 'I'm Muslim and I'm French.' French plus Muslim, that's French, but not very French." Intent on being accepted by the "French, Catholic" people around him, Shayan gave up his Muslim faith and practices.

Since the personal level is within the control of each person, the answer may be clear-cut, even emphatic. Clément, Elise, Hiba, Nassim, and Samuel—all practicing Muslims—grew up in France and vigorously adhere to French values, including *laïcité* and *intégration*. They speak "good" French, and they live, work, and dress in the same manner as the non-Muslims around them. They have the same pride in their country. As far as each of them is concerned, they are both Muslim and French.

The social level is more complicated. The same interviewees feel that many non-Muslims do not see practicing Muslims as truly French, or, put more concretely, they feel that many non-Muslims don't fully accept them. Each reports a deep bias, even fearfulness, on the part of non-Muslims. According to Samuel, "people like to detest Muslims," and some of Hiba's clients feel that "it's the Muslims who cry 'Allahu Akbar' and kill." Clément and Samuel both hide their religion, and Elise tries to keep it from being noticed. But this is often impossible. Nassim, Elise, and Samuel reported that some non-Muslims seem intent on uncovering their secret by checking for foods or beverages they avoid. While the interviewees rarely phrase such experiences in the abstractions of identity (Can a Muslim be French?), the social dynamic underlying their accounts is plain: to be known to be Muslim is to be subject to what Clément called a "completely different look," a "coldness."

This raises an important analytic question: are people of Muslim parentage who grew up in France but who are not Muslims seen as French? Are these people fully accepted? What about Nour, who has always had French values and habits, has always been a "non-Muslim," and has partnered only with "French" men? What of the Shayan of today, who has not only become a "non-Muslim," but also has gravitated toward Catholic people, has married a "French" woman of Catholic origin, and has plans to raise his children to be "totally French"? Or of Nassim in his younger years, who had left Islam behind and was so successful in behaving in the ways expected of French people that his boss called him "the most French person I know"?

These people test what it means to be seen as French. They grew up in France, feel French, and are fully integrated into French values and ways of life, even when it comes to traditional food and drink. For them, there seems to be nothing missing, nothing lacking in what it means to be French. But virtually none of the interviewees said that they are seen as simply or truly French. This is remarkable, almost illogical. Indeed, it suggests that something deeper than all these behavioral attributes is central to being seen as French. But what is it? This pivotal question is addressed in the conclusion of this book.

NOTES

1. A brief history of these attacks is set out in chapter 1 above. Terrorist attacks attributed to Muslims continue through the present.
2. Here, as elsewhere, I follow the interviewees' way of speaking. When talking about Muslims, interviewees spoke far less about religious faith than whether someone is a "practicing" Muslim. Abdel, who was raised in a Muslim family, said, "I don't consider myself Muslim because I drink alcohol and eat pork. It would show a lack of respect to others and myself to say that I'm Muslim when I don't follow the practices."
3. Islam does not prohibit the eating of meat other than pork, but religious law requires that the slaughter of each animal is conducted according to religious dictates. This renders the meat halal, or "permitted." Because French restaurants and "French" people rarely, if ever, serve halal meat, many practicing Muslims forgo all types of meat on social occasions.
4. To keep the variety of people and perspectives from overwhelming readers, I have selected a dozen interviewees. Others who are either Muslim or assumed to be Muslim include Abbas, Abdel, Achraf, Asma, Djibril, Karim, Khira, Lina, Mohamed, Olivier, Salma, Youssef, and Zhora. Discussions of each of these people can be accessed by checking the Appendix, where page references for interviewees are listed.
5. This accords with my own experience in France. Although I do not drink alcohol, I have never been asked why.
6. Depending on the country, the percentage ranges from 98 percent to 99.9 percent (Statista 2019).

7. Samuel said that "they don't realize that only 10 percent of Muslims are Arab." As it turns out, his estimate is not far off: apparently 15 to 20 percent of Muslims worldwide are Arab (see PBS Website n.d.; Georgetown University 2022; Huda 2018).
8. The assumption that non-Maghrebis are not Muslim is not absolute. Abbas and Amina, both Muslims from sub-Saharan Africa, point to their Arab first names. According to Amina, "a Black with an Arab name is necessarily a Muslim." But because Muslims originating from sub-Saharan Africa are not thought to be violent (Ndiaye 208: 238) and being Black is so salient in their dealings with "French" people, their religion hardly seems to matter. Another exception arises from physical proximity. When Fatih was growing up in a French village, there were a number of other Turkish families living there. The fact that others in the village knew they were Muslim is illustrated by a painful memory from Fatih's childhood. When he went to a "French" friend's home for a family dinner, the "adults were mean. They did it intentionally, serving pork, for example, to create a situation. It happened many times." Now that Fatih lives in a city and mixes with "French" people, he is not assumed to be Muslim.

CONCLUSION

Intégration has been a leitmotif of these interviews. At least twenty interviewees used this word, often repeatedly, in discussing their success in fitting in. While this book is replete with such statements, there were many more. Fouzia said that "I integrated myself into French society," and Ibrahim claimed that "I've done everything to integrate myself." For Shayan's parents, "speaking perfect French was essential for their children to fully integrate themselves," and being non-religious helped Youssef "to integrate quickly into French society."

But do the interviewees feel accepted by the "French" people around them, even seen as French? In no case is the answer a simple yes. While they have been able to find a place in the French economy and the daily life around them, the great majority describe, at the least, a conditionality in being accepted. In some contexts, and with some people, the interviewees feel a level of acceptance, but even then rejection can be signaled with just a few words. One need only review the profiles of Samuel, Jean, Thomas, Zhora, Lucas, and Vincent—all of whom were born and grew up in France—to get a sense of these moments of marginalization and the pain they engender. Almost as soon as I turned my recorder on, memories of humiliation by "xenophobic" schoolteachers, of discovering that they were not "in the same category of person" as their friends, of being shunned by others seemed to pour out.

How are the interviewees different from people who *are* fully accepted, who *are* seen as truly French? Does one need to be descended from generations of French people? This cannot be so. Nicolas Sarkozy's family roots in France are shallower than those of some interviewees, and yet he was French enough to be President of France. And then there is Mariana, the Airbnb host from Portugal. Seven years old when her family moved to

France, Mariana attended French schools, learned French, and participated in French life. Now twenty-nine, she feels completely accepted by the people around her; indeed, people at work don't know she was not originally French. How is Mariana different from the other interviewees? That she is Catholic cannot be the answer, because many of the interviewees are lifelong Catholics. Neither can it be her excellent French and way of life, since most of the interviewees can match her there. Her name is European, but that also cannot be the answer: her name is rare among native-born French people, while many of the interviewees have typical French names. She is well educated, but that is common among the interviewees too. In fact, there is only one thing that sets Mariana apart from the interviewees: her European *faciès*.

This stark fact is brought home when one compares Mariana with Nour. Nour has always spoken French, has always felt French, and has always lived like the "French" people around her. She's a "non-Muslim," she said, who eats pork and drinks wine. She adheres to French values to the point of marching with her son in support of freedom of the press following the terrorist attack at the *Charlie Hebdo* magazine office, and she has always participated in the social life of "French" people. As a child, she even attended catechism school with her Catholic friends. Nour is so French, she said, that the word *intégration* makes "no sense" in her case: "My frame of reference is France. I was born in France and grew up in government schools with the values of the Republic." Indeed, Nour has a stronger claim than Mariana to being seen as French, because Mariana didn't come to France until she was seven. And yet, Nour said, "Because of my first and last names and my *faciès*, people make very clear to me that I'm not French." But even Nour's name cannot be pivotal, since many of the interviewees have French first and last names.[1]

One could acknowledge all this and still push back. Does it really matter? According to the interviewees, very much so: people with a non-European *faciès*, especially those categorized as Maghrebi or Black, must contend with stereotypes, biased behavior, and outright discrimination. Many suffer psychologically.

Interviewees reported a raft of stereotypes about Maghrebis (and "Arabs" generally) in the media, from politicians, and in their own interactions with "French" people. Maghrebis are thought to be backward and antisocial. Maghrebi men are said to subjugate the women in their families, beating their wives and forcing their wives and daughters to veil themselves. The young men are said to be lowlifes who curse, jostle, and abuse whomever they come across. Some are thought to be violent, even potential terrorists. Maghrebis are said to stick together in dirty slums, far from respectable "French" people.

These stereotypes are deeply troubling for Maghrebi interviewees. Some think they are unfair, while others are bothered less by the stereotypes themselves—some of which they think may be accurate for Maghrebis living in run-down housing projects—than with the tendency of "French" people to apply the stereotypes to *them*, putting them, as many said, "in the same sack" as those Maghrebis.

Although it is immediately obvious from their language, dress, and behavior that the Maghrebi interviewees do not conform to these stereotypes, they reported insults and demeaning treatment from "French" people. The incidents go on and on: Zhora and Samuel during parking disputes; Mohamed, Ibrahim, and Karim in stores; Youssef, Mohamed, Samuel, and Karim on the street and in public transportation; Samuel at city hall. Lina sees "the look, the hatred" from "French" people on the street and in supermarkets. Although Zhora speaks accent-free French (having lived her entire life in France), she reported being told, "Go back to your own country, dirty *bougnoule*."

Most painful for Maghrebi interviewees has been their presumed association with terrorism. Following the 2015–16 terrorist attacks, "French" people asked Ibrahim, "Why do you do this?" Nassim had to assure his colleagues—people with whom he'd worked for years—that, no, "I'm not a terrorist." At the company where she works as an IT professional, Rania reported, "everyone came to me as if I were responsible." Ayoub was arrested and interrogated for ten hours after confronting a "French" man for harassing a fellow Maghrebi at a bar, purportedly because that man told the police that Ayoub said he had a "bomb that would explode."

Perhaps reacting to such misunderstanding and mistreatment, Maghrebi interviewees reported a deep sense of estrangement. Samuel—born in France, fully participating in French society, and eager to be seen as French—said that people like him don't belong: "We look for a place for us, but there is none. We're lost." After a lifetime in France living and working among "French" people, Zhora despairs: "I don't feel I'm in a country. I don't feel that I'm of any country." Concerned that his son will be shunned because of his dark skin, Mohamed fears that he won't feel French, and if his son "is not French, then what is he? It's enough to make a person schizophrenic."

The stereotypes about Blacks are equally painful. Much as Ndiaye describes in his study of "the Black condition" (see 2008: 205), interviewees reported that Blacks are caricatured as monkeys or gorillas, and as naturally stupid, lazy, and dirty. The Blacks of today are supposedly descended from the "savages" whom France went to civilize not so long ago. But they are not considered dangerous: a generally pliant lot, they're thought to be naturals for the menial jobs that "French" people spurn.

Unlike the Maghrebi interviewees, who think that the stereotypes apply to a different kind of Maghrebi, Black interviewees feel that the stereotypes are directed at *all* Blacks. The calumny that Blacks are inherently inferior must be confronted directly. As Isabel's father said, "a Black must prove that 'I'm intelligent,' that 'I'm not what you think.'" If Amina's business school classmates "thought I'd come down from a tree, that I couldn't be as intelligent as them," she said, "the only way to prove that we're equal is to beat them in school." Decades later, as a business consultant, she said, "I'm in the same battle. My sole revenge is to succeed." A number of Black interviewees disprove the stereotypes by excelling in ways "French" people cannot dispute. Charles and Ariel, like Amina, got university degrees in technical fields and then careers where, as Charles puts it, "intellectual competence, not skin color, is what's valued."

The situation is different among the third group of interviewees, those who are neither Maghrebi nor Black. The older Asian interviewees grew up in the France of the 1950s through the 1970s, when East Asian countries were thought to be backward and the people there were seen, as Grégoire put it, as "nearly savages." Times have changed. China and other East Asian countries have become wealthier, and "Asians are seen better" than before. These days, Paul said, "racism against Asians is very, very, very rare." Having grown up in recent decades, the younger Asian interviewees report positive stereotyping, focusing on Asians' purported intelligence, hard work, and discretion in their private lives. Not surprisingly, Asian interviewees reported far less biased behavior toward them than either Maghrebis or Blacks.

Alone among the interviewees, people who trace their origins to South or Western Asia reported a near-absence of stereotypes. "French" people don't seem to care where they're from, nor do they have preconceptions about what they are like. Although subject to occasional biased behavior and discrimination arising from their non-European *faciès*, they are not assumed to be antisocial or inferior, as Maghrebis and Blacks are.

This is not to say that people of the third group—Asians and others—are seen as French.[2] Although he has a "French" parent and a fully French name, Henri is seen as different because of his "Chinese face." People of South or Western Asian origin are likewise differentiated by their *faciès*. As Shayan said, "my hair is black, my eyes are brown, and I have a dark complexion." Even the child he hopes to have with his "French" wife would not be considered "a true Frenchman" by some.

A number of interviewees try to avoid rejection by becoming "more French than the French" (or "more royalist than the king"). Judging from their accounts, this is ultimately a losing strategy. At any moment, even without a misstep on their part, a "French" person can say something demeaning. But even when this doesn't happen, interviewees can feel diminished by the constant effort to fit in: Olivier likened *intégration* to "submission," and Vincent sees the danger of exclusion as inextricable from his efforts at *intégration*. Ultimately, those who try the hardest can feel the most let down. "One day," Karim said, "you realize that French people won't ever truly accept you. It's unjust, it's unjust to have thought you had to be like that to belong, but in the end you realize that you'll never, ever belong."

Finally, a fundamental social reality is confronted by all interviewees: they know that millions of "French" people think they shouldn't even be in France. Many spoke about the National Front's longtime slogan "France for the French." Even among those born in France, like Fouzia and Markus, the meaning is clear: for many "French" people, France is only for people with a European *faciès*. Clément got a taste of this attitude as a twelve-year-old, when a group of National Front adherents burst out laughing after they had him photographed with them.

The twin issues of whether people feel French and whether they feel others see them as French were included in the nationwide Trajectories and Origins survey. The results, as reported by Patrick Simon (2012) and Cyril Jayet (2016), would not surprise the people I interviewed. A substantial majority of "second generation" people (those born in France of at least one immigrant parent) who originate from non-European countries report that they "feel French" (Simon 2012: 9, Table 3), but far fewer feel that they are "seen as a French person." While the relevant percentages are not broken out in either of the published reports, Jayet notes that, while second-generation people of European origin feel they are seen as French at an even higher rate than they feel French (one thinks of Mariana here), second-generation people of non-European origin are far more likely to feel French than to feel they are seen as French (Jayet 2016: 129, Table 7). Simon reports that, while 10 percent of the "white (European)" immigrants and their children feel they're not accepted as French, four times as many of the others surveyed—non-White, non-European immigrants and their children—feel this way (Simon 2012: 14). The difference is particularly marked among the second generation. "The rejection of Frenchness," Simon reports, "affects those descendants whose origins"—unlike those of "the white (European) group"—"are highly visible in the public space" (15).

There remains the issue of outright discrimination. Perhaps not surprisingly in light of the stereotyping and biased attitudes about them, Maghrebis and Blacks also reported chronic problems involving employment. These begin when one seeks a job. As Fatih said, "I've seen a lot of prejudice in recruitment. I see it all the time." People will say, "A Black, no, that's not possible. And this guy's an Arab, that won't do." Many Maghrebi and Black interviewees complained that their résumés kept them from being even considered for jobs. The tip-off is the photo on the top—revealing their non-European *faciès*—and, for those with a non-European name, their name.

Some interviewees had trouble being considered for positions commensurate with their qualifications, as when Mohamed was channeled toward restaurant work after finishing his bachelor's and master's degrees. As with Khira, salaries may also be significantly lower than what "French" people earn for the same work.

Interviewees who reach a position with authority report additional problems. "French" members of Nour's team insulted her Maghrebi identity, and Salma has had to ask "French" attendees at her business seminars, "Do you want competence, or do you want a 'French' person?"

Workplace discrimination applies to everyone with a non-European *faciès* when a position involves interaction with the public. As Fatih (who is of Turkish origin) said, "There's always a barrier, especially for positions with direct contact with clients." Henri, who is Asian, was rejected for such a position three times over. A member of the selection panel later told him why: "The administration in France needs to remain White. It's illogical for you to think otherwise, for you to attempt to gain that position." When Anna worked for the national train company, she sought an onboard position, but was offered the only job without customer contact.

Such reports of employment discrimination raise an important question: If discrimination is such a problem, how have most of the interviewees found work above—some far above—the level of menial labor? Part of the answer arises from the way the interviewees were selected for this project. Because I sought people who rent an Airbnb room or apartment, I effectively chose those who, through ability, drive, and good fortune, have made their way into the middle class. Another answer arises from their education and choice of career. The majority had attended French universities, many in marketable, skills-oriented fields like information technology, engineering, and business. Many run their own small businesses offering specialized services to companies or individuals; such independence frees them from the bias experienced within corporate hierarchies. Finally, a few work for the government, where jobs are safe and advancement is based largely on uniform testing. In sum, most of the interviewees have used advanced education and an astute choice of career to minimize discrimination.

As already noted, the Trajectories and Origins study shows that high levels of discrimination are reported by Maghrebis and Blacks. But this is not just the case generally; as shown in chapters 1-3, it extends to people like the interviewees, and the aggregate effect of discrimination is enormous. As one expert notes, "there is now a broad consensus in the French social science literature that discriminatory mechanisms are key factors of ethnic inequality, be it in education, employment or socioeconomic status more generally" (Aeberhardt et al. 2015: 586). One article that draws upon this study concludes that people "from North and sub-Saharan Africa and the [overseas *départements*], and their descendants, whether or not they have a successful working career, are still targets of explicitly racist and discriminatory behaviour" (Hamel, Lesné, and Primon 2018: 245).

While stereotyping, biased behavior, and discrimination at the hands of "French" people—external facts of life the interviewees encounter in their daily lives—were extensively reported in chapters 1–3, interviewees' internal experience of feeling inferior or fearing rejection merited a freestanding chapter. The patterns uncovered in chapter 4 were striking. While a few of the interviewees who originate from former colonies reported feelings of inferiority toward "French" people, none of the interviewees who originate from countries that had not been European colonies reported feeling this way. Chapter 4 also revealed a seemingly paradoxical pattern: the majority of interviewees who speak of experiencing demeaning stereotypes, bias, and discrimination have *not* internalized these experiences. They do not feel inferior or fear rejection on the part of "French" people. For these people, there is a basic disjunction between their external experience (the demeaning social environment they live with) and their internal experience (their feelings of worth).

This raises two questions. First, how can so many interviewees face demeaning behavior in their daily lives and still feel good about themselves? As seen in chapter 4, the interviewees have developed at least ten strategies for maintaining self-respect. The second question is broader, and cannot be answered within the scope of this project: is the strength of character among most of the interviewees widely shared by the millions of other people with a non-European *faciès* in France, including those living in the poor and isolated *banlieues*? Since this project focused on a cohort of relatively prosperous people, their success in sloughing off the demeaning attitudes and behavior of others may also be atypical.

The interviewees' choice of romantic partners, spouses, and long-term partners revealed much about how they feel about themselves and their place in France. As reported in chapter 5, a wide range of men spoke of their intense desire for "French" women. Many women interviewees dated "French" men, although for reasons relating more to values and personality than to a particular attraction. The preference for "French" people among both men and women continued as the interviewees entered into more enduring relationships: the majority who married or partnered with anyone did so with a "French" person. Most of these relationships have endured among interviewees who feel more accepted by "French" people, but the opposite pattern is evident among interviewees who tend to feel rejected. All of these people have seen their relationships break apart.

Chapter 6 took up the issue of being Muslim, or just being seen as Muslim, in France. As Shayan said, people "don't distinguish between Muslims and Maghrebis." This tight association of Maghrebis and Muslims—and vice versa—and the antisocial, even violent, behavior attributed to Maghrebis as Muslims discussed in chapter 1 raise a delicate question: might Maghrebi-Muslim constitute a *racial* category in France? As discussed in the introduction, Stuart Hall argues that the "more 'ethnicity' matters, the more its characteristics are represented as relatively fixed, inherent within a group, transmitted from generation to generation, not just by culture and education, but by biological inheritance" (Hall 2000: 223). While further study is required on this issue, it is worth noting that two experts describe the combined Maghrebi-Muslim identity in racial terms. Paul Silverstein argues that the French stereotype of the violence-prone Maghrebi Muslim arose from the history, both in France and its colonization of the Maghreb, of France's "violent *racialization* of North African immigrants and their children as 'Muslims'" (2008: 4, emphasis mine). This stands in contrast to the stereotype of Muslims from other former French colonies. As Pap Ndiaye notes, the Muslims of sub-Saharan Africa are not associated with "radical Islam" and so escape "one of the central components of anti-Arab racism today" (Ndiaye 2008: 238).[3]

Maghrebi or not, are practicing Muslims less French than other people? Elise's predicament is instructive. She was born and educated in France, was raised to be French, has a purely French name, dresses and looks, she said, like a "normal" French woman, and is a champion of French values. But when she declines wine or a pork dish, alarm bells go off: she is "automatically" asked if she is Muslim and then forced to "justify" herself: "It's a battle every day." Does this make her less French? Put more concretely, since the sharing of traditionally French food and drink is an important part of the social life around her, is Elise's repeated refusal to participate a refusal to be truly French? She has had such thoughts herself, she admitted: "I'm in France, and it's part of French culture. It's almost denying your culture not to drink." As Shayan said in explaining his gradual abandonment of Muslim practices, "French plus Muslim, that's French, but not very French."

If the interviewees represent a test case in *intégration*, as I would argue, what are the results of this test? For one thing, *intégration* continues to be a goal for many people, even in its older sense (once called assimilation), by which immigrants and their children absorb the language, values, and ways of life of the people they accept as unquestionably French.[4] Many of the interviewees have taken this path. Then there is the issue of personal identity. With the possible exception of Lucas, all of the interviewees who grew up in France—and even many who came to France as teenagers or young adults—consider themselves French. And all of the interviewees who have had children are raising their children (or have already raised them) to be French.

The interviewees have also made enormous progress in integrating themselves, as many put it, "into French society." To the extent that bias and discrimination have not intervened, they have become participants in the economy and daily life of the country. Most interviewees attended French universities and have solid, in some cases professional, jobs. Most also live in neighborhoods and work with those of varied backgrounds, particularly "French" people. Many have also partnered with or married "French" people.

But there's more to *intégration*. Do the interviewees feel that they are accepted by the people they see as indisputably French? Certainly, they feel accepted in certain circumstances and among certain people. But in all the complexity, variability, and nuance involved in feeling accepted or rejected, one near-constant among the interviewees stands out: the vast majority do not feel that they are seen as truly French. When Emmanuelle tells people "I'm French," she said, some of them "look at me as if to say 'hunh.'" Jean said, "Yes, I'm French," but "I'm no fool. I fully understand that in the eyes of many people I'm something else."[5]

The interviewees' way of speaking reflects and reinforces this limitation on acceptance. As noted in the introduction and evident throughout the interviewees' accounts, only a certain kind of person is referred to as French. This is someone with a European *faciès*, what many of the interviewees call White. As Didier and Eric Fassin have observed, "people called 'French' turn out to be 'white'" (2006: 9). People who are seen as having a non-European *faciès*—even those who have spent their entire lives in France and consider themselves to be French—are not referred to as French. They are instead Maghrebis, Blacks, Asians, or simply *d'origine*.

Labels aside, to the extent that interviewees feel they're not seen as French, what are they? For many of the interviewees, the answer is simple: any person with a non-European *faciès* is seen as a foreigner. "One thing is certain," Amina said: "If you have a different skin color, whether Black, *métis*, Maghrebi, you're a foreigner." Abbas expressed the concept as a social rule: "To be a foreigner is not whether you are a foreigner or not, but whether someone sees you as a foreigner." It's "a matter of skin color," he insisted, "that's a fact." For François, "Black equals foreigner. It's a reflex." And Leila explained, "Sadly, you can be born here, but if you have dark skin, you can't really be French. People with dark skin are foreigners." It's the opposite for people who come from elsewhere in Europe. As far as "French" people are concerned, Leila explained, "that's Europe, that's good, they're not foreigners."

For many interviewees, this is far from an abstraction. Samuel, Thomas, Karim, Vincent, and Fatih all grew up in France. When Samuel was young, he remembered, people "didn't see me as French" but as "a foreigner" and later, when he was out with his "French" girlfriend, French men didn't like seeing her "with a foreigner." Thomas said, "I know that there are French people who consider me a foreigner. They make clear that even if you were born here, you're a foreigner. You remain a Black.'" Even if Karim is "more French than the French," for most people, he explained, "I'm a foreigner. That's on my face."

Vincent, a third-generation French citizen, also feels he has seen as a foreigner. He works to set "a counterexample to what others say about foreigners," fearing that any misstep might end with him being called "dirty foreigner." Fatih feels that the police and various teachers and professors treated him shabbily because they saw him as a "foreigner." Aya's cousin has spent his entire life in France and "doesn't even know how to say *Bonjour* in Arabic," but he's "nevertheless considered a foreigner."

Interviewees spoke mournfully about their children. Although Karim's children have "French" mothers and have spent their entire lives in France, they are seen as "foreigners" because they "have kinky hair." Similarly, François said, "Take the case of my children, who are *métis*. When one sees them, one doesn't say they're White. The *métis* are Black," and Blacks are "always foreigners." Although Leila's children have always lived in France, are fluent only in French, and "consider themselves 100 percent French," they are seen as "foreigners."

In sum, even interviewees who have spent their entire lives in France and adhere to the norms of the "French" people around them typically don't feel that they are seen as French. The reason is simple: their *faciès* is seen as non-European. And not being seen as French, they don't really belong. In the words of many, they are foreigners—foreigners in their own country. This is both ironic and, for the interviewees, deeply painful.

There remain vast and vital areas of study beyond the bounds of this book. What would an intensive interview project of people with what is seen as a European *faciès* reveal about their feelings toward people like the interviewees? While the basic questions may be simple (such as, "Do you consider them French?"), these people's feelings will surely be complex, variable, and hard to reach. And what about people in France who have non-European *faciès* but are different from the interviewees, particularly those who are deeply marginalized? How do such people feel about acceptance and French identity? While, as noted in the introduction, invaluable ethnographies on such issues have been written, there is much more to learn, especially when personal, recorded interviews are studied carefully and the scope of study is widened beyond individual categories of people (like Maghrebis) and specific locations (such as the Paris area).

Even within the scope of this ethnography, further study is merited. Of particular interest is the intersectionality of the interviewees' identities as Maghrebi, Black, Asian, etc., with their other identities.[6] These include gender and religion, as in Amina's description of herself as "a woman, Black, and a Muslim." While implicitly recognized throughout this book, the intersectionality of such identities as Maghrebi, Black, or Asian with social and economic class also deserves closer attention.

Still more broadly, how are other White-majority countries different—or not so different—from France? What is it like to be non-White in each country? Of course, there is an extraordinary amount of literature on these issues. One notable example is Fatima El-Tayeb's 2011 book *European Others: Queering Ethnicity in Postnational Europe*. An expert on Germany (where she grew up), El-Tayeb's argument concerning Europe generally is similar to the conclusion about France reached here. Indeed, the first chapter of her book is entitled "Stranger in My Own Country." The UK has recently seen substantial research on this issue, and the US case has generated whole libraries of scholarship. However different the American and French experiences may be, as Pap Ndiaye (2008) and Tyler Stovall (2021) have shown, comparing the two experiences may generate a richer understanding of each.

I take the liberty of ending this book with comments from two people who are living the lives I have tried to report. A young woman of Maghrebi origin in France who recently reviewed chapter 1—the chapter that focuses on people like her—wrote that, "Thanks to reading this, I am slowly realizing how powerful systemic racism is." While it is not my place to weigh her words, I'm honored that a person in her circumstances would find value in this work.

And then there is what Thomas said at the end of his interview, as quoted in the introduction to this book:

> It has given me pleasure to share my experiences. I hope you recount them. And if what you write helps people to be open-minded, that is the ultimate goal: to be open-minded and avoid psychological barriers. It would be as if I succeeded along with you.

This is to thank Thomas and express the hope that, when he reads this book, he will think we have both succeeded.

NOTES

1. These include Caroline, Charles, Emmanuelle, Henri, Grégoire, Isabel, Jean, Lucas, and Mathieu.
2. Paul is an outlier in this group. Of Korean parentage, Paul says that his adoptive "French" parents raised him to be like them—he thinks of himself as White—and he believes people see him as French once they hear his unaccented speech and totally French name.
3. Being a matter of stereotypes, this dichotomy takes little heed of factual counterexamples, like the 2015 hostage-taking and murder at a kosher food store in Paris by a Muslim of Malian origin.
4. This is hardly the only approach to *intégration* that one might take, especially today. The founder of the *Parti des indigènes de la république* (Party of the Indigenous of the Republic), Houria Bouteldja, proclaims that "We abhor anything that seeks to integrate us into whiteness" (El-Tayeb 2018: 95, quoting "Dieudonné au prisme de la gauche blanche ou comment penser l'internationalisme domestique?" (2014)).
5. In apparent contrast to the interviewees' reports, Pap Ndiaye asserts that "there are many 'French Blacks' in the eyes of society in general" (Ndiaye 2008: 41), but he also says that Blacks "by their skin color" are seen to have an "ineffable foreignness" (163). Patrick Lozès is categorical on this subject: Blacks "are still perceived as foreign to French society. . . . It is skin color that turns a French person into a foreigner" (Lozès 2012: 107).
6. See, e.g., S. Mazouz (2015); Lépinard and S. Mazouz (2021).

APPENDIX

THE INTERVIEWEES

Note: Since the interviews took the form of open-ended conversations, some demographic details (such as age upon arrival in France and specific educational level achieved) were discussed only generally and are only approximated below. In addition, to protect the privacy of the interviewees, I have listed some information in the form of general categories rather than fine-grained specifics.

Maghrebis

Abdel (male, 25). Pages 13, 16, 29, 40–42, 50, 58, 60, 65, 67nn10-11, 169, 170, 172, 173n6, 217, 220n2, 220n4
Country of origin/parentage: "French" father, mother from Morocco
Grew up in France
Education: college
Employment: tourism

Achraf (male, 63). Pages 52–53, 173n6, 189–90, 217, 220n4
Country of origin: Tunisia
Came to France as a teenager/young adult
Education: university degree
Employment: entrepreneur and business owner

Asma (female, 60). Pages 13, 47–48, 62, 64, 159, 161, 190, 220n4
Country of origin: Tunisia
Grew up primarily in France
Education: high school
Employment: social services

Aya (female, 31). Pages 1, 173n6, 186, 233
Country of origin: Tunisia
Came to France as a teenager/young adult
Education: graduate studies
Employment: remains a student; various jobs to support studies

Elise (female, 27). Pages 12, 13, 16, 40–42, 50, 59, 168, 171, 209–11, 212, 213, 214, 215, 216, 217, 218, 219, 230–31
Country of origin/parentage: "French" father, mother from Morocco
Grew up in France
Education: undergraduate and business school degrees
Employment: investment banker

Fouzia (female, 50). Pages 14, 29, 45–46, 65–66, 170–71, 173n6, 184, 222, 226
Country of origin: Algeria
Grew up in France
Education: nursing school
Employment: nurse (now disabled)

Hiba (female, 49). Pages 11, 12, 17, 54–56, 173n6, 188, 205, 212, 215, 219
Country of origin: Morocco
Grew up in France
Education: high school
Employment: small-scale property management and/or childcare

Ibrahim (male, 42). Pages 59, 63, 64, 159–60, 215–16, 222, 224
Country of origin: Morocco
Came to France as a teenager/young adult
Education: some high school
Employment: various

Karim (male, 50). Pages 10–11, 14, 59, 64, 147, 148–51, 157, 159, 168, 171, 190, 217, 220n4, 224, 226, 232, 233
Country of origin: Morocco

Grew up in France
Education: undergraduate studies, professional training
Employment: IT at government research institute

Khira (female, 60). Pages 12, 54, 58, 61–62, 173n6, 188, 212, 215, 220n4, 227
Country of origin: Algeria
Grew up in France
Education: high school
Employment: retired secretary

Leila (Paris) (female, late 60s). Pages 66n6, 232, 233
Country of origin: Syria (Arab, but not Maghrebi)
Came to France as a teenager
Education: middle school or high school
Employment: office work (retired)

Lina (female, 49). Pages 12, 40–41, 50-51, 59, 157, 169, 173n6, 212–13, 215, 220n4, 224
Country of origin: Morocco
Came to France as a teenager/young adult
Education: college
Employment: interpreter

Mohamed (male, 41). Pages 59, 61–62, 63, 64, 154–55, 156, 163, 173n6, 180, 182, 213, 214–15, 221n4, 224, 225, 227
Country of origin: Morocco
Came to France as a teenager/young adult
Education: graduate degree
Employment: social services

Nassim (male, 30). Pages 3, 42–44, 60, 61, 64, 163, 168, 180–81, 196, 204–5, 213, 214, 215, 217, 219, 220, 224
Country of origin: Algeria
Grew up in France
Education: undergraduate studies, technical program
Employment: IT/business

Nour (female, 49). Pages 12, 17, 29, 44–45, 62–63, 171, 173n6, 184, 189, 196, 201–2, 213, 217, 219, 223, 228

Country of origin: Algeria
Grew up in France
Education: university degree
Employment: team supervisor in government agency

Olivier (male, 24). Pages 1, 3, 4, 12, 46–47, 48, 58–59, 64, 161, 168, 177, 179n4, 226
Country of origin: Morocco (father a French citizen)
Came to France as a teenager/young adult
Education: current undergraduate studies
Employment: student

Rania (female, 28). Pages 48–50 168, 202–4, 212, 213, 215, 224
Country of origin: Tunisia
Came to France as a teenager/young adult
Education: graduate degrees
Employment: high-level IT

Salma (female, 46). Pages 51–52, 168, 173n6, 220n4, 228
Country of origin: Morocco
Came to France as teenager/young adult
Education: multiple graduate degrees
Employment: self-employed business consultant

Sami (male, 50). Pages 12, 56–57, 171, 173n6, 188, 205–6, 212, 215, 216
Country of origin: Tunisia
Came to France as a young adult
Education: some high school
Employment: small business owner

Samuel (male, 43). Pages 4, 13, 14, 17–18, 29, 38–40, 58–59, 64, 65, 159, 160, 171, 175–77, 178, 180, 190, 196, 199, 200–1, 213, 214, 215, 217, 219, 221n7, 222, 224, 232
Country of origin/parentage: father from Morocco, "French" mother
Grew up in France
Education: high school
Employment: entertainment industry (at high level)

Youssef (male, 46). Pages 59, 167–68, 173n6, 179, 180, 190, 196, 217, 220n4, 222, 224
Country of origin: Morocco
Came to France for graduate studies
Education: doctorate
Employment: seeking professorship

Zhora (female, 52). Pages 29, 30–36, 37–38, 55, 58, 62, 64, 65, 67n7, 169, 173n6, 177, 184–85, 190, 217, 220n4, 222, 224, 225
Country of origin: Algeria
Grew up in France
Education: some college
Employment: subject matter specialist in government agency

Blacks

Abbas (male, 32). Pages 1, 14, 104, 108, 109, 154, 156, 157, 173n6, 216, 217, 200n4, 221n8, 232
Country of origin: Senegal
Came to France for graduate studies
Education: master's degree
Employment: office work/administration

Amina (female, 39). Pages 90, 94–96, 101-6, 168, 169, 173n6, 186, 206–7, 212, 214, 215, 217, 218, 221n8, 225, 232, 234
Country of origin: Cameroon
Came to France as a teenager/young adult
Education: undergraduate business degree and graduate IT degree
Employment: independent business consultant

Anna (female, 31). Pages 17, 77, 83–85, 102, 104, 106, 110, 168, 169, 171, 173n6, 185, 196, 228
Country of origin/parentage: father from Burkina Faso, "French" stepmother
Grew up in France
Education: undergraduate studies
Employment: office work/administration

Ariel (female, 35). Pages 90, 103, 104, 161–62, 168, 173n6, 183, 193, 194–95, 225
Country of origin: Madagascar
Came to France as a teenager
Education: undergraduate and graduate degrees in IT
Employment: IT professional

Caroline (female, 40). Pages 10, 77, 85–86, 105-6, 110, 112, 177, 185, 189, 196, 233n1
Country of origin: France (Guadeloupe, then mainland France)
Grew up in France (until 3 in Guadeloupe, thereafter mainland France)
Education: high school, professional training
Employment: government agency

Charles (male, 47). Pages 90–92, 103, 104, 105, 112, 162, 168, 169, 170, 173n6, 180, 182–83, 193, 194–95, 225, 233n1
Country of origin: France (Martinique, then mainland France)
Grew up in France (Martinique)
Education: undergraduate IT degree
Employment: IT professional/management

Clément (male, 36). Pages 13, 17, 77, 80–83, 102, 103, 104–8, 113n9, 158, 160, 171, 177, 191–92, 193, 209, 215, 216, 217, 219, 226
Country of origin: Senegal
Grew up in France
Education: high school
Employment: small business owner

Daniel (male, 29). Pages 90, 98–99, 108, 109, 153–54, 156, 163, 169, 173n6
Country of origin: Ivory Coast
Came to France as a teenager/young adult
Education: high school or university degree
Employment: team leader in factory

Djibril (male, 24). Pages 101, 103, 104, 154, 156, 157, 167, 173n6, 217, 220n4

Country of origin: Senegal
Came to France as a teenager
Education: high school, some professional school
Employment: under/unemployment; Airbnb host

Emmanuelle (female, 30). Pages 72, 102, 103, 104–5, 106, 108, 109, 110, 112, 169, 171, 173n6, 231-32, 235n1
Country of origin: France (Guadeloupe, then mainland France)
Grew up in France (Guadeloupe)
Education: graduate/professional degree
Employment: self-employed physical therapist

François (male, 48). Pages 4, 11, 13, 16, 72, 77, 88–89, 104, 108, 153, 154, 156, 171, 179–80, 190, 196, 232, 233
Country of origin: Gabon
Came to France as a teenager/young adult
Education: business school graduate
Employment: social services

Isabel (female, 41). Pages 17, 90, 92–94, 101, 102–3, 104, 106, 107, 168, 169, 173n6, 188–89, 225, 235n1
Country of origin: Congo-Brazzaville
Came to France as a teenager
Education: high school, professional school diploma
Employment: small business owner

Jean (male, 30). Pages 10, 11–12, 14, 77, 78–80, 104, 106, 108, 110, 112, 157, 158, 159, 160, 171, 180, 181–82, 196, 197n5, 222, 232, 235n1
Country of origin: Haiti
Grew up in France
Education: high school
Employment: artist

Lucas (male, 38). Pages 60, 72, 77, 86–88, 103, 104, 107, 110, 112, 160, 197n7, 222, 231, 235n1
Country of origin: France
Grew up in France
Education: high school, technical training
Employment: small business owner

Marie (female, 50). Pages 90, 96–97, 103, 104, 105, 168, 173n6
Country of origin: Cameroon
Came to France as a teenager/young adult
Education: degree in midwifery
Employment: midwife

Markus (male, 19). Pages 90, 96, 97–98, 106, 112, 170–71, 173n6, 226
Country of origin: parents from different sub-Saharan African countries
Grew up in France
Education: senior in high school
Employment: student

Philippe (male, 33). Pages 90, 99–100, 104, 105, 113n11, 163, 169, 173n3, 173n6
Country of origin: Guinea
Came to France as a teenager/young adult
Education: undergraduate and graduate degrees in law
Employment: middle school counselor

Thomas (male, 29). Pages 4, 72–77, 89–90, 101, 102, 103, 104, 105, 107, 108, 109, 110, 112, 113n7, 158, 167, 168–69, 170, 171, 173n6, 180, 222, 232, 234
Country of origin: Congo-Kinshasa
Grew up in France
Education: undergraduate degree in IT engineering
Employment: small business owner

Neither Maghrebi Nor Black

Emily (female, 30). Pages 121, 127–28, 138, 139, 165, 168
Country of origin: China
Came to France as a teenager/young adult
Education: graduate degree
Employment: engineering/management

Eric (male, 33). Pages 165, 188
Country of origin: China
Came to France as a teenager/young adult

Education: doctorate
Employment: IT technician

Fatih (male, 33). Pages 60, 130, 132–33, 137, 138, 139, 143n11, 164, 166, 172, 207, 213, 214, 217, 218, 221n8, 227, 228, 232, 233
Country of origin: Turkey
Grew up in France
Education: graduate degree
Employment: business/company management

Grégoire (male, 68). Pages 121–24, 138, 139, 156, 163, 191, 192–93, 225, 235n1
Country of origin/parentage: "French" father, Vietnamese mother
Grew up in France
Education: high school
Employment: government agency (retired)

Henri (male, 71). Pages 12, 13, 17, 121, 122-24, 139, 140, 156, 163, 188, 189, 193, 226, 228, 235n1
Country of origin/parentage: "French" father, Vietnamese mother
Grew up in France
Education: high school
Employment: government agency (retired)

Kana (female, approx. mid-30s). Pages 121–22, 125, 165, 166, 182, 193–94
Country of origin: Japan
Came to France as young adult
Education: undergraduate degree
Employment: full-time parent; small side-business

Mathieu (male, 38). Pages 121–22, 124–25, 138, 139, 171, 173n6, 180, 182, 193–94, 235n1
Country of origin/parentage: father mixed "French"-Vietnamese; mother Vietnamese
Grew up in France
Education: undergraduate degree
Employment: owner of small business

Nima (male, 68). Pages 130, 135–37, 139, 164, 165, 188, 217, 218
Country of origin: Iran
Came to France for graduate school
Education: graduate degree
Employment: small business owner

Paul (male, 43). Pages 67n7, 121, 128–29, 138, 139, 141, 165, 166, 171, 178, 180, 189, 225, 235n2
Country of origin/parentage: Korean; adopted by "French" parents
Grew up in France
Education: high school
Employment: military career

Rémy (male, 72). Pages 121, 125–27, 139, 141, 156, 169, 188, 189
Country of origin/parentage: father from Vietnam, mother "French"
Grew up in France
Education: high school, professional studies
Employment: division head, National Police training academy (retired)

Shayan (male, 33). Pages 17, 130–32 137, 139, 140–41, 143n11, 164–65, 166, 168, 174, 177, 178, 180, 189, 196, 208, 212, 213, 215, 216, 217, 218, 219, 222, 226, 230, 231
Country of origin: Iran
Grew up in France
Education: undergraduate degree
Employment: IT/management

Tsiory (male, 29). Pages 11, 12, 152–53, 154, 156, 159, 162, 172n5
Country of origin: Madagascar, but with Malayo-Indonesian *faciès*
Came to France as a teenager/young adult
Education: graduate degree
Employment: IT technician

Usman (male, 47). Pages 130, 133–35, 137, 139, 141–42, 155, 156, 163, 168, 178–79, 180, 189, 190, 196, 208–9, 213, 217, 218

Country of origin: Pakistan
Came to France as young adult
Education: doctorate
Employment: high-tech entrepreneur

Vincent (male, 51). Pages 4, 13, 115–20, 130, 139, 140, 141–42, 161, 171, 179, 180, 190, 196, 216, 217, 222, 226, 232–33
Country of origin: French colony of Pondicherry; now part of India
Grew up in France
Education: undergraduate degree
Employment: IT/management

Yuka (female, 30). Pages 14, 121, 127–28, 138, 139, 143n7, 165, 185, 189, 190
Country of origin: China
Came to France as a teenager/young adult
Education: undergraduate degree
Employment: full-time parent; self-employed craftsperson

OTHERS/SPECIAL CASES

Interviewees of European origin

I interviewed a small number of people of European origin (either because I had mistakenly assumed they would be of non-European origin or because they were spouses or partners of my principal interviewee). While some of these interviews did not yield information relevant to this project, two did:

Mariana (female, 29). Pages 37, 222–23, 227
Selma (female, 40s). Pages 29, 61, 71–72

Airbnb hosts from before interview project began, but mentioned in book

Ayoub (male, 30s). Pages 59–60, 138, 198, 217, 224
Nawab (male, 40s). Pages 104, 107

Sole interviewee who declined to have interview recorded

Alejandro (male, 40s). Pages 103, 104, 113n8

Interviewees of non-European origin mentioned only briefly in book

Tarek: (male, 28). Page 4
(Tarek's interview focused on the severe persecution he'd suffered before coming to France.)
Florence (female, 28). Page 142n2
(Florence's interview focused on family and interpersonal issues.)

Interviewees of non-European origin not mentioned in book

Certain people were interviewed but are not mentioned in this book. For each, the principal reason for their absence in these pages is noted in parentheticals: **Jacques** (personal disabilities the focus of his interview); **Yen** (had arrived in France only two years before; had not learned French); **Minji** (had arrived in France seven years before at age 45, and has had limited contact outside her home); **Pauline-Hawa** (personal issues the focus of her interview).

REFERENCES

Aeberhardt, Romain, Roland Rathelot, Mirna Safi, and Catriona Dutreuilh. 2015. "Ethnic Origin or Residential Location: Educational Labour Market Attainment of Young People of Immigrant Background in France." *Population, English edition* 70 (3): 567–60.

"Airbnb. Plus d'un million de personnes n'ont pas voulu signer une charte de non-discrimination." Ouest-France. 11 November 2020. https://www.ouest-france.fr/economie/entreprises/airbnb/airbnb-plus-d-un-million-de-personnes-n-ont-pas-voulu-signer-une-charte-de-non-discrimination-7053487. Retrieved 10 December 2022.

Bancel, Nicolas, and Pascal Blanchard. 2017a. "The Republican Origins of the Colonial Fracture." In *The Colonial Legacy in France: Fracture, Rupture, and Apartheid*, eds. Nicolas Bancel, Pascal Blanchard, and Dominic Thomas, trans. Alexis Pernsteiner, 43–52. Bloomington: Indiana University Press.

______. 2017b. "The Pitfalls of Colonial Memory." In *The Colonial Legacy in France: Fracture, Rupture, and Apartheid*, eds. Nicolas Bancel, Pascal Blanchard, and Dominic Thomas, trans. Alexis Pernsteiner, 153–64. Bloomington: Indiana University Press.

Banton, Michael. 2005. "Historical and Contemporary Modes of Racialization." In *Racialization: Studies in Theory and Practice*, eds. Karim Murjin and John Solomos, 51–68. Oxford: Oxford University Press.

Beaman, Jean. 2017. *Citizen Outsider: Children of North African Immigrants in France*. Oakland, California: University of California Press.

Beauchemin, Cris, Christelle Hamel, Maud Lesné, Patrick Simon, and L'Équipe TeO. 2010. "Discrimination: a question of visible minorities." *Population and societies* (2010): 1–4.

Beaud, Stéphane, and Gérard Noiriel. 2021. *Race et sciences sociales: essai sur les usages publics d'une catégorie*. Marseille: Agone.

Blanchard, Pascal, Hadrien Dubucs, and Yvan Gastaut. 2016. *Atlas des immigrations en France: histoire, mémoire, héritage*. Paris: Éditions Autrement.

Bleich, Erik. 2004. "Anti-Racism Without Races; Politics and Policy in a 'Color-Blind' State." In *Race in France: Interdisciplinary Perspectives on the Politics of Difference*, eds. Herrick Chapman and Laura L. Frader, 162–88. New York: Berghahn Books.

Bosa, Bastien, Julie Pagis, and Benoît Trépied. 2019. "Le *passing*: un concept pour penser les mobilités sociales." *Genèses*, 114 (1): 5–9.

Boucher, Manuel. 2010. *Internés du ghetto: ethnographie des confrontations violentes dans une cité impopulaire.* Paris: L'Harmattan.

Bowen, John R. 2007. *Why the French Don't Like Headscarves: Islam, the State, and Public Space.* Princeton: Princeton University Press.

______. 2010. *Can Islam be French? Pluralism and Pragmatism in a Secularist State.* Princeton: Princeton University Press.

Breuil-Genier, Pascale, Catherine Borrel, and Bertrand L'hommeau. 2011. "Les immigrés, les descendants d'immigrés et leurs enfants." *Portrait Social Edition,* 2011: 31–39. Retrieved 29 December 2022. https://www.insee.fr/fr/statistiques/1373887?sommaire=1373905.

Brinbaum, Yaël, Mirna Safi, and Patrick Simon. 2018. "Discrimination in France: Between Perception and Experience." In *Trajectories and Origins: Survey on the Diversity of the French Population,* eds. Cris Beauchemin, Christelle Hamel and Patrick Simon, 195–222. Cham, Switzerland: Springer.

Cartographie des mémoires de l'esclavage. 2005. *Nutrimaine and Y'a bon Banania.* Retrieved 29 April 2023. https://www.mmoe.llc.ed.ac.uk/en/action/nutrimaine-and-ya-bon-banania.

Centre National de Ressources Textuelles et Lexicales, Portail lexicale, Lexigraphie, "bougnoule." https://www.cnrtl.fr/definition/bougnoule, retrieved 9 December 2022.

Chine informations. n.d. *Chinetoque.* Retrieved 29 April 2023. https://chine.in/guide/toque_4042.html.

Chuang, Ya-Han. 2021. *Une minorité modèle?: Chinois de France et racisme anti-Asiatiques.* Paris: La Découverte.

______. 2022. "Racisme 'anti-asiatique,' ou le dénigrement d'une minorité." *Pouvoirs,* 181 (2): 109–17.

Cohen, Mathilde. 2021. "The Whiteness of French Food: Law, Race, and Eating Culture in France." *French Politics, Culture & Society* 39 (2): 26–52.

Cohen, Mathilde, and Sarah Mazouz. 2021. "A White Republic? Whites and Whiteness in France." *French Politics, Culture & Society* 39 (2): 1–25.

Domergue, René. 2010. *Intégration des Maghrébins dans les villages du Midi.* France: R. Domergue.

Du Bois, W. E. Burghardt. 1903. *The Souls of Black Folk.* Chicago: A. C. McClurg & Co.

Durmelat, Sylvie. 2015. "Colonial Culinary Encounters and Imperial Leftovers." *French Cultural Studies,* 26 (2): 115–29.

El-Tayeb, Fatima. 2011. *European Others: Queering Ethnicity in Postnational Europe.* Minneapolis: University of Minnesota Press.

______. 2018. "Oppressed Majority: Violence and Muslim Communities in Multicultural Europe." In *With Stones in Our Hands: Writings on Muslims, Racism, and Empire,* eds. Sohail Daulatzai and Junaid Rana. Minneapolis: University of Minnesota Press.

Fanon, Frantz. 1986 [1952]. *Black Skin, White Masks,* trans. Charles Lam Markmann. London: Pluto Press.

Fassin, Didier. 2006a. "Du déni à la dénégation, Psychologie politique de la représentation des discriminations." In *De la question sociale à la question raciale?: représenter la société française*, eds. Didier Fassin and Eric Fassin, 141–65. Paris: Découverte.

______. 2006b. "Nommer, interpréter, Le sens commun de la question raciale." In *De la question sociale à la question raciale?: représenter la société française*, eds. Didier Fassin and Eric Fassin, 27–44. Paris: Découverte.

______. 2010. "Ni race, ni racisme. Ce que racialiser veut dire." In *Les nouvelles frontières de la société française*, ed. Didier Fassin, 147–72. Paris: Découverte.

______. 2011. "Racialization: How to Do Races with Bodies." In *A Companion to the Anthropology of the Body and Embodiment*, ed. Frances E. Mascia-Lees, 419–34. Malden, MA: Wiley-Blackwell.

______. 2013. *Enforcing Order: An Ethnography of Urban Policing*. Cambridge: Polity Press.

Fassin, Didier, and Eric Fassin. 2006. "Preface. Des questions 'bonnes à penser.'" In *De la question sociale à la question raciale?: représenter la société française*, eds. Didier Fassin and Eric Fassin, 5–11. Paris: Découverte.

Fernando, Mayanthi L. 2014. *The Republic Unsettled: Muslim French and the Contradictions of Secularism*. Durham: Duke University Press.

Ferry, Jules. 1897. *Discours et Opinions de Jules Ferry*, ed. Paul Robiquet. Paris: Armand Colin & Cie.

Fleming, Crystal Marie. 2017. *Resurrecting Slavery: Racial Legacies and White Supremacy in France*. Philadelphia: Temple University Press.

Gal, Susan, and Judith T. Irvine. 2019. *Signs of Difference: Language and Ideology in Social Life*. Cambridge: Cambridge University Press.

Georgetown University Berkley Center for Religion, Peace, and World Affairs. 2022. "Demographics of Islam." Retrieved 21 December 2022. https://web.archive.org/web/20201009120840/https://berkleycenter.georgetown.edu/essays/demographics-of-islam.

Guillaumin, Colette. 1995. "The Specific Characteristics of Racist Ideology," trans. Andrew Rothwell and Max Silverman. In *Racism, Sexism, Power, and Ideology*, 29–60. London; New York: Routledge.

Hall, Stuart. 2000. "Conclusion: The Multicultural Question." In *Un/settled Multiculturalisms: Diasporas, Entanglements, 'Transruptions,'* ed. Barnor Hesse, 209–41. London; New York: Zed Books.

______. 2021. "Race, the Floating Signifier: What More is There to Say about 'Race'?" In *Selected Writings on Race and Difference*, eds. Paul Gilroy and Ruth Wilson Gilmore, 359–73. Durham: Duke University Press.

Hamel, Christelle, Maud Lesné, and Jean-Luc Primon. 2018. "The Place of Racism in the Study of Discrimination." In *Trajectories and Origins: Survey on the Diversity of the French Population*, eds. Cris Beauchemin, Christelle Hamel and Patrick Simon. 223–48. Cham, Switzerland: Springer.

Huda. 2018. "The World's Muslim Population – Statistics and Key Facts," World Religions website. Retrieved 21 December 2022. https://www.learnreligions.com/worlds-muslim-population-2004480.

Institut national d'études démographiques (INED). "Divorces." Retrieved 20 December 2022. https://www.ined.fr/en/everything_about_population/data/france/marriages-divorces-pacs/divorces/.

Jayet, Cyril. 2016. "Se sentir français et se sentir vu comme un Français. Les relations entre deux dimensions de l'appartenance nationale." *Sociologie* 7 (2): 113–131.

Kastoryano, Riva. 1986. *Etre Turc en France: réflexions sur familles et communauté.* Paris: CIEMI, L'Harmattan.

Keaton, Trica Danielle. 2006. *Muslim Girls and the Other France: Race, Identity Politics, and Social Exclusion.* Bloomington: Indiana University Press.

Killian, Caitlin. 2006. *North African Women in France: Gender, Culture, and Identity.* Stanford: Stanford University Press.

Kobelinsky, Carolina. 2010. *L'accueil des demandeurs d'asile: une ethnographie de l'attente.* Paris: Editions du Cygne.

Ladepeche.fr. 2007. "5 millions de blondes en France, dont 50 percent de fausses." Retrieved 20 December 2022. https://www.ladepeche.fr/article/2007/10/19/88933-5-millions-de-blondes-en-france-dont-50-de-fausses.html.

Larchanché, Stéphanie. 2020. *Cultural Anxieties: Managing Migrant Suffering in France.* New Brunswick: Rutgers University Press.

Lépinard, Eléonore, and Sarah Mazouz. 2021. *Pour l'intersectionnalité.* Paris: Anamosa.

Lozès, Patrick. 2012. "The Invention of Blacks in France." In *Black France/France Noire: The History and Politics of Blackness.* eds. Trica Danielle Keaton, T. Denean Sharpley-Whiting, and Tyler Stovall, 104–09. Durham: Duke University Press.

Lozès, Patrick, and Bernard Lecherbonnier. 2009. *Les Noirs sont-ils des Français à part entière?* Paris: Larousse.

Mahut, David. 2017. *Le déclassement social dans la migration: ethnographie d'une petite bourgeoisie bamakoise installée à Paris.* Paris: L'Harmattan.

Mazouz, Mohammed. 1988. *Les marocains en Ile-de-France.* Paris: CIEMI, L'Harmattan.

Mazouz, Sarah. 2015. "Faire des différences. Ce que l'ethnographie nous apprend sur l'articulation des modes pluriels d'assignation." *Raisons politiques*, 58 (2): 75–89.

______. 2017. *La République et ses autres: politiques de l'altérité dans la France des années 2000.* Lyon: ENS éditions.

______. 2020. *Race.* Paris: Anamosa.

Meurs, Dominique. 2018a. "Employment and Wages of Immigrants and Descendants of Immigrants: Measures of Inequality and Perceived Discrimination." In *Trajectories and Origins: Survey on the Diversity of the French Population*, eds. Cris Beauchemin, Christelle Hamel and Patrick Simon. 79–106. Cham, Switzerland: Springer.

______. 2018b. "The role of discrimination in immigrant unemployment." *Population and societies* (2017): 1–4.

Ndiaye, Pap. 2008. *La condition noire: essai sur une minorité française*. Paris: Calmann-Lévy.

______. 2009. "Questions de couleur. Histoire, idéologie et pratiques du colorisme." In *De la question sociale à la question raciale?: représenter la société française*, eds. Didier Fassin and Eric Fassin, 46–62. Paris: Découverte.

Noiriel, Gérard. 1996. *The French Melting Pot: Immigration, Citizenship, and National Identity*, trans. Geoffroy de Laforcade. Minneapolis: University of Minnesota Press.

______. 2006. "'Color blindness' et construction des identités dans l'espace public français." In *De la question sociale à la question raciale?: représenter la société française*, eds. Didier Fassin and Eric Fassin, 166–82. Paris: Découverte.

______. 2010. "Aux sources de la question raciale. Doctrines racistes et domination sociale." In *Les nouvelles frontières de la société française*, ed. Didier Fassin, 27–51. Paris: Découverte.

Open Society Foundations. 2009. *Profiling Minorities in Paris: Disproportionate Stops of Blacks and Arabs*. Retrieved 17 December 2022. https://www.justiceinitiative.org/publications/profiling-minorities-study-stop-and-search-practices-paris.

Pan Ké Shon, Jean-Louis, and Claire Scodellaro. 2018. "The Living Environment of Immigrants and Their Descendants: Perceived Discrimination and Segregation." In *Trajectories and Origins: Survey on the Diversity of the French Population*, eds. Cris Beauchemin, Christelle Hamel and Patrick Simon. 143–170. Cham, Switzerland: Springer.

Parti des indigènes de la république website. "Dieudonné au prisme de la gauche blanche ou comment penser l'internationalisme domestique?" 2014. Retrieved 10 January 2023. https://indigenes-republique.fr/dieudonne-au-prisme-de-la-gauche-blanche-ou-comment-penser-linternationalisme-domestique/.

PBS Website. "What are the Typical Misperceptions and Stereotypes Westerners Hold about Islam and the Middle East and Vice Versa?" *Global Connections the Middle East*. Retrieved 21 December 2022. http://www.pbs.org/wgbh/globalconnections/mideast/questions/types/index.html.

Provencher, Denis M. 2017. *Queer Maghrebi French: Language, Temporalities, Transfiliations*. Liverpool: Liverpool University Press.

Rathelot, Roland. 2014. "Ethnic differentials on the labor market in the presence of asymmetric spatial sorting: Set identification and estimation." CReAM Discussion Paper Series 1411. Retrieved 10 December 2022. https://ideas.repec.org/p/crm/wpaper/1411.html.

Rigaud, Marie-Hélène. 2010. *Enfants de migrants lao: transmission et réinterprétation culturelles*. Paris: L'Harmattan.

Ruscio, Alain. 2020. *Des racines coloniales du racisme "à la française": petit dictionnaire des insultes racistes*. Paris: Les Indes savantes.

Selby, Jennifer A. 2012. *Questioning French secularism: Gender Politics and Islam in a Parisian Suburb*. New York: Palgrave Macmillan.

Silverstein, Michael. 1976. "Shifters, Linguistic Categories, and Cultural Description." In *Meaning in anthropology*, eds. Keith Basso and Henry Selby, 11–55. Albuquerque: University of New Mexico Press.
Silverstein, Paul A. 2004. *Algeria in France: Transpolitics, Race, and Nation.* Bloomington: Indiana University Press.
______. 2008. "The Context of Antisemitism and Islamophobia in France." *Patterns of Prejudice* 42 (1): 1–26.
______. 2018. *Postcolonial France: Race, Islam, and the Future of the Republic.* London: Pluto Press.
Simon, Patrick. 2008. "The Choice of Ignorance: The Debate on Ethnic and Racial Statistics in France." *French Politics, Culture & Society*, 26 (1): 7–31.
______. 2012. "French National Identity and Integration: Who Belongs to the National Community?" Migration Policy Institute. Retrieved 7 January 2023. https://www.migrationpolicy.org/research/french-national-identity-and-integration-who-belongs-national-community.
Simon, Patrick, Cris Beauchemin, and Christelle Hamel. 2018. "Chapter 1. Introduction." In *Trajectories and Origins: Survey on the Diversity of the French Population*, eds. Cris Beauchemin, Christelle Hamel and Patrick Simon, 1–10. Cham, Switzerland: Springer.
Slooter, Luuk. 2019. *The Making of the Banlieue: An Ethnography of Space, Identity and Violence.* London: Palgrave Macmillan.
Sourou, Benoît. 2016 *Stratégies identitaires chez les migrants turcs en France.* Paris: L'Harmattan.
Statista. 2015. "Distribution of annual income levels of Airbnb hosts in the United Kingdom (UK) from November 2014 to November 2015." Retrieved 10 January 2023. https://www.statista.com/statistics/510128/income-level-airbnb-hosts-united-kingdom-uk/.
______. 2019. "African countries with the highest share of Muslims as of 2019." 2022. Retrieved 20 December 2022. https://www.statista.com/statistics/1239494/share-of-muslim-population-in-africa-by-country/.
______. 2022. "Divorce Rates in 2020 in Europe, by Country." Retrieved 20 December 2022. https://www.statista.com/statistics/612207/divorce-rates-in-european-countries-per-100-marriages/.
Stovall, Tyler. 2021. *White Freedom: The Racial History of an Idea.* Princeton: Princeton University Press
Tetreault, Chantal. 2015. *Transcultural Teens: Performing Youth Identities in French Cités.* Malden, MA: John Wiley & Sons, Inc.
Tin, Louis-Georges. 2008. "Who is Afraid of Blacks in France? The Black Question: The Name Taboo, the Number Taboo." *French Politics, Culture & Society* 26 (1): 32–44.
Tribalat, Michèle. 2015. "Une estimation des populations d'origine étrangère en France en 2011." *Espace populations sociétés:* 2015 (1-2). Retrieved 10 December 2022. http://journals.openedition.org/eps/6073.
Vergès, Françoise. 2014. "Trouble in the Republic, Disturbing Memories, Forgotten Territories." In *Colonial Culture in France Since the Revolution,*

eds. Pascal Blanchard, Sandrine Lemaire, Nicolas Bancel, and Dominic Thomas, trans. Alexis Pernsteiner. Bloomington: Indiana University Press.

———. 2022. "Décolonisation." In *La société qui vient*, ed. Didier Fassin, 843–59. Paris: Éditions du Seuil.

INDEX

www.ingramcontent.com/pod-product-compliance
Ingram Content Group UK Ltd.
Pitfield, Milton Keynes, MK11 3LW, UK
UKHW021850250826
8166IPUK00004B/64

9 781807 581053